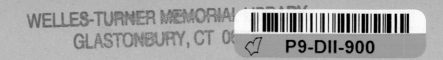

Simple Food for Busy Families

SIMPLE FOOD
FOR BUSY FAMILIES

The Whole Life Nutrition Approach

Jeannette Bessinger, CHHC,
and Tracee Yablon-Brenner, RD, CHHC

CELESTIAL ARTS
Berkeley | Toronto

Celestial Arts
an imprint of Ten Speed Press
PO Box 7123
Berkeley, California 94707
www.tenspeed.com

Distributed in Australia by Simon and Schuster Australia, in Canada by Ten Speed Press Canada, in New Zealand by Southern Publishers Group, in South Africa by Real Books, and in the United Kingdom and Europe by Publishers Group UK.

Design by Katy Brown

Library of Congress Cataloging-in-Publication Data

Bessinger, Jeannette.
  Simple food for busy families : the whole life nutrition approach / Jeannette Bessinger and Tracee Yablon-Brenner.
    p. cm.
  Includes bibliographical references and index.
  Summary: "An accessible guide to nutrition and healthful meal planning for busy parents, including recipes and tips for preparing wholesome meals and teaching children good eating habits for life" —Provided by publisher.
    ISBN-13: 978-1-58761-335-7
    ISBN-10: 1-58761-335-2
    ISBN-13: 978-1-58761-336-4
    ISBN-10: 1-58761-336-0
  1. Cookery (Natural foods) 2. Nutrition.
I. Yablon-Brenner, Tracee. II. Title.
  TX741.B47 2009
  641.5' 636—dc22
                                    2008030939

Printed in China
First printing this edition, 2009

1 2 3 4 5 6 7 8 9 10 — 13 12 11 10 09

Dedication

This book is lovingly dedicated to my grandmother, Jeannette Lee Porter, who, at 90 years old, is still cleaning up at the bridge table and faithfully going to water aerobics. With her simple, wise approach to life, she's raised an amazing family that spans four generations and holds many of my best friends. I believe there is no greater gift or legacy than a strong family. Thank you, Grandma.

Special thanks, also, to my husband, Jay, and my children, Jesse and Julian, for their sweet love, friendship, encouragement, tolerance, and fabulous senses of humor. You are my dearest loves.

—Jeannette Lee (Mom)

I dedicate this book to my parents, whose poor health and busy lifestyle set me on my journey to find answers and better options for a healthier, longer life. And also to my daughters, Emily and Alana, whose constant love is my source of inspiration to teach others the benefits of eating nourishing food.

Special thanks to my friends and family for their unconditional support, motivation, and love.

—Tracee

Contents

Part II. Everyday Cooking: Keeping It Real 107

Foreword

Each of us was born into a family. Our families taught us how to live, what to eat, and where we fit into the world. If you talk to almost anybody today, you will discover that his or her personal health, relationship to food, level of self-esteem, and achievements have all been influenced to some degree by childhood experiences. Families form the foundation of our communities and our country, and so it is crucial that we find ways for them to be as happy and healthy as possible.

In the past thirty years or so, a new style of family life has developed in America. Parents are incredibly busy, running around, working multiple jobs, and trying to get the kids to their next activity. Children listen to iPods, talk on cell phones, and do their homework all at the same time. Typical household foods come in plastic packages and are high in white flour, fat, and sugar. Most family dinners are nuked instead of cooked with care and love. We see children eating fast food and parents on fad diets. Most people don't have time to sit down and figure out how to feed the people they want to nourish most.

From a health perspective, this lifestyle is not really working. Rates of obesity and diabetes are rising in both adults and children. Inappropriate food, plus an overbooked and sedentary lifestyle, has created a health crisis that severely threatens the health of the next generation of children. Most parents have no idea where to turn for real solutions. Post-modern families need a post-modern approach to nutrition that is sensible and easy to implement.

Jeannette and Tracee, graduates of the Institute for Integrative Nutrition, have taken up this challenge. They are experts at helping busy parents make sense of the confusing world of nutrition and wellness. In their roles as mothers, health-care professionals, and writers, they provide deep understanding and practical wisdom to today's struggling families. Their book presents a flexible, easy-to-follow approach that can help any parent create a healthier family lifestyle.

This is a crucial and timely book. Children are the adults of tomorrow. They require healthy bodies and minds in order to reach their goals and fulfill their dreams. If we want to build a better future, we need to give our children the best nourishment possible. I appreciate Tracee and Jeannette for writing a wonderful book that will give American families the support they need and move us one step closer to the healthy, happy future we all deserve.

—Joshua Rosenthal, MScEd
Founder and Director, Institute for Integrative Nutrition

Acknowledgments

We wish to thank everyone who contributed to this project. We're very grateful for your help in bringing *Simple Food* to life.

To the team at the Institute for Integrative Nutrition: Without you, there would be no book. Thank you for your deep support, guidance, and encouragement as we created a working manuscript together. Special thanks to Jen Rosenblum for your discerning editor's eye; to Jennifer Thorpe, for being the original design visionary; and to Joshua Rosenthal and Suzanne Boothby, for helping us find our wings.

To Coleen O'Shea, our incredible agent, for your steadfast belief in the promise of this book, your patience with our stumbles, and your cheerleading throughout the process.

To Brie Mazurek, editor, for your friendly guidance and crystal clarity.

To the Ten Speed Press design team, for the beautiful images and clean, modern look of the book.

To AM Graphics: Many thanks for the gorgeous, full-color manuscript copies. You gave us a beautiful face for the publishers.

To Lora Ruffner and Neil Beaty, for our delicious business websites.

To the fabulous folks at the Aquidneck Grower's Market, Nature's Goodness, Northvale Organica, and Damico Farms: Many thanks for your commitment to producing and selling beautiful and delectable organic foods. And to the Green Grocer team, John Wood and Aly Marks-Wood, thank you for your well of wisdom and for providing ethically treated, high-quality animal foods (among many other delicious groceries!).

From Jeannette: To Jonny Bowden, my mentor, my nutrition rock star, my #1 cheerleader, and most important, my beloved friend for the past twenty-five years; I can never repay you for all you've done for me, but I will try! To Judi Smith and Jim Sattel, for your personal support and tireless efforts in working toward a healthier Newport County. To my mom, the true writer in the family, for cooking always—even in the solo years. To my extended family and all my friends (my second family), thank you for your love, encouragement, and inspiring examples of great family living in the 2000s.

From Tracee: To Barbara Anne Prince and Sandy Rousso, thank you for your constant encouragement and guidance that helped me make this book a reality. To my family, for their continued support, and to my special friends, who are like family, for always being there and continuing to inspire me to push through when the journey gets tough.

Introduction

You're busy, right? You want to create the best possible health for yourself and your family, but your endlessly full days seem to keep getting in the way. Sound familiar?

Families today are *busy*. Their most precious commodity is time. Yet many parents are beginning to realize that their most *valuable* commodity is health. Too often, in the name of saving time, they are straining their families' health to the breaking point with poor daily food and lifestyle choices. When saving your health becomes more important than saving time, what can you do?

This book grew out of countless requests for help that we receive from parents asking that very question. These parents are trying to make healthy lifestyle changes, but they feel overwhelmed. They don't know how to make the time or where to begin. They want to know the truth about food, but they are confused by all the trendy nutritional advice that never seems to work. They want to feed their families well, but they don't want to go on any radical diets. Often they are scared of "health food." Will it smell funny? Taste awful? Be too hard to cook? What if the kids hate it?

In our experience, American kids and families will thrive on diets of natural foods and loving, consistent routines. But to get there, parents desperately need simple and practical solutions. They want to be shown what they can do in their regular lives, right now, to become healthier. That's what we offer them, and that's what we will try to offer you in this book. As holistic health counselors (and a registered dietician), our daily work is taking individuals and families through step-by-step processes to improve their ways of eating and balance their busy lifestyles. As working moms, we've spent years developing real strategies that work in the real world, for our own families and for others.

We call our approach Whole Life Nutrition, because it truly looks at your whole life. As a parent, you spend so much time trying to patch up your family's health; you become exhausted trying to fix a million little symptoms. "What can I take for my migraines?" "How can I get my son to fall asleep at night?" "What's the quickest way to get rid of my 'muffin top'?" (For those of you without preteen daughters, that's what you call the roll of fat that spills over the top of your low-rider jeans!) Whole Life Nutrition addresses the foundation of health, not the symptoms, and helps you build new routines to balance and support that foundation in gentle, practical ways. Although this approach requires an investment of time up-front, once you are out of the cycle of chasing symptoms you will save yourself a lot of time and anxiety.

This book is a practical guide to getting families with school-age children on that simpler track to better health. Half lifestyle-balancing guidelines and half innovative cooking tools, the book contains all that you need to get started on a healthy path that you and your family can sustain for a lifetime.

Part I introduces you to our five principles of Whole Life Nutrition: Quality, Balance, Seasonality, Quantity, and Routine. We'll explore the roots of modern health problems and demonstrate how, when these five principles are applied to your diet and lifestyle, many of the challenges you struggle with can simply vanish. You'll also learn the crucial difference between Standard American Diet (SAD) Eating and Natural Eating and figure out how to transition from one to the other without turning your world upside down. Each chapter begins with a Noteworthy Nourisher, a food we feature for its nutritional benefits that can help you make that transition. Chapter 8 is your practical guide to implementing all the principles. There you'll find simple recommendations, a timeline, and lots of options that can be tailored to whatever works best for your family.

In part II, we set you up with everything you need to make simple, healthy cooking part of your everyday life. We provide a guide to vegetables, grains, beans, and spices that will familiarize you with natural, plant-based foods. There is also a guide to setting up a great pantry, and a descriptive list of key kitchen equipment. The heart of this section is our Mix and Match charts. They are innovative tools to support those of you with little experience in the basics of cooking; they will build your speed, confidence, and intuition in the kitchen. They are also great time-saving alternatives to standard recipes. For more seasoned cooks, the charts provide new ideas for creating simple, palate-pleasing meals, snacks, and sweets.

As you read this book, keep a few things in mind. First of all, you don't have to do everything at once. By making one or two positive changes at a time, and taking it slowly, you'll encounter less resistance and have more success. Also, you know your family better than anyone else. These suggestions have worked well with our children and the families of our clients, but they may not all fit your life perfectly. If a suggestion isn't working, modify it or move on to something else. Creating a healthier lifestyle isn't easy, but it is simpler than you think, and we'll help you all we can in the following chapters. We applaud you for any healthy changes you choose to make. Your family is definitely worth it.

PART I | Whole Life Nutrition

The Big American Picture

Families Under Pressure

A strong family is a national treasure. Families come in all shapes and sizes, and they are the best vehicles we have for raising healthy, vibrant children. It may sound corny, but it's true: children are the future. And in America right now, families are under a tremendous amount of pressure.

In the past, families were founded on marriage, with children raised by two parents and supported by extended family and friends living nearby. Today's family looks very different. More than half of all marriages end in divorce; some couples never marry, and some individuals choose single parenthood. One in three American families is comprised of a child or children with only one parent. Often parents move to follow jobs far away from their birth families, so they are without the support of grandparents, aunts and uncles, or cousins. Instead of living in a close-knit community, many people don't even know the names of their next-door neighbors.

As family structures and our society change, every family member is suffering under levels of pressure never before experienced. Work demands are at an all-time high: people are expected to produce more with less support in less time. Mothers are working *and* managing homes *and* raising families; some fathers are doing this too, and even some grandparents. More is being demanded of school children: they have more structured activities, more academic demands, and less free playtime.

The increasing pressures and pace of family life create significant stress on the mind and body that must somehow be alleviated. Anything that promises to help families get more done in less time, that gives them a moment to relax and put their feet up, is almost irresistible. So it is no surprise that many parents and children are turning to fast food and fast-paced entertainment to help them balance that stress.

Consumers' demand for speed, ease, and stress relief has led to remarkable changes in how they eat, what they buy, and how they use their time. Consider the following:

- People eat out at restaurants more than any other time in the history of modern life.
- Young mothers don't learn how to cook because they don't have to: American grocery stores stock more than 30,000 products, most of them processed, refined foods that require minimal preparation.
- Portion sizes are exploding. The average dinner plate at a typical family restaurant chain today would have fed a family of four fifty years ago. You can buy a 64-oz *single serving* soft drink; that's almost ten times the size of the average soda in the 1950s.

NOTEWORTHY NOURISHER

Pumpkin Seeds

- 1 oz roasted (142 seeds) contains 1 gram of fiber and 148 calories; raw has 153 calories
- Contain high amounts of chlorophyll, zinc, omega-3 fatty acids, and carotenoids
- Have a bittersweet flavor
- Are great for snacking, especially as an alternative for those who are allergic to nuts
- Contain mostly monounsaturated fat, which does not raise blood cholesterol
- Boil raw, unhulled seeds for 5 minutes, then roast or lightly pan-fry seeds during the Halloween season to get the most out of your pumpkin
- Roasting raw pumpkin seeds removes any harmful *E. coli* bacteria from their surface

- Cable and satellite TV and radio provide hundreds of channels of programming.
- iPods can hold several TV episodes so people can watch *CSI* on a 2-inch screen whenever they have a two-minute break.
- The Internet allows anyone to access an infinite amount of information instantaneously.

All these changes in food and entertainment technology feed the modern need for stress relief and speed.

Kids' Health Epidemic

Let's look at other developments that have taken place as life has gotten busier. The prevalence of overweight and obesity in US children has *quadrupled* since the 1960s. According to recent data from the US Centers for Disease Control and Prevention, 32 percent of American children between the ages of two and nineteen years are overweight; about half of those (16 percent) are obese.[1] *That's more than 23,500,000 kids.*

American kids are getting fatter every day. The problem isn't just weight, either; there is also an alarming increase in type 2 diabetes, even in the very young. This disease was called "adult-onset" diabetes for a long time because it was seen only in older generations. Today, however, adolescents and even some preadolescents are being diagnosed with it. According to the American Academy of Pediatrics, the prevalence of type 2 diabetes newly diagnosed in children jumped from less than 5 percent before 1994 to 30 to 50 percent since then.[2] Today's children are also at risk for other "adult" imbalances that go along with being overweight, such as hypertension and elevated levels of triglycerides and LDLs (the "bad" cholesterol). This was almost unheard of in our youth population even twenty years ago.

American children are among the first generation in modern history that will likely have shorter life spans than their parents. This is shocking. No one wants these health problems for their children, so how on earth did it get so bad? The connection between the advent of the high-pressure American lifestyle and the decline of our children's health is not coincidental. As families have become busier, their quality of food, exercise, sleep, and self-care has decreased. It used to be that the cheapest and easiest food was the healthiest, but now the opposite is true: too much inexpensive, fast, and processed food is harming our children It used to be that family home entertainment involved the whole family and was truly entertaining. Now it keeps kids inside, sitting on their butts in front of the TV or video games. Sadly, in the health of this generation of children, we now see the results.

Overindulging in quick and easy "junk" food and "junk" entertainment has become a favorite escape from modern-day stress for both kids and parents. But this collective "solution" isn't working. It's actually adding to the pressure by making everyone slower, heavier, and sicker. We call this new problem the Standard American Diet (SAD) Lifestyle.

The SAD Lifestyle is one that includes:
- Fast food, junk food, family-style restaurant food, or processed store-bought food as regular sources of nourishment
- Screen entertainment (television, DVDs, computer time, video games) as a significant part of every day
- Stress as a regular part of daily life

The SAD Lifestyle is missing:
- High-quality, natural foods as the foundation of the daily diet
- Ongoing healthy lifestyle practices (getting enough sleep, exercise, play, relaxed family time, etc.)
- Daily structure or routines for those practices

How Did We Get Here?

The negative long-term effects of passively indulging in the SAD Lifestyle have crept up on us slowly. Although there are reports in the media about the epidemic of childhood obesity and the increase in lifestyle illnesses that go along with it, much of the nation is still unaware of the depth or seriousness of the problem.

The situation is like that of the frog and the boiling water. If you drop a frog into a pot of boiling water, it will sensibly jump right out. But if you put it into cold water and heat the water very slowly, it will stay in and eventually get cooked. Right now, America is a nation of such frogs: unknowingly getting cooked by junk food because we haven't noticed that the diet-related health crisis is heating up to a dangerous degree.

America has been in this situation before, with the smoking crisis of thirty years ago. Eating lots of junk food today, like smoking cigarettes thirty years ago, is accepted and not considered a cause for alarm. This acceptance is deeply entrenched in our culture and will require a long-term, comprehensive approach to change the cultural tide, similar to the approach taken to curb smoking.

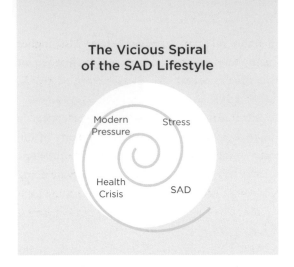

**The Vicious Spiral
of the SAD Lifestyle**

Modern Pressure

Stress

Health Crisis

SAD

Early advertising touted smoking as a healthy activity. Maybe you've seen one of those older ads: someone on a mountain talking about how he never would have made it to the top without the help of his trusty cigarette! It took a long-term, exhaustive campaign by national and state health departments to convince the American public that smoking was truly unhealthy and to "kick the habit." That campaign continues today with a multilayered effort to discourage kids from taking up smoking in the first place.

As with smoking cigarettes in the past, people today are consuming a lot of manufactured food products without fully understanding their effects. In part, that responsibility should be taken up by corporations and the government to ensure that foods on the market are truly safe and healthy. But to a larger extent, this is a matter of education. *Many American families simply are not aware of the fundamental connection between what they eat, how much they eat, and their health and well-being.* So many of the illnesses faced by American children are essentially diseases of food and lifestyle. But some parents still think, "What's the harm in

a Happy Meal?" They do not deeply consider what they feed, or do *not* feed, to their kids because they don't understand the health effects.

Other parents out there *are* aware of the impact diet and lifestyle has on their kids, but they feel a sense of powerlessness or hopelessness about the situation. Perhaps you *know* that your children are unhealthy or overweight, but you believe that because you are overweight, or because your parents were, that your kids are doomed to the same condition: "There's nothing I can do, so why try?" Or you may feel isolated and overwhelmed when faced with trying to make changes in your family's health, especially after years of being stuck on the SAD Lifestyle treadmill.

You have more power than you know. The fact is that nearly all of the health problems we have mentioned are reversible, or can be alleviated by making some basic changes in the ways you nourish yourself, move your body, and help your kids do the same.

We definitely don't want to sound fatalistic here; national consciousness *is* rising, and the tide is starting to turn. It is possible to turn our kids' health crisis around and to make healthier diets and lifestyles an important national priority. Just take a look at the smoking issue. In many states it is now illegal to smoke inside any public buildings; there are ongoing lawsuits against tobacco companies; and smoking is much less socially acceptable than it was in the past. In the same way, the hazards of the SAD Lifestyle can be recognized and reversed.

The fact that you picked up this book is a good sign. You must know something is out of balance and want to make some changes. You are not alone. Many families are starting to think differently about food and lifestyle choices. With a gradual and sustained effort, you can make changes that will dramatically improve the quality of your family's health and daily life. This book will show you how.

We don't pretend that these changes are easy. It's going to take hard work on your part. Your family's health is not the responsibility of schools or the government or advertisers in the media—it is yours. Those institutions are probably not going to help you—they may even resist you. But you can do it. The real question is, what do you want your family's life and health to look like a year from now? The next year is going to pass anyway, right? On your next birthday you will be one year older, whether you and your family are in the same "SAD state," worse, or improving. Why not go for it?

Whole Life Nutrition: An Alternative to the SAD Lifestyle

This book offers an antidote to the SAD Lifestyle: Whole Life Nutrition. This is a holistic approach to nourishing your family's bodies and minds in a way that is more in tune with the natural rhythms of life. It allows your family to enjoy the conveniences and pleasures of modern life in a balanced way, while reconnecting with simple foods and tried-and-true practices that have kept humans healthy throughout time.

The wonderful thing about the Whole Life Nutrition approach is that, although it takes deliberate effort and investment (which can be hard to muster if you have an overly busy life), it will pay for itself, and more, in the long run. Implementing new routines now might take extra time and organization, but you'll be rewarded with a healthier and

therefore more manageable life later. Also, higher quality food might cost more, but you'll save a lot over time in doctor bills, chiropractors, sleep aids, and diet pills.

If you make the effort to change, you'll not only improve your family's health and quality of life right now, but you'll also help prevent the development of disease later. Not enough families are doing this yet, so your children will likely be among the healthiest in their adult peer groups, and thus even more important to our future.

This book represents our effort to share an approach that has helped our own families and our clients meet today's challenges with success. But we recognize that your family is unique and that no one has perfect solutions for what families face. We are all in process, all working together on the problem. For this reason, Whole Life Nutrition is a flexible approach; we encourage you to dive in and experiment with our suggestions yourself and to see what works best for you.

You Are Not Alone

We want you to know that you are not alone. Here are some stories from dedicated parents who have made positive changes in their families' lives using the Whole Life Nutrition approach.

- Sally, an overworked and overweight mother of three rambunctious boys, felt her eating and her children's behavior were completely out of control. "I'm so scared they are going to end up fat like me!" Simply by restructuring her day to include a regular schedule of mealtime, bath time, and bedtime routines, Sally cut down the "whine time" that was the theme of all her evenings to almost nothing. Her stress levels decreased radically as her children became more deeply rested and their frantic, oppositional behaviors calmed down a little. It became much easier for her to "get her face out of the chip bag" in the late evenings, and her weight gradually began to decrease.

- A couple of young professional parents with two "very finicky" girls (a toddler and a preschooler) came looking for help. They wanted to get their children to start eating vegetables and to boost their own energy levels. Mom "wasn't much of a cook" and lacked confidence in the kitchen, so she often resorted to feeding her family with restaurant food and prepackaged meals. After being walked through some basic cooking techniques, and educated about the less familiar whole foods such as grains, greens, and beans, both parents began experimenting with creating home-cooked meals. As their cooking

Imbalances Caused by the SAD Lifestyle

Here are some typical symptoms of the SAD Lifestyle seen in children and adults. Note that other factors and situations can produce these symptoms; whenever you have a health concern, you should see your doctor.

- Craving all forms of sugar, including all of the white foods such as alcohol and simple carbohydrates
- Regularly craving salty foods such as chips, pretzels, nachos, etc.
- Regularly craving fatty foods such as pizza, french fries, ice cream, etc.
- Feeling hungry even when your belly is full
- Frequently asking for juice boxes or soda (children)
- Alternating between eating or craving salty and sweet snacks
- Preferring sweet and salty tastes over all others
- Disliking vegetables
- Experiencing mood swings or "crashing" if you go too long without food
- Having behavior meltdowns when meals are late (children)

- Feeling shaky or irritable if a meal is late (adults)
- Feeling lethargic
- Wanting to eat or snack late into the night
- Not feeling hungry in the morning: wanting to skip breakfast
- Experiencing irregular elimination, especially constipation
- Having brittle or dry hair, skin, and nails
- Having poor skin or frequent breakouts
- Having a pasty or sallow skin color
- Being overweight or obese
- Experiencing chronic low energy or burning out quickly when playing
- Preferring sedentary activities over physical ones
- Preferring "screen time" to any other form of entertainment
- Erratic sleep patterns, such as difficulty falling asleep or waking up
- Needing stimulants to get going in the morning or alcohol to relax at night (adults)
- Having tension headaches
- Having poor attention spans

confidence grew, they brainstormed many ways to make vegetables more appetizing to their girls, as well as many methods for "sneaking the veggies in." In time, both girls were eating a much wider variety of healthy vegetables, often without even knowing it! The parents found their energy improved to such a degree that they were both able to reduce their heavy caffeine habits.

- Another overweight mother working with the principles of Whole Life Nutrition helped her young daughters learn to tune in to their bodies' hunger cues for guidance about their food choices and portion control. She delightedly reported that, after checking whether her daughter was "truly hungry again—dinner was just an hour ago," her daughter thought about it and said, "Actually Mommy, I'm hungry for bed!"

- Maria, a busy, working mother of four, needed guidance about how to improve her children's diets, especially those of the teenagers. Maria had a very healthy diet herself and was a competitive athlete. She also had a job that would sometimes keep her away from home in the afternoons and evenings for hours at a time, even overnight. She was worried that her children, without enough supervision, were starting to eat too much "junk" on a regular basis. Maria gradually transformed her pantry from a junk-food warehouse to a storeroom of delectable, high-quality snack and meal choices. By slowly increasing the quality of the foods she was offering her kids, she found that their palates began to change, and their cravings for the overly salty and sweet foods on which they had been bingeing decreased. She also got two of them very interested in cooking, and eventually they took over half of the evening meal preparation for the family!

As the authors of this book, we are with you in your everyday struggles to lead a healthier life. We don't have it all figured out ourselves. We work daily on our own challenges within our own families, learning as we go. But we deeply believe in the power of American families to heal themselves, and we have committed our professional lives to supporting that effort. Families are precious. They are a vital part of the American culture. They help us pass on the things that are most important: love, values, traditions, and dreams. By nourishing your family well, you will help create a rich and vibrant future for everyone.

Top Takeaways

- Many people are caught in the spiral of the SAD Lifestyle, characterized by poor-quality food and too much screen time, which increases rather than alleviates stress on families.
- America's children are getting heavier and sicker every day; it's time to work hard to relieve the extra stress imposed by the SAD Lifestyle.
- The Whole Life Nutrition approach can help parents restore health and vitality to their families' lives.
- It's up to parents to take on the challenge to make changes. With a collective, determined effort, parents can make a difference in our future.

FOR YOU

- Are you or your kids under a lot of pressure at home, at work, or from school?
- How do you manage your stress right now?
- How often do you eat fast food each week? How about at "family style" restaurants such as Applebee's or 99 Restaurant?
- Do you know how much TV your kids watch each day? How much time do they spend on the computer?
- Is your family living the SAD Lifestyle?
- What is one activity that is not food-related and not passive you could start doing as a family right now to decrease some of the stress you feel?

FOR YOUR KIDS

- Ask your children if they feel pressured by anything at home or at school and really listen to their answers. Don't be judgmental or impose consequences for what they say.
- Ask them what they like to do for fun. You might think you already know this, but you may hear something that surprises you.
- Ask them what they like best about watching TV and using their computers. With them, start to brainstorm a list of ways for them to get similar kinds of pleasure and benefits in other, more active ways.

The SAD Eater versus the Natural Eater

Whole Life Nutrition principles rest on a single, simple premise: you, as a human being, are an animal, and like an animal you have a body that has an inherent and beneficial synchronicity with its habitat, the natural world. It might be a little shocking to think of yourself as an animal, but an animal you are. (Of course, if you have, say, a ten-year-old son, the animal thing might make a lot more sense.)

Human beings (and their domesticated pets and livestock) are the only animals that no longer live their lives and eat their food in alignment with the natural world. We have built a "world within our world," placing cultural and technological barriers between ourselves and nature. Americans' growing lifestyle and health problems (which we now see the world over, especially in technologically advanced nations) have their origins in this basic separation from nature's rhythms and riches.

From this perspective it's very easy to understand why some children are so unwell. What do you think would happen to the fox population if you fed them Sour Patch Kids instead of mice? Would you feed a camel two mocha lattes and a Dunkin' Donuts croissant and expect it to make a long trek across the desert?

Humans are not foxes or camels, you might argue. But we ask you: what animal *would* thrive while continually eating these kinds of foods? The answer is: no animal would, including the human one. Perhaps because the human animal is so amazingly adaptable to all kinds of foods and conditions, because people can and do eat things such as Sour Patch Kids, we have made the simple mistake of thinking that those kinds of foods can replace what we're actually *designed* to eat—namely, plants and animals. In this country especially, people don't yet truly believe that they are suffering significant ill effects from eating these nonfood foods.

It's really only been in the past thirty years or so that humans have even been *producing* things such as Sour Patch Kids. Fifty years ago, most Americans ate primarily whole, natural, minimally processed foods that were growing in season. Fifty years before that, they generally slept when the sun was down and woke when the sun came up. In the colder winter months

Collard Greens

- 1 cup cooked greens contains 5 grams of fiber and has 49 calories
- 1 cup cooked greens contains 226 mg of calcium (almost as much as cows' milk: 210 to 301 mg per 8-oz serving)
- 1 cup cooked greens contains 38 mg magnesium; magnesium helps regulate sleep patterns and stress in the body
- Are high in chlorophyll, and the highest leafy-green source of omega-3 fatty acids (alpha-linoleic acid)
- Are high in iron, which enriches the blood and helps treat anemia
- Are high in antioxidants: vitamins C and E, and beta-carotene
- Are high in the trace mineral manganese, which helps the body activate and utilize vitamin C
- Are high in folate, vitamin B6, riboflavin, and niacin, which helps decrease high cholesterol
- Are high in vitamin A and zinc, which boost the immune system
- Are high in sulforaphane, which aids in special protection for those with colon cancer
- Benefit the liver with a high concentration of pro-vitamin A, which is essential for the correct metabolism of protein
- Are a member of the brassica family—collards contain glucosinolates, which seem to be cancer preventive
- See page 139 for more about collard greens

they stayed mostly indoors and did less, and were more active when it was warmer outside, just like all the other (diurnal) mammals living around them. In short, people used to live more in synch with the natural world, just as all animals are designed to do.

The Natural Eater

Before processed foods dominated the dinner table, before daily routines were dictated by the corporate treadmill and TV schedules, people's eating habits reflected their close connection with nature. In fact, until about fifty years ago, the norm in this country was to be what we call a "Natural Eater." There are some Natural Eaters still around today, though they are a rare breed. What does life as a Natural Eater look like? Here's an example:

Meet Jane: her mom had a balanced constitution and a healthy pregnancy. She was a Natural Eater herself and provided for all of Jane's fetal nutritional needs. After Jane made her grand entrance, her mother *still* continued to eat well; her foods, moods, breathing, and movement provided abundant nutritional, physical, and emotional nourishment for both mother and child. Jane was breast-fed when she was hungry and allowed to stop when she was satisfied. She was gradually weaned off breast milk, on her own timing, and was offered a variety of healthy foods, beginning with very simple staples that her small body could digest easily, such as rice cereal. (This is a great "recipe" for growing a human being who will naturally eat to stay healthy throughout life. Children born like this, who are offered a variety of whole natural foods that are mostly prepared at home, will usually grow up to be Natural Eaters.)

As an adult, Jane hears her body's internal cues and heeds them automatically. When she is hungry, she'll eat; when thirsty, she'll drink. When she is satisfied, she will stop eating. Jane will naturally migrate toward certain foods at certain times, unconsciously led by her body's subtle desires for certain elements of different foods. She might be a natural seasonal eater, tending toward heavier, warming foods in the fall and winter, more greens in the spring, and fresh berries in the summer.

Natural Eaters like Jane tend to be in generally good health, with a good temperament, and they usually have a healthy weight. They eat intuitively, maintaining the health of their slender bodies without having to consider a lot of external eating guidelines. Though you may know some people like this, you probably don't know many. But if you do meet one, it can be very enlightening to follow him around for a while and watch him eat.

That's right: stare unabashedly at the Natural Eaters as they are offered food, or as they prepare food and eat. Chances are you will see them do things like this: breathe and talk before they take their first bite at a meal, pause between bites, leave some things on their plate, or maybe even turn down dessert *without seeming to care that much about it!* Or perhaps they'll say, "Oh, it's chocolate soufflé, my very favorite!" and eat the whole thing without gaining a pound.

Why can Natural Eaters delve into that heavy dessert without consequences? In the weeks leading up to that dessert and the days directly following, *the Natural Eater intuitively eats in a way that balances the extra sugar, fat, and calories in the dessert,* allowing her body to assimilate it organically without taking a harsh toll on her system. Jane might eat that soufflé on "girl's night out," but she will usually have eaten a very light lunch earlier in anticipation of a special treat at the gathering. The next day she'll continue to eat lightly, probably avoiding anything oily or sugary to help her body restore its natural healthy equilibrium.

Watch young Natural Eaters, too: these children might eat like they have a hollow leg for several days, and then eat what looks like only a few tablespoons of food at their mealtimes for a week. They might eat all watermelon at breakfast, and then want only the beans at the lunch meal. They may sometimes decline the cake and ice cream at a birthday party, and munch on the carrot sticks instead. (And yet, they seem to be enjoying the party just as much as their friends!) As we will explain in more detail later, these children are following their natural internal cues about what nutrition and how much of it their body needs.

If you are very lucky, perhaps you were born as a Natural Eater, and then raised to keep it up. In that case, you can follow the simplest guidelines: the signals sent by your own body. You don't need a diet book, or any nutritional book to guide your eating. But today, Natural Eaters are the exception rather than the rule. In the past fifty years, the state of our national nutritional health has been declining at a rapid pace, and happy, Natural Eaters have become fewer in number.

The rest of us, those who are *not* Natural Eaters, are also guided by signals from our bodies: hungers, cravings, etc. But these internal cues no longer necessarily point us in the right direction. They have been thrown off balance by the overconsumption of sugar, salt, unhealthy fats, and chemicalized foods, all of which interfere with our digestion, metabolism, and entire chemical makeup. Eating the Standard American Diet (SAD), including those

Sour Patch Kids, is not only less "natural" itself, but it also prevents us from being the happy, Natural Eaters we were designed to be.

The SAD (Standard American Diet) Eater

There are so many Americans out of balance now that we have literally become a nation of SAD Eaters. Here's one you might know:

Meet Joe, a typical SAD Eater. Joe is nine years old and fairly thick around the middle. He was a thin toddler, but started to put on extra weight when he was about four years old. When Joe wakes up in the morning, he's usually not very hungry. But if his mom offers him Cap'n Crunch, he'll eat two bowls. His lunch box typically has a pack of Oreo cookies, a soda or a juice box, a mini-bag of potato chips, maybe an apple or an orange, and sometimes a sandwich. The sandwich is always on white bread and is usually peanut butter and jelly or an Uncrustable (premade sandwich "pie" by Smucker's). Joe might trade his apple for a bag of Teddy Grahams, and he usually won't finish his whole lunch. The leftover Teddy Grahams will probably go for a ride in his pocket when the lunch bell rings.

He is famished when he gets home from school and goes right to the fridge for a soda or juice box and a pudding cup because he wants something cold. He doesn't settle down easily to do his homework, preferring instead to play a video game for a while. By 4:30 he is hungry again, and might be getting a little cranky. At dinnertime he'll complain about the meal unless it's a hamburger, chicken nuggets, white spaghetti, a hot dog, or pizza. He'll ignore all the veggies and have extra rolls. He'll ask about dessert before the meal is over. If he stays up late watching TV, he will likely ask for another snack by about 8 P.M.

When Joe gets to his teenage years, he will probably be overweight, but he may be thin if he's growing a lot. His eating routines won't have changed much, except that he'll either pack his own lunch now or buy pizza and Tater Tots in the school cafeteria. He might be able to go for long periods of time without eating much, but he will usually drink sodas or "energy drinks" such as Red Bull throughout the day. When he does eat a meal, he will likely eat to excess, perhaps priding himself on getting through two or three Wendy's combo meals when he goes out with his friends. He might stay up late and in the morning wake with difficulty, and he might start to use coffee to get him through his school day.

As an adult, Joe will definitely be overweight. He will need coffee to get him going in the morning, and maybe a latte around 4 P.M. He will unwind with a few beers every night after work. From time to time he might decide to "get in shape" and buy some kind of weight machine for the house, or join a gym. This kind of weight-lifting phase usually lasts a few days to a few weeks, and then is gradually forgotten. His favorite meals will likely include some kind of red meat or pizza, and he will usually have dessert. He will probably not enjoy vegetables, and will complain when the food is unfamiliar.

Joe will be warned by his doctor that his cholesterol isn't good and told he needs to lose some weight. He will experience chronic bouts of indigestion or constipation, and have a medicine cabinet well stocked with over-the-counter remedies for those annoying problems. Maybe he will be concerned about his weight, but he probably won't

A Word about Emotional Eating

It's important to acknowledge that hunger and cravings are not simply biological functions. Although we tend to think of them as three separate entities, the mind, the body, and the feelings are all deeply interconnected—so much so that it actually makes more sense to think of them as one cohesive system. We call that system the "bodymind."

Many cravings have an emotional basis. Everyone has, at times, eaten food as a substitute for something else the bodymind wants. For instance, if you are feeling really angry, your bodymind might need to "cool down," and so it could send you a craving for ice cream. What does ice cream offer in the feeling-realm? It's sweet, smooth, and cold—all properties that might soothe "hot," disgruntled feelings. So that craving could be more about emotions than about any purely nutritional need. It's important to be aware that some of your intuitive food cravings might be your body's way, or child's body's way, of trying to balance out *emotional* as well as nutritional imbalances.

For a deeper exploration of this issue, see *Rescuing the Emotional Lives of Our Overweight Children: What Our Kids Go Through—And How We Can Help* by Sylvia and Eric Rimm, or *Eating in the Light of the Moon* by Anita Johnston.

really get the relationship between his eating and exercise habits and the risk for heart disease his doctor talks about.

Joe might have chronically low energy and might be slightly depressed. He will be so used to feeling uncomfortable in his body—either due to a digestive complaint, his joints or back hurting, or his belt cutting into his belly all day—that he will look and feel much older than his forty-two years. He might know something is "wrong," but it might be a vague feeling of unease that he isn't sure he can do anything about.

As you can see from the statistics in the SAD Facts list on page 18, many people in this country eat too many extreme foods (foods with added sugars and too much salt, such as poor-quality restaurant food), and not enough of the foods they need, especially vegetables. For most people, eating extreme amounts of salt, sugar, and poor-quality, fatty foods and not enough nourishing foods eventually leads them into the SAD state. When you look at Joe's history and the likely state of his body as an adult, it is easy to understand what's happening to the health of Americans today, and why it has crept up on us so slowly. *The most common health struggles that you and your children may face—overweight, obesity, diabetes, heart disease—are often a direct result of living the SAD Lifestyle.*

From SAD Eater to Natural Eater

About 80 percent of what we do in our health counseling practices is help adults and children such as Joe transform from SAD Eaters into happier, more Natural Eaters like our ancestors of only a few generations back. By aligning their eating with what

SAD Facts

AMERICAN SUGAR INTAKE

In this country, 16 percent of our daily caloric intake comes from added sugars.[1] According to USDA data, between 1994 and 1996, children ages 6 to 11 got more than 18 percent of their total calories from added sugars; between 1996 and 2005, teenagers (ages 12 to 19) got 20 percent of their total daily calories from added sugars; and in 1999, the average teenage boy ate or drank more than 109 pounds of sugar every year.[2]

AMERICAN SODA INTAKE

According to the CDC's 1999–2000 National Health and Nutrition Survey, soda (carbonated soft drinks) is the single most consumed food in the American diet, providing about 7 percent of our total caloric intake.[3] If you include noncarbonated soft drinks, the total rises to 9 percent. In addition, 13 percent of teenagers' daily calories come from sodas and noncarbonated soft drinks. Americans spent $66 billion on sodas in 2004, and billions more on noncarbonated soft drinks. That's about $850 per household, per year.[4] In the past two decades, soda consumption has increased by 300 percent. More than half of our school children drink at least one can of soda every day.[5]

AMERICAN SALT INTAKE

A normal child ages 4 to 8 typically needs about 1,200 mg per day of salt. The average American child consumes at least 2,800 mg per day.[6]

AMERICAN VEGETABLE INTAKE

Researchers estimate that fewer than half of all American children meet the USDA's My Pyramid recommendations for vegetable consumption. The percentages range from 48 percent of children ages 2 to 3 getting their recommended number of servings per day, to only 0.7 percent of teenage boys eating their recommended number of servings. The proportions of older age groups meeting all their My Pyramid dietary recommendations range from 1 to 17 percent. On average, the number of servings of dark green and orange vegetables and legumes consumed is less than one-third of the recommended amounts. The average number of servings of other vegetables is about one-quarter to three-quarters of the recommended amounts. On the other hand, Americans are eating too many starchy vegetables, especially white potatoes: the average number of servings was above recommended levels for 12 out of the 15 groups studied.[7]

AMERICANS EATING OUT

In 1970, Americans spent 26 percent of their food dollars on restaurant meals and other meals prepared outside their homes.[8] That number has risen dramatically since then to the point where Americans spend almost half of their food dollars at restaurants. Almost half of all American adults eat or get takeout at a restaurant every day. Americans over the age of 8 years eat an average of 218 restaurant meals per year. When they're at a restaurant, children eat almost double the number of calories they eat when they're at home. According to Steven Gortmaker, professor of the practice of health sociology at Harvard School of Public Health, on any given day, 30 percent of American children ages 4 to 19 years eat fast food, and older and wealthier children eat even more. Overall, 7 percent of the US population visits McDonald's each day, and 20 to 25 percent eats in some kind of fast-food restaurant.[9]

was growing in nature, and their daily routines with the cycles of the sun and the seasons, our ancestors were able to harness a powerful source of natural health. In our practices, we help our clients realign the routines of their daily lives with the rhythms and foods of the natural world, so they too can access this simple, organic source of health and well-being.

Although it may sound like a challenge, aligning your family's routines with nature actually makes your life simpler. It is like paddling *with* the current: you get farther, faster, with less effort. Most of us spend most of our time paddling upstream, against the natural flow of how our bodies were designed to function: in cooperation with our planet, its climates, and its foods. Going against the stream is much harder and takes much more time, and it's much easier to go off course; this is why staying healthy and keeping your kids healthy "upstream" can be such a struggle. This book is designed to help you end that struggle, turn your boat around, and flow in the direction in which your body really wants to go.

To make it easy to understand, we have boiled down this philosophy into five primary principles:

Quality: The quality of your food directly affects your health. Moving from "wrappers" to real food will help you look better and feel better without necessarily changing the kinds of meals you eat.

Balance: Food can be broken down into five primary components called macro- and micronutrients. Getting a healthy balance of those vital nutrients can release you from a whole host of imbalanced cravings that make it almost impossible to eat in a healthy way.

Seasonality: The foods that grow in each season are a natural tonic for the physical and emotional challenges that come with the changes of season.

Quantity: Understanding the human body and how much fuel it needs at different ages and stages can help guide you to healthier meal sizes and natural portion control.

Routine: Aligning the routines of your eating, sleeping, working, and playing with the natural cycles of the day can restore ease and vibrant energy to everything you do.

Together we call these the Whole Life Nutrition Principles. They are five concepts that promote living in the most health-enhancing way possible, with the least amount of effort. They are simple and cut through the confusing array of trendy nutritional information and diets in the media. In the next several chapters, we will discuss what, how, how much, when, and where to eat using our five basic principles. By following these guidelines you will be able to shift your family from being SAD Eaters to more Natural Eaters.

Top Takeaways

- Humans are animals. Your body is part of the natural world and is meant to thrive on natural foods.
- The health problems of the SAD Lifestyle are relatively recent; until about fifty years ago, people lived and ate very differently than they do now.
- The effects of SAD eating are cumulative, leading to more imbalance, illness, and discomfort over time.
- The five Whole Life Nutrition Principles of quality, balance, seasonality, quantity, and routine can help you harness the power of your body and the natural world to rebalance your health and your life.

FOR YOU

Are you a Natural Eater or a SAD Eater? Consider the following:

- Do you eat based more on internal cues, such as hunger, or more on external cues, such as the clock or an advertisement for a Big Mac?
- Do you stop eating when you feel satisfied, or when the food runs out?
- Can you pass up dessert if it doesn't look delicious or you've had enough to eat? Or do you feel cheated if you don't have anything sweet after a meal?
- Do you like to eat the same foods year-round, or do your tastes and eating habits change with the seasons?

FOR YOUR KIDS

Are your kids Natural Eaters or SAD Eaters? Pay close attention to your children's eating and drinking habits for a week:

- What do they eat and drink each day? When? How much?
- Ask them exactly what they ate or drank while they were away from you at school, too. (Remember: no penalties for total honesty.)
- Do they have any cravings?
- Do you think they eat based on internal or external cues?

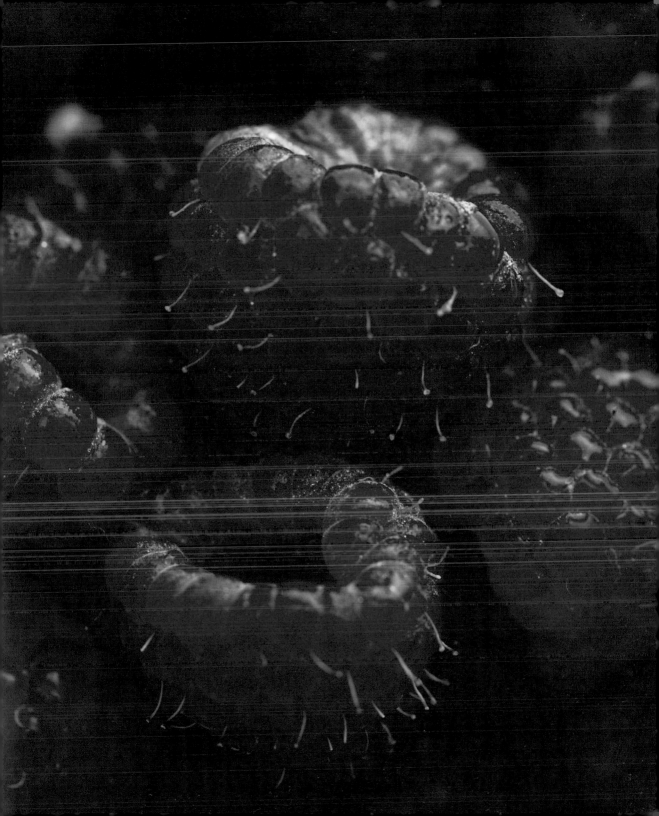

What We Eat: Food Quality

From Wrappers to Real Food

When you consider changing your eating habits, your first thoughts may be about eating more good food, eating less bad food, using power food, avoiding junk food, eating a balance from all of the food groups, etc. In other words, changing the specific foods now in your diet. However, because nutritional science is always changing, and the media continually oversimplifies the latest studies into "sound bites," there are a lot of conflicting messages about what's "good" for you and what's "bad" for you. How do you know what you should be eating? Eggs are "bad": they contain too much cholesterol. Eggs are "good": they are an excellent source of protein. It can get confusing very quickly. Also, calling foods "good" or "bad" sets up a kind of moralistic thinking about food that is even more confusing for kids.

Fortunately, there is a much easier place to begin than changing all the family menus at once, and that is to improve the overall *quality* of the foods you are already eating. By working with your food quality, you won't have to totally overhaul your entire diet, but rather look at the kinds of foods that work well for you and your family and then simply begin to upgrade them.

For us, food of the highest quality has several important characteristics. It is:

- In its original, natural state (or close to it)
- Fresh
- Intact (a "whole" food, minimally processed)
- Organic, or at least not full of a lot of additives and preservatives

Low-quality food, by contrast, is characterized by the opposite qualities. The lowest quality food is:

- Not in its original state, but altered by extreme refinement or processing
- Commercially "prepared" in a way that has compromised its natural vital energy
- Broken down, and its important nutrients stripped away

- Full of unhealthy chemicals, additives, preservatives, or "extreme" salts, simple sugars, or poor quality fats
- Produced through intensive factory farming, grown with harmful pesticides, or the result of damaging food-growing processes

NOTEWORTHY NOURISHER

Agave Nectar

- Has a consistency close to honey but thinner and more easily dissolved, like a combination of maple syrup and honey
- Is harvested from the blue agave or salmiana plants, both desert succulents native to Mexico
- Has a low glycemic load (see chapter 4), so it will not raise blood sugar levels as quickly as other sugars do. For brands that have been certified as low glycemic or safe for diabetics, look for the Glycemic Research Institute's seals
- Different manufacturers have different levels of sweetness. Try various brands to see which ones you like
- Use in baking; as a sweetener in tea, coffee, or iced drinks; or on waffles or pancakes
- When baking, substitute 3/4 cup of agave nectar for 1 cup of sugar, and reduce liquids by 1/4 cup and reduce oven temperature by 25°F

The quality of your food choices, whatever they are, has a direct and sometimes immediate effect on how you feel, think, look, and behave. Imagine two people who are confined to eating only one thing for two weeks: green peas. One of them is given peas from a bulk packing company; the peas are canned in a giant vat with a little salt and a preservative. The second person is allowed to pick her peas from organically grown pea plants on an organic farm at the peak of their growing season.

Nutritional science would have us believe that there is no qualitative difference between the foods in those two scenarios: peas are peas, right? They all have pea vitamins and pea minerals and pea calories, and nothing else much matters. But what do your instincts tell you about how these two folks will fare? How would you feel eating the canned peas day after day? The fresh? Think of the difference between how the two types of peas look: canned peas are a little gray and very uniform; fresh peas are vibrant green and come in all sizes. Canned peas are mushy and taste salty and flat. Fresh peas pop open in your mouth and taste like . . . well, summer: very fresh and sweet.

The canned peas have lost most of their natural life energy. Eventually, they would make you feel like they look: pale and mushy! The fresh peas, picked at the height of their ripeness, however, would be full of vibrant energy from the plant itself. Also, because they could be consumed immediately after harvesting, they would still contain much more of their natural nutrient content. Although you would never want to live on peas alone, you would have more natural energy and feel more satisfied on the fresh peas for a much longer period of time.

Definitely don't try this at home; that's a lot of peas! But really, you do versions of this experiment every day. With each meal you eat, you are choosing high-quality or low-quality foods, and if you pay attention, you can really notice the difference in how those foods make you feel. Jeannette's family members eat high-quality foods most of the time, and they are used to getting a lot of nutritional "bang for the buck" in their regular diet. A few years ago, they took a road trip to Florida and drove for twenty-four hours straight. Have you ever traveled along Route 95 through the East Coast states? Suffice it to say, they didn't find very many health food stores. They never ate so much fast food in their lives. By the end of the trip everyone felt cranky, bloated, and exhausted. If you travel, you have probably experienced some version of this with your family too, right? It can really drive home the impact that high- or low-quality eating can have on how everyone feels.

Imagine for a moment how your family might feel if you all ate primarily fresh, intact organic food on a daily basis. What impact might that have on your children's energy? On their moods? On their weight and overall health? This is the gift of eating higher quality, real food, rather than prepared food in wrappers.

So when you look at the foods in your family's diet, how do you know whether they are high quality? Start with this question: are they *real* foods, from a plant or an animal, in a natural state? If so, you're on the right track. Think of things such as fresh apples, crisp sugar snap peas, a warm bowl of whole grain rice, or a lean cut of fish—all pretty close to how you might find them in nature. Now what about Skittles: a high-quality food? Definitely not: no Skittle trees, right? Skittles are a prime example of a food in a "wrapper." So is a microwaved, fried apple pie from a fast-food drive-thru,

or a frosted Apple Cinnamon Pop-Tart. These products have apples in them, yes, but they're a long way from the tree and are now "wrapper" food.

It can be a real challenge to see through all the exciting advertisements and time-saving promises of "ready to eat" wrapper foods in order to get to higher quality foods for your family. This chapter will help you really understand the difference by exploring three basic distinctions: fresh versus preserved food, whole versus processed food, and organically versus industrially farmed food.

Fresh versus Preserved Food

Dr. Liz Lipsky puts it simply: "The life in food gives us life."[2] The energy in food gives you energy. The fresher a food, the more life energy it contains. When you cut flowers for your mantel, they are vibrant and straight for the first day or two, right? Then the color begins to fade, the stems begin to droop, the leaves rot, and the petals fall off. By the end of the week, the life energy in that plant is basically gone. This is exactly what happens to your food. Eating tired old food makes you feel tired and old!

The sooner something is eaten after it has been harvested, the more life energy and nutrient content it will naturally contain. In our food culture, however, it is extremely difficult to purchase fresh produce (fruits and vegetables) and animal products immediately after they are harvested. Most people in this country get the bulk of their food from the supermarket, and the supermarket gets its food from all over the world. Even if you have local farming in your community, chances are good that the green beans in your grocery store come from a commercial farm in another area of the country, or even another country altogether, rather than from your neighborhood farm!

Because of the commercial food industry and the fact that there are very different growing seasons in different parts of the United States, there is usually a long transit time between a food's harvest and when it reaches your table. Two methods commonly used to preserve the shelf life of fresh produce for months, or even years, are freezing and canning.

FREEZING

Of the two, freezing involves less processing—fewer changes to the original food—so we consider frozen foods to be of higher quality than canned. They are also very convenient: frozen vegetables of all kinds are inexpensive, are readily available, and can be cooked quickly to add to a meal. The highest quality frozen produce is organic with no preservatives, salt, or sugar. (There is a more detailed description of the term *organic* later in this chapter.)

The High Cost of Low Quality

One of the most striking nutritional research projects is the early work of Weston Price in the 1930s. He was a dentist who became interested in the fact that indigenous children's dental health seemed to change radically within one generation of being introduced to a more refined "modern" diet. He embarked on a 100,000-mile journey around the world to study several different native cultures, whose lifestyles had not yet been significantly impacted by what he called the "influence of the white man." He studied people in areas as varied and far apart as Africa, Polynesia, and northern Canada.

Without exception, Price found that the average person in each native group was stunningly healthy in every way. They had fantastic straight teeth with no decay, strong supple bodies, and none of the degenerative "lifestyle" diseases that are so common today. His findings were very different when he studied groups from similar cultures who were less isolated and had access to the "white man's store"—refined trade foods brought in by industrialized societies. These people exhibited the same types of dental decay, immune system weakness, and degenerative diseases that were common in the modern Western cultures.[1]

So what were these native people eating that was making them so healthy? Here's the most interesting part of what Price discovered: the actual diets typical of each culture were as different as they could possibly be: meat-eating, vegetarian, dairy-based, etc. But, without exception, when each of these cultures was exposed to more refined, industrially farmed foods, their health began to disintegrate *within one generation.* The moral of this story is that the "perfect diet" can vary greatly from culture to culture or from person to person, but it almost always includes high-quality natural foods. On the other hand, it does not take long for *poor-quality foods* to rob us of our health. You can read more about Price's work (and see the incredible photographs, too) in his book, *Nutrition and Physical Degeneration.*

SIMPLE FOOD FOR BUSY FAMILIES

The freezing process turns the water in the food to ice, which slows down natural food decay and inhibits bacterial growth. Typically, produce is frozen very soon after harvest, so it's able to retain more of its natural life energy. But you need to keep a frozen food at a temperature of 0°F or lower for the food to remain unchanged. Frozen produce will "keep" in your freezer for months, but if it thaws and refreezes, its texture will be soggy and a little chewy when you cook it—not very appealing. One way to tell whether a frozen food's temperature has been compromised, or it has simply gotten too old, is to check for freezer burn or a thick layer of frosty ice surrounding the fruit or vegetables. Usually, freezer-burned or frosty food is still safe to consume, but its quality and taste will be reduced.

CANNING

Although we consider commercially canned foods to be of lower quality than fresh or frozen foods, canning isn't a bad thing. In fact, it's a real convenience for hardier plants such as beans (most legumes hold their energy and nutrients really well when cooked and stored properly): canned beans can save you several hours of preparation. But in general, canned foods tend to have far less life energy and fewer nutrients than fresh foods do.

Canning vegetables often requires fairly rigorous processing to make the food safe for the consumer to eat months or even years later. Processing can mean many things. Foods may be peeled by a machine using steam or lye. After peeling, food might be boiled at a high temperature with large quantities of salt or other various additives. Corn from a can that you ate last night may have been picked and processed years before you had it for dinner. Indeed, the average shelf life for Libby vegetables is twenty-four to forty-eight months![3]

Again, we want to emphasize that canned vegetables *are not bad for you*, and they are certainly better for you than no vegetables at all! But if you are subsisting on preboiled, chemically peeled vegetables that were picked four years ago, how much "life" can they be giving your body? It is a matter of quality.

Whole versus Processed Food

We hear more and more about whole foods (and whole food diets) lately. Although this concept used to be relegated to bad 1970s food co-ops, in this age of thousands of prepared foods, it is resurfacing as a useful guide for how to eat in a healthier way. What exactly is a whole food? It's simply food that is as close to its intact, natural form as possible. For instance, whole grains are grains that are essentially complete: they contain the original hulls (casings) and germs that grow naturally in the plant. When determining whether or not something is a whole food, consider whether it is intact versus refined and natural versus prepared.

INTACT VERSUS REFINED FOOD

Refined foods are foods that have been broken down by some kind of preparation or packaging process. If you take wheat berries (the whole head of grain from a wheat plant), strip them of their hard outer casings, remove the germ, grind what's left into a powder, and bleach it so it looks snowy white, the result is common white flour. Add back in a few vitamins that have been lost and you can call it "enriched wheat flour," which *sounds* more like a whole food, but really isn't. This white flour is a staple in most American diets, and it is a highly refined food. Here are some other examples of intact foods and their refined counterparts:

INTACT	REFINED
Apple	Apple juice
Oat groats	Instant oatmeal
Pinto beans	Refried beans in a can
Pork chop	Hot dog
Potato	Potato chips
Sugar cane	Powdered sugar
Turkey breast	Turkey jerky or pressed turkey "loaf"
Wheat berries	White flour
Whole brown rice	Instant white rice

There are different degrees of processing. For instance, taking that wheat berry and simply grinding it into a powder without first removing the germ and casings is a form of processing that results in whole wheat flour (also called "stone ground" wheat flour). This product, though processed, is *less* refined than enriched white flour, because more of the whole original plant (and the attendant fiber and nutrients) is present. Therefore it is of higher quality. There are more and more of these "whole wheat" or "whole grain" products available on the market, including breads, pastas, and baking flours.

To eat wheat in its truly whole, totally unrefined state would be to eat the wheat berries. Wheat berries are part of the cereal grains family. (This name refers to the group of grains people typically eat, not just what you have in the morning with milk!) Cereal grains include wheat berries, oat groats, all forms of brown or wild rice, quinoa, millet, amaranth, and many others. (See chapter 12 for descriptions and preparation directions for these grains.) When these grains are whole, they are hard and dry, requiring rinsing, soaking, and usually an extended cooking time before they are digestible. These are not "fast foods"—they require some forethought and advanced preparation if you wish to enjoy them at a meal, but they are excellent sources of high-fiber carbohydrate, some protein, and many vitamins and minerals.

Having companies process those whole grains definitely saves time in the kitchen: no rinsing or presoaking is necessary, and it takes less time to cook milled grains. However, the greater the degrees of processing, the less healthy the food is for you. Take oats, for example: oat groats are the most complete and therefore highest quality version of oats to eat. Crack those hard groats into smaller chunks and you have "steel cut" oats that take less cooking time; press those pieces flat and you have the "rolled oats" that look like what you thought oats actually were. If you break those down even further you get "instant" oatmeal, to which you simply add boiling water and have a bowl of hot cereal in moments.

Once inside your body, those instant oats break down very quickly into glucose (a form of simple sugar) in your blood. Glucose is like our bodies' gasoline, our primary source of energy. The more refined any grain is, the faster it converts into glucose, and the faster it hits your bloodstream. The more "complex" (whole, intact) a grain is, the harder your body has to work to break it down and convert it into sugar, and thus the slower it enters your bloodstream as fuel. In this situation, slower is better: think of whole grains as a gentle IV drip of glucose, providing your body with a gradual, sustained source of energy over time. In contrast, refined grains provide a fast, intense glucose "dump" into your bloodstream, elevating your blood sugar and energy levels briefly, then letting them crash.

When you eat white flour, white rice, white sugar, etc., the sugar (glucose) explodes like a bomb into your system and can put your body into crisis mode. When you eat the less refined versions of the "whites," whole grain pasta, wild rice, sprouted grain bread, etc., you provide your body with gentler forms of sustained energy. So even though oat groats take longer to cook, they are healthier and more energizing over the course of your day than the "instant" oatmeal.

So when you eat processed grains (especially flour products), try to choose the less refined versions. For instance, upgrade from your current white spaghetti to a whole wheat version (or brown rice or quinoa or any of a number of milled *whole* grain pasta products). The flavor is richer and the texture a bit rougher. It can take some getting used to for some family members. Personally, we much prefer the flavor of the whole grain varieties. There are even some products available now that are half white, half whole wheat flour—these could be a good place to begin. You can do the same with your breads: gradually choose less and less refined products until your family is accustomed to the textures of whole grain, or even sprouted whole grain, breads. We have had clients who started with

The Bread Quality Spectrum

Stores carry a full spectrum of breads, from lowest quality to highest quality. Here's the range you might see, along with some common brands.

Organic Sprouted Grain Bread (Ezekiel)

Organic Stone Ground Whole Wheat Bread (Matthew's)

Commercial Whole Wheat Bread (Arnold)

Commercial White Bread (Wonder)

sandwiches of one white slice and one whole wheat slice for their kids!

Also, it is fairly easy to make the switch from white flour to whole grain flours in your baking. The most similar to white in taste and texture is whole wheat pastry flour: it's made from the whole grain of the wheat, but milled very finely so it will behave in a manner similar to that of white flour. We have found it to be virtually interchangeable with white. The end product will be a little denser, but again, with more overall flavor. Another newer product on the market is white wheat whole grain flour. Because the color will be more familiar, this is also a good one to start with, and it is readily available in most supermarkets.

There are several other varieties of grain flours available. Two of our favorites are barley flour and brown rice flour. Many people actually have a mild to moderate sensitivity to wheat itself, so these flours are less likely to affect your body adversely.

Even if you have no problems with wheat, experimenting with different grain flours lends a different taste, texture, and vitamin and mineral "palette" to your cooking. Further, the pizza crusts, breads, and other pastries you can make with them are often more delicate and flavorful than those made from traditional wheat flour. You have to work with these different flours for a while to figure out their different properties for yourself. It can be helpful to work from a recipe specifically calling for a different flour first, before you try substituting it in a recipe that calls for wheat flour, just to get a sense of the right proportions and how to work with it. But, if you don't need to serve your cookies to the president or anything, you can just try switching the flours you use and notice what happens.

NATURAL VERSUS PREPARED FOOD

When you take a whole food in its original state, strip parts of it away, and then grind it up or chemically peel or boil it at very high heat, much of its natural life energy is lost. It also loses much of its original vitamin and mineral content, its flavor, and even its color. After heavy processing, most foods look pale or grayish—not very appealing to the average consumer, especially children! That's where "prepared" foods come in.

Make no mistake, food manufacturers are in business for profit, so they have an interest in making their food products appealing to consumers. How do they make heavily processed foods look appealing? It's pretty simple, really: they add some strong colors and flavors back in! They must also add preservatives to make the food last, because most food production companies couldn't possibly get their foods processed, shipped to grocery shelves, and sold before it decomposes. Enter the chemical, the artificial, the experimental, and the generally scary. The result is shelves and shelves of prepared foods—jars, cans, bags, and boxes of heavily flavored and preserved food products.

This may seem like manufacturing "progress" to some, but it isn't healthy for your body. The lack of fiber and added sweeteners and other nonfood preservatives means these foods also hit your system like a "sugar bomb," just like very refined grains do. This is not a good thing: it can start you on a lifelong negative blood sugar cycle (see chapter 4 for more about this). Plus, these prepared foods contain chemicals that your body neither needs nor knows what to do with.

Do yourself a favor: go find that box of snacks that your kids beg for—we'll probably get into trouble if we mention any specific companies here, but you are likely familiar with many of them, and probably have at least some of their products in your pantry. Read the ingredients list of one such product. Read the whole thing. It's long, isn't it? Why is it so long? When you make cookies from scratch, the ingredients list is about six items long, including all the spices. But what are all those ingredients at the end of the list on the package? Can you even pronounce those words?

The number of additives and preservatives in our food is astounding. How do we know what they are and whether they are safe? Every food product that goes on the market in this country has to be approved as safe for human consumption by the federal Food and Drug Administration (FDA)— and we're glad there is an agency like that in place. But don't depend entirely on the FDA; use a little common sense of your own. For example, what exactly is tartrazine? Does it grow on a tree? Did it even exist fifteen years ago? Tartrazine gives food a yellow color. It's a coal-tar derivative, not even *from* a food. Do you think it's a good idea to put that into your children's growing bodies on a regular basis? These kinds of chemical additives and preservatives are a relatively recent phenomenon in the food industry, and there's not a lot of data on their long-term impact on health, especially children's health. The FDA makes sure that the product won't kill your child, but it doesn't check thoroughly for its impact on things such as mood, weight, energy level, and attention span. It is up to parents to regulate how many of these chemicals go into their kids' bodies.

Chemical and artificial colors, flavors, and preservatives aside, what *else* gets added to those processed and prepared foods? They usually include an excess of one or more of these three ingredients: salt (otherwise known as sodium), sugar (otherwise known by many names—see the chart on page 32 for some of them), and poor-quality fat (otherwise known as hydrogenated or partially hydrogenated oil: trans fats).

Americans are known for their love of salty and sweet foods. Many don't seem to know that there are any other flavors! And fat has two special properties: it carries the odors and flavors of a food, and it triggers the brain's satisfaction center. Put these

DID YOU KNOW?

Additives and Preservatives

More than 14,000 man-made chemicals are added to the American food supply today.[4] Many of these "additives" are perfectly safe. A few of them are simply vitamins and minerals that can help us meet our daily nutrition requirements. That's usually what a food label means if it says "enriched," as in "enriched wheat flour"—micronutrients have been added. But many additives have no nutritionally redeeming value at all and some may even be detrimental to your health. The additive category that is the trickiest is the preservatives. Preservatives are used the most in the lowest quality foods.

Nitrates, in particular, are harmful. Nitrates convert into nitrites, and when nitrites combine with certain compounds in the stomach, they can form nitrosamines, which were found to cause cancer in laboratory rats. Nitrates are used in processed red meat such as salami, bologna, and hot dogs. They are not used in processed white meat, so if your choice is between processed red or white meat, go for the white.

According to the American Institute for Cancer Research, eating more fruits and vegetables rich in vitamins C and E helps reduce the formation of nitrosamines. Avocado and dark green leafy vegetables have high amounts of vitamin E. Citrus fruits, tomatoes, and broccoli are a few sources of vitamin C.

The Center for Science in the Public Interest recommends avoiding these additives in particular: sodium nitrate, saccharin, caffeine, olestra, acesulfame K, and artificial coloring. Additional information about some of the additives is available at www.cspinet.org.[5]

three elements all together and presto, you have a food "drug": a sugar or salt "injection" transported by fats directly to the pleasure and satisfaction centers of your brain.

This extreme flavor "pop" is especially exciting to children, who are already naturally attracted to sweet tastes. And it more than makes up for the bland, lifeless quality of the processed food itself. Add a few bright, eye-catching artificial colors, and you've got yourself a winner with the twelve-and-under crowd. Run some fun, attention-grabbing advertisements for it several hundred times during their favorite TV programs and that apple and peanut butter snack you're offering will have a heck of a time competing.

Eventually, over time, continual ingestion of extreme salts, sugars, and fats will change the palate of a child, or an adult, for that matter. By comparison, whole foods will begin to taste bland, and the other flavors that occur naturally in real food (the bitter, pungent, sour, or astringent tastes) will seem unpleasant. In a fairly short amount of time, vegetables of all kinds can become completely unpalatable to your child. In fact, when parents come to us with children who "don't like any vegetables," the first thing we ask is how much sugar and/or processed foods they eat. Many more times than not, we hear that they have grown up on highly processed foods such as juice boxes or sodas, processed snacks, cereals, candies, frozen dinners, and restaurant "kids' meals"—all of which provide the kind of notorious sugar-salt-fat "injection" that we are discussing here. Does this diet sound familiar? That's right. It's the SAD kids raised on this low-quality diet who can easily develop one or more related imbalances (what we call SAD imbalances) that lead to health problems such as imbalanced blood sugar, constipation, and even obesity. (See chapter 4 for specific information about the SAD imbalances.)

To restore health and balance, parents need to help their kids wean off these prepared food "drugs." Although it's definitely easier to train the palate of a young child than to change the tastes of an older child, with patience and gradual adjustments, it can be done. Once your children get a good foundation of higher quality, fresh whole foods in their diets, their tastes will begin to adjust. You will see a slow but steady improvement in their taste buds as they grow older. Eventually, as their palates rebalance, they may even begin to make some healthier food choices on their own.

Organically versus Industrially Farmed Food

One of the nicest benefits of increasing the quality of your food by switching from conventionally farmed foods to organically farmed ones is that organic food tastes better. The fruit tastes sweeter, the meat tastes richer, and the vegetables taste more like vegetables and less like water. A palate that has been bombarded with extreme salts and sugars may respond to organic produce better than less tasty industrially farmed produce. The subtle sweetness of a bright orange carrot or sweet potato, or the natural saltiness of raw celery, *will* come through more strongly in organic as opposed to nonorganic versions of these vegetables.

Organically farmed foods are foods grown without synthetic pesticides, herbicides, growth aids, fertilizers, or feed. They are not allowed to be irradiated, and may not contain any ingredients from a genetically modified plant. You can feed them to your children without any worries about potential

Identifying Organic Foods[13]

The United States Department of Agriculture (USDA) has identified four categories of organic food based on percentage of organic content, and has developed guidelines for manufacturers to use in labeling their foods as organic. The USDA Organic Seal began appearing on shelves in October 2002. The USDA's categories of "organic" and labeling guidelines are as follows:

100 Percent Organic: When 100 percent of a product's ingredients are organic, the packaging may display the USDA Organic Seal on the front.

Organic: When at least 95 percent of a product's ingredients are organic by weight (excluding water and salt), the packaging may display the USDA Organic Seal.

Made with Organic: When at least 70 percent of a product's ingredients are organic, the packaging may display the phrase "Made with Organic," followed by up to three specific ingredients. Such products may not display the USDA Organic Seal.

Products with less than 70 percent organic content may list organic ingredients on the side panel, but not on the front of the package. Such products may not display the USDA Organic Seal.

Upgrading Restaurant and Takeout Options

When upgrading your food, it is obviously much easier to do "quality control" when you make it at home. But the truth is, you are not going to forego all fast food and family restaurants forever. You can do a little damage control by following a few principles:

- Always make the highest quality food choices possible: if there's organic or fresh food available, choose it over processed food.
- Add some fiber: choose a whole grain bun or whole grain rice. If possible, add beans to your meal.
- If you can't avoid processed carbohydrates, add some protein: add a chicken breast, a few shrimp, or a hard-boiled egg.

- Include plenty of vegetables: add a salad, choose a vegetarian option, or get a side of steamed veggies.
- Avoid fried foods: choose baked, steamed, or broiled instead.
- Avoid heavy sauces, which can be loaded with sugar and poor-quality fat: ask for the hamburger or veggies plain, without the extra sauce.
- Limit your portions of low-quality foods: choose only one fried or sweet item. Tell your children they can have a small portion of fries *or* a small milk shake, not both. If you are eating a meal high in sugar, salt, or fat, drink water or milk instead of soda. Or offer the option of a small soda *or* dessert, not both.

problems from chemical additives or treatments. Organic farmers work hard to keep their soil rich and balanced, using methods such as actual tilling and crop rotation. As a result, the produce and animals raised organically are in a more natural state and thus often richer in nutrients than their industrially farmed counterparts.

Organic produce generally has better natural color and is somewhat smaller in size. It may also have a flaw or two in its color or shape. This is because it hasn't been genetically engineered for enormous size and uniformity, or coated with chemicals to keep pests away. Its naturally bright colors indicate freshness and the presence of better flavors and more micronutrients (vitamins and minerals).

In this country, we have national standards for organic foods (also just called "organics"). The standards were developed by the National Organic Standards Board, a team including representatives from the farming, processing, retail, and science industries, as well as environmentalists, all appointed by the United States Department of Agriculture (USDA). These standards were first established in the Organic Foods Production Act (OFPA) in 1990[12] and they help regulate which foods can legally be called organic and which cannot.

UNDERSTANDING INDUSTRIAL FARMING

Produce that is not organic is typically called "conventional" or "industrially farmed." Most of the meats and produce sold in the big supermarket and grocery store chains in this country are products of large-scale, industrial farming. If you ask your children to describe a farm, you'll probably get something like Old MacDonald's place with a cow here and a chicken there. It's a romantic and old-fashioned image. The truth of the matter is that modern industrial farming, especially intensive farming, is a long way from E-I-E-I-O.

Today, most farmers grow monocrops or raise one type of animal—that is, they produce as much of one plant or animal as possible, as quickly as possible, at the lowest possible cost. As a result, produce, meat, and other animal products from industrial farms are of lower quality than those of smaller organic farms.

Industrially farmed produce is typically fed powerful chemical fertilizers so strong that plants can be grown unnaturally close together. They don't need as much sunlight because they are getting so much "fuel" from the fertilizer. The same crops are grown repeatedly in the same soil, fertilized anew each time. As a result of being grown in overused soil, these crops are nutrient deficient.

These crops are also routinely treated with multiple chemical pesticides and herbicides to reduce crop loss from insects and disease. Many of the chemicals remain in the skins of the produce, even after they are well washed. As a result, people consume those chemicals. The Environmental Working Group, a nonprofit watchdog organization, maintains a list of the "Dirty Dozen": the twelve foods with the highest pesticide content. It is best to buy those foods organic if possible. Consumers can download the list at www.foodnews.org/walletguide.php.

Industrially farmed meat comes from animals that are raised indoors with no sunlight, in close, confined quarters, often without enough space even to turn around. The nutrients in the eggs, milk, and meats from these animals have largely been added by artificial means, rather than cultivated naturally by providing the animal with a healthy diet and exposure to the sun.

These animals are routinely fed foods their bodies were never designed to eat. Industrial cattle eat grain, not grass, and it damages their digestive systems, creating health problems that require antibiotics and other medicines. People consume those additives through eggs, milk, and meat, along with unnatural levels of adrenalin and other hormones produced by animals' bodies in response to stresses in their lives and deaths.

We think it's pretty clear that organics are much healthier, higher quality foods to be feeding your children. But we understand that it can be challenging for a parent to switch from industrially farmed foods to organic foods. Although most supermarkets do offer organic foods now, the selection is generally smaller than the conventionally farmed offerings, and the cost is a little higher. But there has been progress already, as consumers become more interested in organics for their flavor and health benefits. And in this consumer-driven society, product availability usually follows popular demand. Fifteen years ago you would have had a hard time finding organic sections in the larger supermarket chains, but today even Wal-Mart is going organic. This is the food industry responding to consumers' shopping habits.

We believe that it is worth it to pay a little more for more natural, high-quality foods, not only because of the myriad health benefits for your family, but also to keep steady pressure on the food industry to continue making positive changes.

Top Takeaways

- Replacing highly processed, poor-quality "wrapper" foods with fresh, high-quality foods will give you and your family more vitality and a healthier nutritional base.
- Real food that is healthiest for your family usually doesn't come in brightly designed boxes, bags, cans, or plastic wrappers.
- Shop the outside aisles of your supermarket, where the produce is located, for the real food.
- Improve your family's health by serving higher quality versions of what they already eat: sandwiches, spaghetti, whatever!
- If you wean your and your family's bodies off highly processed foods, your systems will come into better balance—real food will start tasting better than junk food.
- Protect your kids' health by reading labels, following news about food quality, and learning where your food comes from.

FOR YOU

- What is one junk food item in your pantry that you could throw out today and never buy again?
- What is one "treasured" junk food that you could painlessly replace with a higher quality version the next time you go shopping?
- Which fresh food will you try this week?

FOR YOUR KIDS

- Tell them they deserve good-quality food.
- Tell them that good vegetables taste much better than the ones at the school cafeteria.
- Tell them that their taste buds will change as they grow and their diet improves, so they should keep trying different veggies, even if they think they don't like them.
- Get them to help you peel and wash any fruit or vegetables you use in meals this week.
- Play the vegetable or fruit game with younger kids: name a vegetable or fruit, then have your child take a turn, then take a turn yourself, and so on until one of you can't think of any more. (This is a simple way to broaden children's knowledge of vegetables.)
- Ask your kids to read out loud the ingredient list of the worst processed foods in your pantry. Ask them what some of those ingredients are—are they food?

Genetically Modified Foods[14-15]

In the mid-1990s the first crops of genetically modified (GM) food plants were put on the market for human consumption. GM foods are plants (or animals) that have had their DNA structure deliberately altered in some way to cultivate, strengthen, or weaken a particular trait, such as resistance to cold or certain pests. The most common way food plants are genetically modified is with the introduction of genetic material from a separate organism into the plant, also known as transgenics, biotech, or bioengineering.

Since that time, more than fifty different GM plant foods have been introduced into our food stores. The food crops with the highest percentages of genetically modified versions are soybeans, corn, and cotton. The use of soybean oil, corn syrup, and cottonseed oil is so prevalent that *the Grocery Manufacturers of America estimates that between 70 and 75 percent of all processed foods available in US grocery stores may contain ingredients from genetically engineered plants.*

The genetic modifications to these plants and others like them have been primarily of benefit to the growers of the plants rather than the consumers of the foods. Corn and soybeans have had genetic material introduced that allows them to survive very toxic herbicides that would normally kill everything green. In addition, corn has been modified so that the corn itself becomes a pesticide, directly toxic to certain common crop pests. This technology and most of its research is dominated by a few enormous agribusinesses, and its primary result thus far

has been increased profit for those businesses, rather than any improvement in the nutritional content of food.

Right now the consultation process set up by the FDA to help the biotech developers meet the testing guidelines for plant breeding are voluntary, and they are not specific to bioengineering, but common to all forms of plant breeding. In addition, *in the United States, the food labeling laws do not require any food product to disclose whether it contains a GM food.* In fact, the only way to be sure your food does *not* contain a genetically modified ingredient is to buy certified organic products.

To date, the FDA has found GM foods to be GRAS: Generally Recognized as Safe for human consumption. However, many individuals and organizations have significant concerns about the long-term safety of bioengineered foods. Among the concerns are the potential risk for allergic reactions and the unknown health risks of long-term consumption of these foods. At the moment, there is no effective way to test whether or not these new foods will generate an allergic reaction in consumers, and they have not been on the market long enough to evaluate the potential for long-term health risks. In addition, many growers have voiced concerns about the unintended and uncontrolled cross-pollination of GM plants with unmodified plants. These concerns and others like them are significant enough that several countries and specific counties in the United States have banned the use of genetically engineered foods altogether.

Pesto Pasta (see page 197)

4

More about What We Eat: Nutrient Balance

What to feed your family is one of the most critical and immediate issues you deal with every day. Now that you understand that the quality of your choices is extremely important, what daily food choices will you make to support everyone's health?

Deciding what to eat is easier for Natural Eaters. They have been eating primarily natural, healthy foods their whole lives. Their minds and bodies are in subtle communication all the time, making them naturally desire fresh, balanced foods that will meet their nutritional needs at any given time of the year, month, week, or day. One of the ways we can heal the SAD state and become more like Natural Eaters is to consciously choose foods that have a better nutrient balance than the foods we get on a junk-food diet. Over time, our bodies will respond to these foods and begin to cue us to crave them, bringing us more into a Natural Eating state.

As we've discussed, choosing high-quality foods with good nutritional content does not come as easily to SAD Eaters. They haven't had much practice with it, and they probably can't rely on their internal cues, which create cravings for extreme foods and junk foods. The solution is simple: a little education. Once you know something about the nutrient makeup of foods and how your body uses them, you can consciously choose foods with a good nutrient balance.

Most people are not properly educated about what's in their food and how their body uses those components. Everyone must provide fuel to their bodies, but we were never issued an owner's manual with good advice about fuel choices and regular tune-ups. It's helpful to know at least a little bit about how nutrition works in the body—after all, you get only one body and you should know how to care for it. And as parents, it's up to you to give your children *their* owner's manuals as well.

What's in That Food? A Simple Nutrition Lesson

All foods are made up of five basic components that nutritionists break down into two categories: macronutrients and micronutrients. The macronutrients are carbohydrates, protein, and fat. The micronutrients are vitamins and minerals. "Macro" means big: the bulkier components of your food. "Micro" means small: the trace components.

MACRONUTRIENTS: THE BIG STUFF

Macronutrients are the three main nutritional components you learned about in health class as a kid, and that you often hear stories about in the nutrition news. They are carbohydrates, proteins, and fats.

NOTEWORTHY NOURISHER

Cinnamon[1]

- Tastes sweet and is warming to the body
- Improves glucose and cholesterol balance in people with type 2 diabetes: a recent study concluded that consuming just 1/2 teaspoon of powdered cinnamon daily significantly reduces blood sugar levels in people with type 2 diabetes, and reduces cardiovascular risk factors
- Aids in digestion, and can help relieve congestion
- Relieves menstrual discomfort
- Contains blood-thinning compounds that stimulate circulation
- Is a powerful antimicrobial agent
- See page 128 for more about cinnamon

CARBOHYDRATES

Carbohydrates are the components of food that provide your body with its main source of fuel: glucose. As we discussed in chapter 3, glucose is your body's "gasoline." Carbohydrates (often called "carbs") are found in many foods, but primarily vegetables, fruits, grains, and legumes (beans and peas). All highly refined "white" foods (such as white flour, white sugar, and white rice) have a high carbohydrate content, but not much else. Carbohydrates have four calories per gram.

Carbohydrates provide the primary, most easily accessible source of energy to the body. They also provide fiber, which you can think of as a giant broom that moves through the digestive system, "sweeping" it clean of debris and other toxins. Unrefined (whole) carbohydrates are also the largest source of micronutrients (vitamins and minerals—more on those in the next section). Highly refined carbohydrates, however, have been stripped of their micronutrients and fiber—what's left are simple sugars, which are not good for the body, as we discussed in chapter 3.

Carbohydrates can be divided into two categories: simple and complex. The body transforms simple carbohydrates into sugar (glucose) very quickly during digestion. The body breaks down complex carbohydrates more slowly.

The Glycemic Index (GI) is a system that indicates how quickly a carbohydrate turns into sugar. In this system, each food is assigned a number to indicate whether it has a high GI (70 or more, for foods that rapidly turn into sugar), a mid-range GI (56–69), or a low GI (55 or less, for foods that convert to sugar slowly). More recently, the system was improved by incorporating the food's calories into the equation, which gives a more accurate picture of how the food impacts your body. The new version is called the Glycemic Load. A high glycemic load is 20 or more, medium is 11 to 19, and low is 10 or less. A lower load is preferable.

In general, the "white foods" we've mentioned (white sugar, white flour, white rice, and white potatoes) have the highest glycemic loads. Alcohol and sugary tropical fruits, such as bananas and pineapples, also have high glycemic loads because they transform into glucose so rapidly. Many grains have a middle to high glycemic load—especially refined grains such as white rice—while most beans have low glycemic loads. Green leafy vegetables have the lowest glycemic loads of all carbohydrates. Some less sugary fruits, including berries, apples, and pears, are fairly low in glycemic load as well.

A glycemic load chart can help you categorize the carbohydrates in your diet according to how great a sugar impact they have on your body. There are many charts and calculators available for free on the Internet. If you or your child struggles with sugar cravings, you can start to rebalance your bodies by switching out some high-glycemic carbohydrates for choices that have a lower glycemic load. Later in this chapter you'll learn more about sugar cravings, the SAD blood sugar cycle, and the important role of high quality, low glycemic carbohydrates in improving your health.

PROTEIN

Protein is made up of thousands of different combinations of twenty-one specific building blocks called amino acids. Your body can manufacture about half of these building blocks, but the other half must come from the protein foods you eat. (Nutritionists call macronutrient building blocks your body can't manufacture on its own

My Pyramid

The United States Department of Agriculture's (USDA) nutritional advice is summed up neatly in the Food Pyramid. Have you heard that it has recently been updated? The previous iteration was the Food Guide Pyramid, released in 1992. This was a triangular chart describing the national standard for appropriate daily portions for different types of food. It broke the original four "food groups" (which had been the US standard since 1956) into six more specific categories: grains, vegetables, fruits, milk and other dairy products, meats and beans, and oils.

In 2005, the USDA replaced it with "My Pyramid," which incorporates changes based on the new 2005 Dietary Guidelines for Americans. Our favorite addition is the suggestion that eating scads of sugar *might not be* the best thing for your health. But the biggest change is that it is much more individualized: it has twelve different variations. To discover which of the twelve is "your pyramid," go to www.mypyramid.gov and plug in your age, gender, and average amount of daily physical activity.

We applaud the USDA's attempt to take our bio-individuality into account when recommending food choices and amounts. After all, as we've talked about, one size definitely does *not* fit all. Unfortunately, many of our clients are not yet using My Pyramid, having found it to be too complex and time-consuming.

"essential"—this does not mean that they are more important than the other building blocks; it simply means you must get them from your diet or you will have to do without.)

Protein has two important jobs. The primary job is structural: to build cells (especially muscles, bone cells, and tissue). The secondary job is functional: proteins make up many of the body's "communicators," including hormones and enzymes.

Protein has four calories per gram, just like carbohydrates. Good sources of protein include most animal foods: meat, poultry, fish, and eggs. Some dairy products, such as cheese, also contain protein, but they have much more fat, so they are characterized as such. Good nonanimal sources of protein include legumes (beans and peas), nuts, and seeds. Whole grains also contain some protein. Most of these are considered "incomplete" protein sources, meaning none of them contains all the essential amino acids. However, if you eat them in combination throughout the day—for example, beans at lunch and a grain and some nuts at dinnertime—you get enough amino acids to make a "complete" protein. Quinoa, while botanically not a true grain (it's really a seed), is the exception: it contains eight essential amino acids and is considered a complete protein on its own.

Here's a simple formula to help you remember which foods are mainly carbohydrates and which are mainly proteins (Barry Sears of the Zone Diet gave us this little rhyme in an Institute for Integrative Nutrition lecture): *Carbohydrates grow from the ground, and protein walks around.* Although that's not completely accurate (as we noted, there are many great plant-based sources of protein), it's still a terrific little memory tool, and your kids will get it right away.

FAT

Fat, like protein, is also made up of building blocks; these are called fatty acids. Nutritionists divide fat into two main categories: saturated and unsaturated. Unsaturated fats break down into two further subcategories: polyunsaturated and monounsaturated. Polyunsaturated fats are broken down into two more subcategories: omega-3s and omega-6s. These two omegas are the only fats your body cannot make itself, so they are called essential fatty acids. All types of fat have nine calories per gram, more than double the number in carbohydrates or protein. Most foods that are high in fat have an oily or greasy texture: they will leave an oily stain on a paper bag. For more information about fats and oils, see chapter 6 and appendix D.

Fat has many functions in our system. Because smaller amounts of it pack more calories than the other macronutrients, it serves as a concentrated source of energy. It lubricates and protects the organs, and it is an important part of the membrane of our cells. Certain fats are vital to healthy brain function, and a healthy fat balance in the body contributes to lustrous hair, nails, and skin. "Extra" dietary fat that can't be utilized right away is stored in the body as fat tissue, also known as adipose tissue, also known as the "muffin top"!

Fat also carries the bulk of the smells and flavors of our foods. This becomes very clear when you are cooking with any kind of oil. Consider which smells stronger: garlic in a water-based soup, or garlic sizzling in olive oil? All good cooks understand that to get the biggest impact in terms of aroma, you marry your strongest spices with a fat or an oil. Further, flavors carried on fat taste stronger on the tongue.

Finally, fats help send the satiety (satisfaction) signal to the brain that will tell us we have had enough to eat. Have you ever noticed how hard it is to eat just two fat-free cookies? We know that's the recommended portion size, but most people never have much luck opening that bag, eating two, and then tucking it away. Why is that? For one thing, they are usually very high in sugar (to make up for not tasting very good), so they can quickly put you on the SAD blood sugar cycle (later in this chapter we'll describe how this works). The second reason is precisely that they have no fat, so they don't send a satisfaction signal to your brain. If you eat the whole box, then you might get a little blast of endorphins from overeating and feel slightly more satisfied, but only until the queasiness sets in. Annemaric Colbin, PhD, author of *Food and Healing*, once said, "If you want to eat just two fat-free cookies, try spreading a little butter on them first."

MICRONUTRIENTS: THE LITTLE GUYS WITH BIG JOBS

Micronutrients include vitamins and minerals. The amount of micronutrients required by the body is small, and, correspondingly, food contains only trace amounts. But without them, a body would be unable to sustain life. Each vitamin and mineral has a specific role and function. It is beyond the scope of this book to list each of those roles, but the importance of getting enough micronutrients in your diet cannot be underestimated.

All the systems of the body require that cells function in very specific ways. Several complex processes govern the creation, nourishing, and function of cells, as well as how they communicate and get rid of the waste materials and by-products of their functions. Many of these processes are controlled chemically and require the presence of vitamins and minerals. If a micronutrient isn't present in the body, it may mean that a very important function can't be accomplished, and your health will suffer, sometimes dramatically.

With the exception of vitamin D, which can be produced in the skin with sunlight exposure, the body cannot make its own vitamins and minerals. *They must come from the foods you eat.*

VITAMINS

A vitamin is an organic compound (meaning it comes from something alive) required for life functioning. There are thirteen primary vitamins:

Biotin	Vitamin B6
Folic acid	Vitamin B12
Niacin	Vitamin C
Pantothenic acid	Vitamin D
Riboflavin (B2)	Vitamin E
Thiamin	Vitamin K
Vitamin A	

MINERALS

Minerals are elements that come from soil, water, and rocks, and cannot be made by organic life forms. Plants absorb minerals from soil and water, and then animals eat plants. We receive most of our minerals from plants, and some from animals in this secondhand way. There are fourteen primary minerals:

Calcium	Manganese
Chromium	Molybdenum
Copper	Phosphorus
Fluoride	Potassium
Iodine	Selenium
Iron	Sodium (Chloride)
Magnesium	Zinc

Minerals and Oxalic Acid

Oxalic acid is found in foods such as quinoa, cocoa, plums, beet greens, spinach, and chard. When oxalic acid is released in cooking, it binds with calcium and makes it difficult for the body to absorb the calcium. Eating them seasonally (see chapter 5) is the perfect way to include them in a balanced diet. There is some indication that eating these foods with things like cheese, eggs, or another source of healthy fat may reduce the impact of the oxalic acid. The benefits of eating these foods with oxalic acid far outweigh the compromise to their calcium content.

OTHER MICRONUTRIENTS

Other micronutrients found in food fall into smaller categories than vitamins and minerals. One important category, of which you may have heard, is phytonutrients. These are chemicals that are produced by plants and have beneficial effects on our health when we eat them—but they are not yet considered one of the five "essential" nutrients by clinical dietary standards. Some examples of phytonutrients are carotenoids (found in acorn squash, apricots, carrots, and fresh corn) and lignans (found in flaxseeds, rye, and berries). Fiber is actually considered a phytonutrient as well, but we include it in the carbohydrate discussion because we consider high-quality carbohydrates to be high in fiber.

The higher the quality of a food, the higher the micronutrient concentration will be. A refined and processed food has been stripped of many of its original vitamins and minerals. Although food manufacturers try to put some of them back by adding various micronutrients to highly processed foods such as sugared cereals or orange juice drinks, the forms of those added vitamins may not be recognized by the body as a food, and therefore may not be fully absorbed.

Micronutrient research is still in its early stages, but it seems to indicate that having extra stores of vitamins available in the body may optimize the functions they help support. Although there are some compelling arguments for augmenting the vitamins and minerals we receive from our foods with supplements, we still maintain that the *primary* source of these vital nutrients should be a high-quality daily diet. People are designed to absorb nutrients best from food sources. That said, it's probably a good idea to supplement your children's diets with a good-quality multivitamin and a small amount of high-quality fish or krill oil to assure they are getting adequate amounts of a broad range of vitamins and minerals—especially if your child is a SAD Eater.

MACRO- AND MICRONUTRIENT BALANCE PRINCIPLES

All of the macro- and micronutrients are necessary for the performance of important and distinct body functions. Eliminating a macronutrient, such as carbohydrates or fats, from your diet in order to lose weight or affect your health in some extreme manner is dangerous. It is vital to your health to include an adequate balance of each of the five macro- and micronutrients in your daily diet.

Natural Eaters will usually instinctively be drawn to the right balance of macronutrient and micronutrient foods as they wander the store aisles. But if you are still recovering from the SAD state, here are some simple guidelines for how to select foods that will give your family a good balance of nutrients:

SIMPLE FOOD FOR BUSY FAMILIES

1. When you are shopping, try to include a broad variety of colors and textures: create a rainbow of vegetables and fruits in your shopping cart. You can do the same thing in an individual meal: try to have a good variety of colors and textures on your plate.

2. Use taste as a guide: select a range of foods that provides distinct flavors in your meals. Americans tend to crave sweet and salty flavors, but there are four other tastes recognized by your tongue and brain: sour, bitter, pungent (spicy, with a bite), and astringent (drying, such as beans or pomegranate). (The six tastes are covered in greater depth in chapter 10.) These different flavors correspond to different nutrient profiles in the food. A meal with many flavors provides a good variety of micronutrients.

3. Choose foods that taste good to you. Research demonstrates that the visual appeal and flavor of our foods affect how well we absorb the nutrients contained within them (for more on this, see chapter 6). In a nutshell, if we like how a food looks, if we chew it well and enjoy its taste in our mouths, we will receive a better nutritional "bang for the buck" in that meal. Therefore, you should create meals that will be attractive and delicious to your family. When your family eats, encourage everyone to savor and enjoy the variety of tastes and colors. They will be on their way to getting a better nutrient balance.

Using Nutrition to Heal SAD Imbalances

As we've established, the major difference between children who are Natural Eaters and children on the Standard American Diet is that SAD kids' exposure to processed foods and a life out of rhythm with nature has upset the balance of their internal cues, causing them to crave extreme foods (salt, sugar, and high fats) or more food than they need.

One solution is to gradually reset those inner signals so that your child's body will naturally steer her toward healthier choices. Dieting or restricted eating cannot accomplish this, and can be emotionally and physically harmful to children. To help SAD children become healthier, parents have to intervene in their children's eating patterns. But rather than prescribing a certain type of diet to follow, it is far more effective in the long run to work toward rebuilding the child's natural internal balance.

This can be accomplished simply by upgrading your food quality across the board, and also by increasing certain nutrients in their diet to offset particular imbalances caused by being in the SAD state. The SAD state is characterized by several imbalances in the bodymind system. We have identified three of the most common imbalances and the nutritional antidotes that will correct them. We call these imbalances the SAD Blood Cycle, the Overfed and Undernourished State, and the Flawed Fats Imbalance.

SAD IMBALANCE #1: SAD BLOOD SUGAR CYCLE

The SAD blood sugar cycle is an imbalance in the body's glucose regulation system. The body may not produce enough insulin (an important hormone with many jobs, one of which is to regulate carbohydrate metabolism), or may overproduce it. The body's cells may become insulin resistant, meaning the insulin may be present, but the cells do not respond to it as they normally should. As a result, levels of sugar in the blood are improperly regulated. The SAD blood sugar cycle is a very common imbalance; by some estimates, more than 40 million Americans are suffering from some form of blood sugar imbalance.

In the SAD blood sugar cycle you typically don't feel very hungry in the mornings, crave sweet foods with most meals, and sometimes experience an energy nose-dive between 2 and 4 P.M. You might be inclined to snack on junk foods from dinner to bedtime every night. You typically feel a little weak or cranky when you are hungry, and you may lose your taste for other types of foods, especially vegetables.

Here's what's happening: when most of the carbohydrates that you and your family eat have a high glycemic load, or are simple carbohydrates (white flour, white sugar, white rice, etc.), your bodies experience blood sugar spikes on a regular basis. This creates cravings; you can easily fall into a cycle in which the more sugar (simple carbohydrates) you eat, the more you want.

For example, you eat three Krispy Kreme glazed donuts because they taste so light and delicious; one is not enough. Your blood sugar spikes quickly because Krispy Kremes have a very high glycemic

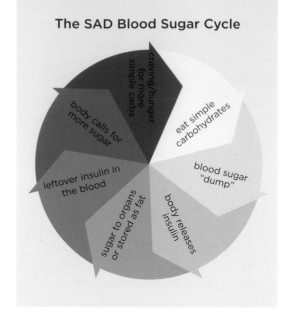

The SAD Blood Sugar Cycle

load. To get all that sugar out of your bloodstream and safely to your cells for fuel, your pancreas releases the hormone insulin. Insulin acts like a key that unlocks cells and allows glucose to pass from the blood into the cells where it's needed. Any extra glucose is stored as fat.

This is a great system when it's working well, but if you have chronically overeaten simple carbohydrates (or if you are one of the unlucky people genetically disposed to having a less-than-perfect insulin lock-and-key system), then the Krispy Kreme sugar rush leaves you with too much insulin in your blood. Too much insulin is like a crisis for the body, and it will immediately need to be balanced out. Your body will call for what it needs in the form of sugar cravings, hunger, jitters, low energy, or other symptoms, regardless of how much food you already have in your stomach. If you respond by eating another donut or drinking a soda or a mocha latte, you'll relieve the insulin problem temporarily,

Finding the Perfect Diet

If you were to scrupulously record exactly what several Natural Eaters ate in exactly what amounts, you'd find it difficult to create a "diet" from this information. You would probably find that what they eat, when they eat, and how much varies greatly from individual to individual. In fact, it would be very hard for you to find much "rhyme or reason" in their eating patterns at all. You would also find that their patterns probably change with the seasons and with different times in their lives.

This is healthy and perfectly natural: people have different ethnic heritages, different bodies, different needs at different ages, and different life demands. It makes sense, then, that our nutritional needs will differ. This bio-individuality makes creating a standard diet, or even guidelines, difficult. As Joshua Rosenthal, founder of the Institute for Integrative Nutrition, is fond of saying: "Nutritional science is the only science where the researchers can empirically prove diametrically opposed positions."

A large body of research-based evidence indicates that eating a diet high in complex carbohydrates and low in animal foods will make you healthy. And yet, when many people try to eat that way, they become spacey, even dizzy, and might gain a lot of weight. Another set of research indicates that reducing your overall carbohydrate intake and increasing your animal proteins will help you lose weight and lower your cholesterol. But when some people dutifully follow that plan, their energy plummets, their cholesterol increases, and they start feeling low, depressed, or even angry! Remember the old maxim? *One man's meat is another man's poison.*

Countless opposing nutrition books and experts, as well as working with clients in both private practice and hospital programs, have led us to the conclusion that there is no one perfect diet. You can only find the diet that works for you through education and experimentation. However, there are definitely "healing diets" that can be very helpful. A healing diet is a temporary, more prescriptive approach to eating that can help individuals who have a significant health issue regain or maintain their natural physiological balance. For example, when a person has had a lot of chemotherapy, his digestive system often becomes toxic and sluggish. For that person, a healing diet could be one that is light, nourishing, completely organic, flavorful, and extremely easy to digest.

A good healing diet is usually short-term, flexible, nonstressful, and adaptable to different individual needs. Some of the recommendations in this chapter, including the SAD imbalance antidotes and the Balanced Plate chart, can be used as healing diets until eating in a healthy way that best suits your body becomes more intuitive.

but immediately cause another sugar spike, followed by another insulin spike, and so on.

If you get caught in the SAD blood sugar cycle for long enough, eventually you can wear the system out, and the lock-and-key system stops working. At this point, the SAD imbalance becomes an actual disease: type 2 diabetes. When you look at the national trend toward the popularity of inexpensive, highly refined foods, the rapid rise of type 2 diabetes in the population is not surprising.

It is, however, very alarming, particularly because type 2 diabetes used to be considered a disease of old age: it used to take the imbalanced system much longer to wear out. But now it is affecting our children in unprecedented numbers. The early onset of prediabetes or type 2 diabetes causes serious complications for children as they age. It is important to understand that the problem is almost completely preventable. Improved nutrition and lifestyle habits can even reverse a child's prediabetic condition and return him or her to a normal, balanced state.

ANTIDOTES FOR BREAKING THE SAD BLOOD SUGAR CYCLE

1. **Avoid triggering a sugar "dump."**

- Eat fewer low-quality "white foods" such as snack cakes, candy, soda, and white pasta.
- Upgrade to more whole grain foods, such as quinoa and whole wheat pasta.
- Snack on lower glycemic-load foods, such as low-sugar fruit or homemade trail mix with nuts and seeds. See chapter 14 for snack and dessert ideas.
- Eat more foods that are naturally high in fiber, especially vegetables and beans. Because it is difficult to digest, fiber slows the breakdown

Are You or Your Child Prediabetic?

One simple way to determine whether you might be prediabetic is to ask your doctor to give you a fasting blood test to measure your glucose level. If your result reads under 100, you have normal blood sugars. Congratulations! If the results are between 100 and 125, you may have a prediabetic condition, and it's very important for you to break the SAD blood sugar cycle. If your levels are 126 or higher on two separate tests, this may indicate that you have developed type 2 diabetes, making it even more imperative to balance your sugars. Your doctor and a registered dietician can counsel you about these issues.

and absorption of carbohydrates into the bloodstream; it acts like a natural "time release" element for the sugars in food.

- Add high-quality protein or fat to meals or snacks with simple carbohydrates. Consuming these fats and proteins at the same time as simple carbs gives your body more to process and slows the release of the sugar into your bloodstream.

2. **Prevent excessive hunger and low blood sugar.** Do not let anyone in the family skip meals or go more than four hours without eating. Encourage everyone to snack on healthy, natural high-fiber foods between meals if they are hungry.

3. **Stay hydrated.** Dehydration can trigger sugar cravings. Encourage everyone to drink plenty of water and reduce or eliminate fruit juice and soda—they add a lot of sugar

to your system and don't quench thirst as effectively.

4. **Always eat breakfast, and include some protein.** When your children start the day with no breakfast, they are falling right into the SAD blood sugar cycle. Little bodies need good fuel, including protein, soon after waking to maintain stable sugars throughout the day. See chapter 13 for some quick and healthy breakfast ideas.

5. **Use physical exercise to break the cycle.** Regular, moderate physical exercise lowers blood sugar levels. This is yet another great reason to get your family moving!

SAD IMBALANCE #2: OVERFED AND UNDERNOURISHED STATE

This state of nutritional deficiency is characterized by the overeating of poor-quality foods. In this imbalance, the foods you eat are high in calories but low in nutrients. Your body may be getting bigger, but it is not getting enough of the right macro- or micronutrients, so it keeps sending you hunger signals and cravings, and you keep eating. But because you aren't meeting your nutritional needs, no amount of food is truly satisfying.

If this is your or your child's challenge, you're probably overweight, or even obese. You have strong cravings and regularly eat more food than you actually need, while still feeling vaguely unsatisfied and low in energy. You may also regularly eat food when you feel full, chronically taxing your digestive system and energy levels. And yet your body may still be starved for higher quality nutrition.

It may be hard to think of overweight kids as undernourished, but many of them are. Because they have been eating a SAD diet high in fat, salt, and sugars, they have become too heavy. And because their diet is so low in quality, they are probably deficient in certain vitamins and minerals. They need more of the other macronutrients, usually high-quality protein, healthy fats, and fiber in order to bring some balance to their systems. Their bodies know they need these vital nutrients, so they cue the children to keep eating, and the cycle continues until it is deliberately interrupted—usually by their parents or a doctor.

In addition to the extra weight and disease risk that goes with it, "overfed" kids can suffer other bothersome health issues as a result of their poorly nourished state. A micronutrient deficiency can result in acne or other skin problems. Heavier kids have more difficulty sleeping and often struggle with chronic headaches, muscle aches, or joint pain. Hormone cycles can be affected, resulting in unpleasant menstrual problems for girls or mood swings in both genders. Digestive complaints such as heartburn, acid reflux, gas, or constipation are also common.

ANTIDOTES FOR THE OVERFED AND UNDERNOURISHED STATE

1. **Increase the quality of your food.** Although increasing food quality is a core Whole Life Nutrition principle, it is most vital of all for children with this imbalance. These kids need to switch their high-calorie, low-nutrient density, refined foods to higher quality real foods. See chapter 3 for a more in-depth discussion of food quality.

2. **Eat more vegetables!** Most people in this state eat mostly bland, white meals: white

The SAD Vegetarian Risk

If your family is vegetarian, your children are especially vulnerable to the SAD blood sugar cycle. Many Americans who become vegetarians simply take the meat out of their diet and don't adequately replace the macro- and micronutrients they would normally get from those animal foods. As a result, their diets are deficient in protein, B vitamins, vitamin D, and iron. Without enough balancing protein and healthy fat, you run the risk of falling into the SAD blood sugar cycle.

Eating combinations of higher protein grains such as quinoa, beans, and nuts and seeds throughout the day will help. Also consider getting protein through soy in products such as tofu and tempeh, or their more processed counterparts, such as Not Dogs and Soysage. We recommend that children not eat too many soy products, however, especially soy protein powder, because they have a high concentration of phytoestrogen, a phytonutrient that mimics estrogen and can upset the hormonal balance in little bodies. If you are not vegans (who eat no animal products at all), you can also incorporate high-quality eggs and dairy products into your diet.

---

pasta, pizza, french fries, iceberg lettuce, rolls, etc. Adding colorful vegetables with different textures and flavors ensures that you get more fiber and a greater quantity and variety of vitamins and minerals in your meals.

3. **Make snacks count: offer balanced mini-meals instead of junk snacks.** Eating a lot of "filler" snacks to curb that empty "hunger" just keeps this cycle going. To interrupt it, try mini-meals with fiber-rich vegetables or fruit and a bit of lean protein and healthy fat. American kids' favorite snacks—crackers, chips, pretzels, Goldfish, Doritos—sabotage their nutritional health. See chapter 13 for some healthy mini-meal ideas.

4. **Encourage your children to eat more slowly and chew their food well.** This will improve digestion and nutrient absorption, and it will also help with natural portion control. The more slowly you eat, the less you tend to consume. See chapter 6 for more tips on natural portion control.

SAD IMBALANCE #3: FLAWED FATS IMBALANCE

This imbalance is due to improper proportions of dietary fat—for example, an overabundance of poor-quality fats, a deficiency in high-quality fats (especially the omega-3 essential fatty acids), or both. It is typical for a fat-flawed person to have elevated "bad cholesterol" levels and low "good cholesterol" levels. He or she is often, but not necessarily, overweight and may crave or eat a lot of high-fat foods such as pizza, chips, french fries, fried foods, deli meats, pies, ice cream, etc. As a flawed-fat person, you may struggle with constipation or diarrhea. Your hair and skin may be too oily or too dry.

There is a lot of confusion around fats: which ones are healthy, how much you need, etc. Let's take a look at two common misconceptions: the "no fat" myth and the "bad fat" myth.

NO FAT MYTH

The "no fat" diet gained popularity in the 1980s as a weight-loss technique. There were also heart disease treatment programs, such as Pritikin, which had great success by lowering the overall fat intake of their cardiac care patients. However, the "no fat" movement has become less popular as it has become clear that, although fat has more than twice as many calories per gram as the other macronutrients, it is *not* true that by eliminating it from your diet you will be healthier. *Remember, your body needs a good balance of each of the five main nutrients.* You cannot leave a whole one out and expect to operate at peak health!

If you eliminate fat entirely from your diet, you may become fat-deficient and might have to deal with one or more of the following symptoms:

- Depletion of the fat-soluble vitamins A, D, E, and K
- Brittle hair or nails
- Dry skin, acne, eczema, or psoriasis
- PMS
- Diabetes
- High cholesterol
- Fertility problems
- Binge eating
- Possible growth retardation and hyperactivity (in children)

On the other hand, *reducing* certain fats in the American diet has been shown to dramatically improve health and assist in weight loss. But this leads to another common misconception about fats: the "bad fat" myth.

BAD FAT MYTH

Saturated fats (the ones found primarily in high-fat animal products such as heavy cream and fatty cuts of meat) have been implicated in coronary heart disease and high cholesterol. As a result, they got a reputation as "bad fats." But high-quality saturated fat is not bad. The body needs small amounts of saturated fat to function efficiently. The real dietary culprit in health issues such as heart disease is an *excessive* consumption of fats in general, especially poor-quality fats from things such as processed meat products and deep-fried foods.

The only truly "bad" fat is hydrogenated or partially hydrogenated oil, which contain trans fat. Partially hydrogenated oil is a man-made product. To make it, vegetable oil is heated to a very high temperature and injected with hydrogen molecules. In this way, perishable liquid vegetable oil is converted into a grayish solid mass of very stable, solid fat that can help preserve the shelf life of certain foods almost indefinitely. This product is not a natural food and should not be consumed by humans or animals.

In this country, we definitely consume too many poor quality and saturated fats, and not enough unsaturated fats, leading us into the flawed fats state. The answer is not to cut out any single type of fat entirely, but to eat them in balanced quantities. The reality is that we each need small amounts of all the natural fats (saturated, monounsaturated, polyunsaturated, etc.). The best way to get them into our diets is through eating high-quality food sources.

1. **Clean up your saturated fats.** Most of these come from animal sources, so try reducing your consumption of high-fat cheeses and meats. Try substituting 2 percent or evaporated skim milk for heavy cream in recipes and your coffee. Choose lower-fat cheeses and ice creams. Trim all visible fat off lean meat cuts. Remember that light meat usually has a lower fat content than dark meat does. Choose low-fat deli meats, such as turkey and chicken breast, over high-fat choices, such as salami and bologna. Avoid fried foods—try baking or steaming instead.

2. **Emphasize high-quality polyunsaturated fats.** Good sources include olives and olive oil, nuts and seeds, and avocados.

3. **Consume more essential fatty acids, especially omega-3s.** Healthy cells need essential fatty acids for membrane formation, to clear cells of plaque, and to aid in vital nutrient absorption and toxin expulsion. For children, who are growing all the time, essential fatty acids are particularly important nutrients, nourishing the nervous system and brain function. Good sources include ground flaxseed and flaxseed oil, and ground hemp seed (which comes in flavored powdered forms for smoothies). The most complete, bioavailable form is found in cold-water fish and fish or krill oil (to make sure it's clean, look for molecularly distilled or certified free of mercury and PCBs).

Trans-Fatty Acids and the Body

There is one kind of fat that should always be avoided: trans fat. Trans fats are found in hydrogenated oils and shortenings and are commonly used in the preparation of fast foods, although currently many restaurants are switching to healthier oils. There are no known health benefits of trans-fatty acids. Here are some of the health risks:

- Lowers the "good" protective HDL cholesterol
- Increases the harmful LDL cholesterol
- Increases risk of diabetes
- Potentially accelerates childhood asthma
- Plays a role in cardiovascular disease
- Disturbs cellular function
- Interrupts the processing of essential fatty acids, leading to essential fatty acid deficiency

Look for food products labeled Trans Fat Free and always check food labels for the presence of partially hydrogenated oils.

IMPLEMENTING THE ANTIDOTES

You now have a better understanding of what is going on inside your and your children's bodies, and you have some tools and strategies for making changes. As we will discuss in chapter 8, don't try to change everything at once. Start by simply considering some of the symptoms in your family. Write down a few of the antidotes we've discussed here and bring that list with you the next time you go food shopping, or review it before preparing your next meal. Experiment with these recommendations and see what results you get. Be patient—it can take several months to a year (and even longer if your child is obese) to rebalance a child's nutrient base and taste buds and to heal the symptoms of imbalance. This is a marathon approach, not a sprint. But it's well worth the effort because the results can last a lifetime.

Don't Be Afraid of Fish[2]

Although our ocean's fish stores are definitely tainted with mercury, PCBs, and other pollution toxins, there are some "cleaner" options. See our Balanced Plate for the SAD State chart on page 54 for choices that, according to KidSafe Seafood (www.kidsafeseafood.org), are safer for children. Recent research indicates that the nutritional benefits of eating the safer fish outweigh the risks. If you are deeply concerned, you can avoid fish, but still offer your child a fish or krill oil supplement that is molecularly distilled and certified as free of the toxins. For more information, see www.mercuryaction.org (sponsored by Physicians for Social Responsibility) and www.cfsan.fda.gov/~dms/admehg3.html (US Department of Health and Human Services and EPA guidelines for pregnant and nursing mothers).

A Balanced Plate for the SAD State

We've given you a lot of information in this chapter about different foods and how they impact the body. How do you take this information and use it to create a healthy meal? On the following page is a tool to help you keep it simple. This chart divides the foods we've discussed into their primary macronutrient categories. To create a nutrient-based plate that will help balance the SAD state, choose one food from each column (Savory Carbs, Sweet Carbs, Protein, and Fat).

If you'll notice, this balance "formula" has vegetables making up half to three-quarters of your plate. Vegetables with low to mid-range glycemic loads are some of the most important food tools for balancing the SAD state, so *eat your veggies!* We recommend hand-based portion sizes of each food—see chapter 6 for a more thorough discussion of portions.

Once you move from being a SAD Eater to more of a Natural Eater, you will not have to think too much about balancing your macro- and micronutrients at every meal in this way. Instead, selecting a healthy balance of foods will become more intuitive. Nonetheless, making deliberate choices for a time can help the SAD Eater stabilize some of her imbalances. It is a form of a "healing diet," but should never become prescriptive or too limited. Use it instead as a general guideline to help your body get into the habit of recognizing foods that are healthy.

MIX AND MATCH: **BALANCED PLATE FOR THE SAD STATE**

Prepare one food from each column (fats can be cooked with the dish or served on the side). The foods listed here are suggestions, not complete lists. Serve your meal according to the portion guide in the table, and enjoy!

NUTRIENT GROUP	SAVORY CARBS OR LOW-GLYCEMIC CARBS	SWEET CARBS OR LOW- TO MEDIUM-GLYCEMIC CARBS
PORTION PER PLATE (see chapter 6 for more details)	size of two hands cupped together	size of closed fist
TRY THESE FOODS	**Leafy greens:** bok choy, broccoli rabe, chard, collards, dandelion greens, escarole, kale, mustard greens, spinach **Other vegetables:** artichokes, asparagus, broccoli, Brussels sprouts, cauliflower, celery, cucumbers, eggplant, fennel, garlic, green beans, leeks, lettuce, onions, peas, peppers, radishes, sprouts, summer squash, tomatoes, zucchini	**Fruits:** apples, blueberries, cantaloupe, grapes, melons, oranges, peaches, pears, raspberries, strawberries, watermelon **Sweet vegetables:** beets, carrots, parsnips, sweet potatoes, pumpkin, turnips, winter squash **Whole grains:** amaranth, barley, buckwheat, millet, oats, quinoa, spelt, whole grain pasta, whole grain rice
NOTES	These veggies contain a lot of fiber and water. They have low glycemic loads and are very low in calories.	Fruit can be served with your meal or right afterward. The fruits listed here are all lower glycemic fruits. Some of the grains have higher than medium glycemic loads. If you are caught in the SAD blood sugar cycle, use them sparingly. Beans, listed in the next column, can also be used as a low–glycemic load carb in this column.

For detailed information on any unfamiliar foods listed here, see the guides in chapters 9 and 10 or appendix B at the back of the book.

PROTEIN	FAT
size of open palm	size of thumb
Beans: adzuki, black, garbanzo, great Northern, kidney, lentils, lima, navy **Dairy:** low-fat cottage cheese, low-fat cow's milk or goat's milk cheese, plain low-fat yogurt, low-fat milk **Meat (lean cuts):** beef, lamb, pork **Poultry or eggs:** chicken, turkey, eggs, egg whites **Seafood (kid-safe):** farmed bay scallops, farmed blue mussels, sardines, tilapia, wild Alaskan salmon **Soy:** edamame, tempeh, tofu, textured vegetable protein products	**Butter:** ghee (clarified butter) or natural, organic butter **Nuts and seeds:** almonds, cashews, chestnuts, hazelnuts, pecans, pine nuts, pumpkin seeds, sesame seeds, sunflower seeds, walnuts, nut butters **Oils:** avocado oil, coconut oil, flaxseed oil, grapeseed oil, macadamia nut oil, olive oil, sesame oil **Spreads:** avocado, guacamole, hummus, pesto
Keep it varied. We recommend soy no more than 4 times per week for kids. Also, milk and beans can be considered half carbohydrate, half protein, so be aware of amounts as you balance your plate. Choose low-fat, organic, hormone-free, antibiotic-free options whenever possible.	Some fats may be cooked into a carb or protein dish; others are best drizzled on top or served on the side of the dish. Choose organic, fresh, unsalted, and raw options whenever possible.

Top Takeaways

- Educating yourself about high-quality "real" foods will help you make good choices to get a plentiful range of macro- and micronutrients.
- You need all the macro- and micronutrients in balance to be fully healthy; cutting out an entire group of nutrients is harmful.
- Although the goal is to become a Natural Eater, there is no such thing as a perfect diet. If you are a SAD Eater, finding and eating the right healing diet for a time may help you get back on track.
- If you or your child has one of the three specific SAD imbalances, follow the antidote guidelines to come back into balance.
- Using the Balanced Plate chart or specific antidotes, a SAD Eater can evolve into more of a Natural Eater.

FOR YOU

- Do you tend to eat a lot of one nutrient, such as carbohydrates, and less of another, such as protein, in your regular daily diet?
- Look at the Balanced Plate chart: do most of your macro- and micronutrients come from those types of high-quality foods, or are you getting the bulk of your nutrients from poor-quality fare?
- How does your typical dinner plate "measure up" for nutrient balance?
- If you believe that you have one or more of the SAD imbalances, choose one of the antidotes, and try it out this week.

FOR YOUR KIDS

- Teach your children about the macro- and micronutrients in their foods. Help them learn to identify foods that are rich in certain nutrients. If they are younger, make it a game: which foods grow from the ground (contain carbs)? Which foods come from things that walk around (contain protein)?
- Try leaving different foods in paper bags to see which ones leave an oily stain. Put an apple in one and a piece of cheese in another: the next day, ask them which food has more fat.
- Avoid begging, bribing, or threatening your child into eating the newly upgraded foods. Remain neutral when offering new choices: putting any extra attention (positive or negative) on a particular food will usually backfire.
- When offering a new food to your child, prepare it in a way that is similar to something familiar. Offer it repeatedly, even if it's rejected. It can take up to 15 exposures before kids are willing to try something new.

Seasonality: Eating in Harmony with Nature

The Benefits of Eating Seasonally

To eat "seasonally" is simply to consume the foods that grow naturally in your local environment in each season. To *not* eat seasonally became an option only in the past hundred years or so. Prior to the turn of the century, people had no choice but to eat what was growing locally in the ground during the current season.

With the advent of electric refrigeration, commercial food preservation, and mass agricultural transport came liberation from the constraints of the local climate: people could keep food for longer periods and have access to foods that were grown in other areas. A more recent development in food availability was the birth of the supermarket chain, which provides continual year-round access to all kinds of foods from all over the world. But with unlimited access to world produce comes a dissociation from the local environment—the land and the climate, and the food it produces.

Most people aren't even aware that there is an organic synchronicity between the plants that grow in the ground and the animals (including us!) that eat them. The human body must adapt in a variety of ways to the challenges presented by each season. *And here's one of nature's secrets: the foods from a particular season can help the body meet those challenges* (such as colds, allergies, weight gain, etc.). Thus, being separated from this system, and eating out-of-season foods from elsewhere in the world, can create an array of health complaints. This is yet another example of how following a typical modern American lifestyle can upset the delicate natural balance of your body.

How does this apply to you as parents? *By adding some local and seasonal foods to your regular diet, your family will be better able to tolerate the changes of each season.* You will become more resilient to the onslaught of things such as winter infections and spring allergies, and your digestion will gradually strengthen and improve. In short, you will be paddling downstream, with the current of physiological changes that occur in nature and in your body each season, not fighting against them.

YOUR LOCAL SEASONS

In the United States, the seasons vary according to where you live. For the purposes of this book, we will cover the fundamental qualities of (and bodily responses to) the four seasons that occur in the climates of the northern, Midwestern, and Mid-Atlantic states: winter, spring, summer, and fall.

Each season generates certain conditions, such as extra heat or moisture, and those conditions have an effect on your body. In turn, eating certain foods can generate similar or complementary "conditions" inside the body, such as cooling or drying. By understanding the specific qualities of each season, you can choose certain foods to balance out that season's impact on your body.

The foods that "antidote" your seasonal conditions may simply be the ones that are growing out of the ground in season in your local area. If you live in an area with more limited growing seasons, you can still choose seasonally balancing foods if you understand which foods generate which internal "conditions" to offset what is happening in your local climate.

Seasonal eating is not an exact science; it is more like a collection of general guidelines. Also, opinions vary somewhat about which foods have which properties. However, once you understand the basic principles, you will be better able to intuit what your family might need at a given time. These days, it is impractical for most people to eat exclusively seasonally (especially for those who live in colder northern areas of the United States with very short growing seasons). You may find that you can get good results by simply including a few more seasonal foods and reducing some of the more exotic, out-of-season fare.

Much of our information here about the seasonal properties of foods is drawn from two excellent books on the subject: *Staying Healthy with the Seasons* by Dr. Elson Haas and *The 3-Season Diet* by Dr. John Douillard. We recommend that you read these books for a more thorough exploration of these concepts.

EASY WAYS TO ADD LOCAL, SEASONAL FOODS TO YOUR DIET

Support your local growers: Look for farm stands or farmers' markets in your area. They grow plants and raise animals on your region's native soil. If that land naturally nourishes those plants and animals well, eating them will nourish you well. As an added bonus, those foods will likely be of high quality, as they will be sold closer to their harvest, and therefore will be fresher. Many farmers' markets participate in state programs for low-income families, such as WIC, so you can even use food assistance checks. Not all farms that participate in farmers' markets are organic farms, so remember to seek out the organic farms first! Buying local produce has an additional environmental benefit: the food does not have to be mass-transported, a conventional farming practice that contributes to global warming.

Look for seasonal produce in your grocery stores: If you have no access to local growers, pay attention to the most plentiful produce in your grocery store. Chances are that if there's a lot of it in the most prominent bins, it's in season! You will also save money by choosing the seasonal produce, because it's usually cheaper.

Grow it yourself: It's actually quite easy to cultivate a small vegetable garden. If you have no yard, check to see whether there are any community gardens in your area. If you don't have access to any land, you can still grow vegetables indoors or on a small patio in growing tubs called EarthBoxes (www.earthbox.com). These containers are simple, reusable, and virtually foolproof. They require very little maintenance and actually produce a mini-harvest.

The boxes come with everything you need except for the plant seedlings and water. Many of Tracee's clients have started little gardens of their own. Gardening has many added benefits for children: it's fun and it teaches them about the connection between nature and food. It seems miraculous to them and they are usually eager to try the foods they have grown themselves. It's also a creative and effective way to introduce them to new fruits and vegetables.

Guidelines for Seasonal Eating

In this section you will learn about the qualities of the four seasons, how they impact your body, and which seasonal foods will help you stay healthy in each season.

WINTER: COLD WEATHER AND YOUR BODY

In the wintertime, the weather is usually cold and dry. The days are shorter, and people are generally less active, burning fewer calories. It is a time for slowing down, for conserving energy. You might notice a natural tendency to want to sleep more or be less active.

Because of the dryness of the cold air outdoors and the heat indoors, your body can become very dry. In response to this dryness, you tend to produce more mucus to keep the body's moist tissues and delicate membranes lubricated. This additional mucus production can lead to more frequent colds and sinus, bronchial, and ear infections.

To balance and counteract some of these seasonal tendencies in your body, you might naturally crave warm, moist foods that are rich in starchy carbohydrates, dense protein, and fat. These richer, higher fat foods will help counteract the cold dryness. They may also add a few pounds to your frame. A slight weight gain in the winter is very natural. (A problem for people who follow the SAD Lifestyle is that they don't change their habits accordingly in the spring to naturally shed that added weight!)

BALANCING WINTER FOODS

Stews and rich soups make terrific winter meals. They give the body a lot of inner warmth.

Warming foods include:

- Apples, pears, and peaches to help combat excess mucus production
- Sour fruits and vegetables to generate internal heat
- Root vegetables to help clear the body of toxins
- Brown rice, buckwheat, and millet for warming winter grains (Tracee's girls love Nature's Path Buckwheat Waffles for breakfast)
- Moderate amounts of high-quality red meat to nourish the heart and circulation
- Cheese for its warming properties—but watch out, because it can also increase mucus production, so use it in moderation (goat's milk cheeses, such as feta, are easier to digest and create less mucus than do cow's milk cheeses)
- Roasted nuts for their very warming qualities and great taste; try them with whole grains, or alone as a snack
- Spices such as cinnamon, cayenne pepper, and garlic to help the body sweat and also for their antiviral and antibiotic properties

Foods to avoid in winter include:

- Cold foods, such as ice cream
- Excessive raw foods, including salads, because they require the body to work to supply extra heat in order to digest them

SPRING: WET WEATHER AND YOUR BODY

In the spring, everything begins to thaw. With the thaw and the spring rains, the earth gets very saturated with moisture. Unsurprisingly, so does your body! It too tends to carry extra "moisture" in the spring, often in the form of leftover winter mucus and extra fat. To counteract this, you can eat some gently drying foods and engage in activities that help rid your body of the excess moisture.

As the weather begins to warm and the earth begins to freshen, it's an excellent time to get outside in the gentle sun and enjoy some moderate regular exercise, such as family walks. Spring is nature's time of renewal, and the green shoots that are the hallmark of this season are packed with nutrients. These early greens also have a bitter, drying quality that is an excellent antidote to the excess fat and mucus in the body.

BALANCING SPRING FOODS

Lighten up your diet after the winter: let go of heavier, more fatty foods and eat more seasonal vegetables, especially leafy greens. If you get outside more, increase your physical activity, and feast on the spring greens, you will trigger your body's natural seasonal fat metabolism, and the extra winter weight will begin to come off on its own with very little effort. Lighter meals such as broiled fish or white meat, cooked greens, beans, and sprouted salads are ideal for the spring season.

Grow Your Own Sprouts

Sprouts are an excellent spring food loaded with nutritional benefits: they contain high concentrations of enzymes, vitamins, and amino acids. Growing your own is easy and can be a fun project to do with the kids. In our experience, when children are involved in the process of growing something or cooking it, they are more willing to try it.

You can find sprouting kits (which contain special screened jar tops; different types of seeds, nuts, or beans; and directions for sprouting) in natural food stores or online (we like www.sproutpeople.com). Or you can just purchase sprouting seeds, nuts, or beans and make your own. Place a large handful of sprouting seeds in a large glass jar covered by a piece of cheesecloth (use a rubber band to keep it snug). Cover the seeds with a 2:1 solution of water and vinegar—at least four times as much water as seeds. (The vinegar's acidity will help kill any preexisting bacteria on the seeds.) Let soak for at least 3 hours and up to 24 hours, depending on the package directions for your type of seeds. Drain the water and rinse with fresh water, leaving the seeds moist, but not wet. Lay the jar on its side, out of the sun. For the next two to four days, rinse and shake the seeds twice a day—the seeds should not dry out. Change to new, dry cheesecloth after each rinsing session. In a few days, they will sprout.

Once they sprout, place the jar in a sunny spot and keep moist in the same fashion. They are ready to eat when they're green on top (filled with chlorophyll). Refrigerate and use them in salads, in sandwiches, atop soups, and as snacks.

Caution: Following a small outbreak of salmonella in a few western states in 2002, the Centers for Disease Control and Prevention (CDC) issued a warning about eating raw sprouts. The two dozen reported cases were traced back to alfalfa sprouts produced by one company, which withdrew that product from the marketplace.[1]

Because of the moist growing environment necessary to cultivate sprouts, they can harbor bacteria. These bacteria can be particularly harmful to people with compromised immune systems, such as children, the elderly, and those with chronic illness. But actual recorded cases of salmonella or *E. coli* from sprouts are very rare, especially in comparison to the number of cases caused by meats and other animal products.

Drying foods include:

- Clean, fresh water to help flush out the excess mucus and fats
- Bitter spring greens, such as collards and turnip greens, because they are drying and stimulate digestion. Other greens as well for their detoxifying effects
- Young salad vegetables, such as baby turnips and radishes, for their tonifying effect on the body
- Sprouts of all kinds for enzymes and rich nutrients such as chlorophyll, a power pack of vital energy
- Beans of all kinds, especially lentils and limas, for their cleansing and drying effects
- Lighter, less fatty meats, such as fish, poultry, and lean cuts of pork, as good sources of protein
- Pumpkin seeds, sunflower seeds, and hazelnuts for their nutrients and lighter fats
- Turmeric for its anti-inflammatory benefits
  Foods to reduce or avoid in spring include:
- Excess salt, because it causes the body to retain moisture
- Saturated fats or heated oils, because your body needs to rid itself of its excess winter fat
- Rice and yeasted bread and crackers, because they increase moisture in the body (dry, yeast-free breads and crackers are drying, however)

SUMMER: HOT WEATHER AND YOUR BODY

In the summer, the temperature heats up, so your body will want to cool down. You might experience cravings for cold, sweet, or raw foods. You might feel lighter and more energetic than in the colder months, enjoying more outdoor play. Your children will benefit from cooling water play on the hottest days, at the beach or under a sprinkler.

If you were able to metabolize the extra winter fat in the spring, your body will be in balance, ready to receive the higher sugar levels of the summer fruits. If, on the other hand, your fat metabolism didn't get triggered and your internal balance restored, your system will still be carbohydrate- and fat-overloaded and, when you eat summer sweets such as fruits and cooling treats such as ice creams, you'll be more susceptible to the SAD blood sugar cycle.

BALANCING SUMMER FOODS

Lunch or dinner salads make excellent summer meals. It's a good time to eat raw foods. Cooking techniques that work well in the summer are grilling, simmering, steaming, and fast sautéing. In the summer, it is natural to eat a little more lightly than in the colder months: this has a balancing effect after heavy winter meals. You may find that you or your children are simply less hungry when it's hot outside.

Cooling foods include:

- Melons, especially watermelon
- Berries
- Salads and salad vegetables, such as cucumbers and jicama
- Cooling teas, such as chamomile and mint
- Tahini (a spread made from sesame seeds); tahini is delicious on cold sesame noodles, in salad dressings, and as a dip for vegetables
  Foods to reduce or avoid in summer include:
- Sour foods, such as buttermilk and olives, because they increase heat in the body

- Fried or high-fat foods, such as pizza and fatty meats, because they are too heavy for these "lighter" months

AUTUMN: COOLING WEATHER AND YOUR BODY

Autumn is a natural time of harvest and preparation for the cold hard months of winter. You may feel a kind of busy energy in the fall season, as if your animal body is feeling the urge to put away food for the winter. Throughout most of the country, children return to school, and families enter into a more regular routine after the less structured, longer days of summer. As you adjust to these societal transitions, so too does your body adjust to the cooler temperatures of fall after the heat of summer, preparing itself for a gradual transition to the more extreme cold of winter.

BALANCING AUTUMN FOODS

In the fall it's time to shift your cooking techniques and break out slow cookers and roasting pans. Great fall meals include roasted root vegetables and the dark green leafy vegetables that thrive in the initial cold snap of the harvest season, such as kale and collard greens. Warm grain and bean dishes are great meals that will help you move into the heavier soups and stews as the weather gets colder.

Transitional warming foods include:
- Winter squashes, such as acorn, butternut, and pumpkin
- A variety of cereal grains, such as barley, amaranth, oats, and sweet brown rice
- Lean red meat to help build up the iron in the blood
- Cheeses, butter, ghee, and soured dairy products such as yogurt, kefir, and light sour cream to help start the warming process in the body

Foods to reduce or avoid in autumn include:
- Sweet summer fruits, such as berries and melons
- Tropical fruits, such as bananas, which can have a congesting effect and cause constipation

Can you see the natural wisdom of eating foods according to the seasons? Autumn and winter foods bring cooling relief from the intense heat of summer. Spring foods bring a reprieve from the cold dryness of winter. And summer foods provide heat to dry up the waters of the spring. It's beautiful in its simplicity, really. The more you follow Mother Nature's lead by eating the foods that grow during these seasons, the more harmoniously you can move through the transitions and challenges the changing weather has on your body.

Top Takeaways

- Eating foods that are grown in season, especially on local land, will help you and your family stay healthy through the natural transitions of the year.
- Attuning to the particular physical demands of each season can give you clues about which kinds of foods will balance the challenges of excess heat, cold, moisture, and dryness.
- Let your choices of cooking techniques be responsive to the seasons; prepare lighter, cooler dishes in the warmer months and more roasts, casseroles, and slow-cooked foods in the colder months.

FOR YOU

- Call your local Chamber of Commerce for a listing of local farmers' markets in your area. Ask about their seasons and times of operation. Plan to visit them to see what they offer.
- Do you have any farm stands where you live? If they are fairly close by, try visiting one of them, rather than your supermarket, for your fresh produce this week.
- Look into local growers' co-ops. Many small farms sell shares of a season's crops to families. Having a "farm share" is fun and easy: most farms designate days and locations where you pick up your share. (When you invest in a local farmer in this way, you share his or her risk: depending on the weather and other environmental factors, you might not get a great tomato return, but you could have plenty of early lettuce.) See www.localharvest.org/farms for a listing of co-ops, CSAs, and farmers' markets.

FOR YOUR KIDS

A few times a year, try to schedule a fun event that will help your children understand the connection between their food and the local climate and farms.

- In the fall, take them to an orchard to pick apples. Attend a harvest fair and look at the prize-winning vegetables.
- In the winter, have them help you peel a bunch of root vegetables, such as sweet potatoes, beets, and parsnips, and roast them together with a little olive oil to make your own "sweet veggie fries."
- In the spring, tour a small local farm. Many offer hayrides, petting zoos, and fun farm stands.
- In the summer, help your children grow some sunflowers outside. If you can't grow things outside, get a mason jar and follow the sprouting directions earlier in this chapter to harvest a mini-crop of fresh, crunchy sprouts.

Dairy[2-3]

Many people are confused about the proper role of dairy in their diet. Dairy is heavily promoted in this country as being key for bone health. What really creates strong bones is a balanced diet, weight-bearing exercise, proper trace nutrient intake, and hormonal health. Here are some facts about dairy:

- The USDA recommends that adults drink 3 cups of cow's milk per day. This supplies two-thirds of the day's recommended protein, leaving less room to consume a variety of other high-quality protein foods, such as beans and fish, which provide vital nutritional benefits.
- Cow's milk is designed to promote the growth of baby cows: it is very high in protein to help build calves' fast-growing bodies and slower developing minds. A calf is supposed to quadruple in weight during its first six months, while human infants' weight should only double.

- Lactose, the sugar in cow's milk, is difficult to digest. Many people are lactose intolerant, especially people of Asian and African descent.
- Women of Asian countries such as Japan and China, where dairy is rarely consumed, have fewer fractures and fewer incidents of osteoporosis than women from milk-drinking countries, including the United States and Scandinavian nations.
- Fluorine, a dietary mineral, helps strengthen immunity, teeth, and bones; raw goat's milk is one of the best sources of fluorine; fluorine is almost ten times higher in goat's milk than in cow's milk. The chemical version, sodium fluoride (in our water supply), does not have the same nutritional value as dietary fluorine does.
- Another advantage of goat's milk over cow's milk is its smooth curd and tinier fat globules, which make it more digestible.
- Excellent nondairy sources of absorbable calcium include collard greens, kale, mustard greens, dried beans, nuts, corn tortillas, and tofu.

Vegetarian
Naked Quiche
(see page 187)

6

How Much We Eat: Food Quantity

We've been talking a lot about the "whats" and "hows" of eating; in this chapter we'll look at the important topic of how *much* to eat: portion sizes. There is no perfect formula for accurately determining a healthy quantity of food. How much to eat, like what to eat, is a very individual decision. It depends on factors such as your age, weight, level of physical activity, and which particular foods you are eating at a given meal.

For a Natural Eater, the decision of how much to eat is guided simply and automatically by that person's hunger and satiety (satisfaction) signals. In a balanced system, when the body needs to eat, it will naturally send cues and signals that the fuel tank is low and needs to be replenished. True hunger signals (not imbalanced cravings) usually occur when there is no more food digesting in the stomach from the last meal, and the body needs another "tank" of food to manufacture its fuel.

We understand that hunger and portion size can be very sticky issues to approach with your children, especially if they tend to overeat because of one or more of the SAD imbalances. If you are a SAD Eater, then it is probably already challenging for you to consistently eat healthy portions yourself, never mind helping your children to do the same.

To help your children figure out how much is enough, you'll need a safe and friendly way to communicate with them about food. We have found that educating kids about their body's way of "talking to them" can be an effective approach. If you put the emphasis on hearing the body's natural signals, rather than on the food itself, you can diffuse some of the natural defensiveness and shame your children might experience when talking about how much they eat and why. Obviously, this kind of communication will look different if you are talking with a kindergartener or a tenth-grader, and you can modify your approach so that it is always age appropriate. (See the end of this chapter for some practical suggestions.) The best place to start is to learn about the mechanisms of hunger and satiety and how they occur in your own body.

Sweet Potato

- 1 medium baked sweet potato with skin (2" x 5") contains 2 g protein and 4 g fiber, and has 103 calories
- Is a naturally sweet, nutritious root vegetable
- Is high in vitamin A and a good source of vitamin C, manganese, copper, fiber, potassium, vitamin B6, and iron
- Is high in antioxidants, which eliminate free radicals in the body and are anti-inflammatory
- Is high in carotenoids, which may help lower insulin resistance
- Helps increase calcium absorption: eat sweet potatoes two to three hours after taking calcium supplements
- Should be firm without bruises, cracks, or soft spots
- Store loose, in a cool, dark ventilated area; will stay fresh for up to ten days
- Can be prepared in many ways: baked whole in skin, baked as french fries, puréed with cinnamon and maple syrup, steamed, and added to muffins, pies, pudding, or bread. Try substituting sweet potato for white potato to improve the nutritional quality of any dish
- See page 149 for more about sweet potatoes

Hunger Cues

Actual physical hunger is a polite sensation at first. It can manifest in many ways. It can be a hollow or empty feeling just below your rib cage. (That's where your stomach is: right below the solar plexus. It's not behind the belly button, as many people think—that's your intestines, or "gut.") Some people experience it as a mild ache. Sometimes your belly will sing for its supper, emitting a series of Pooh-bear-like growls and grumbles (if these growls are above your belt line, they're generally signaling hunger; if they are below, they are usually the result of digestion or gas). Some people don't actually feel physical sensations in the stomach, but rather an overall sense of being empty. Other people feel a little shaky or lightheaded from the lack of fuel, but that usually manifests when they are more than just a little hungry.

As we said, hunger sensations are polite at first: they will visit you for only about fifteen minutes. If you don't respond with food, the hunger "pains" will often subside for twenty to forty-five minutes, and then will arise again. Usually they increase in intensity each time they arise until you eat something. If you wait too long, you will eventually feel a sense of weakness, or even fatigue, and a strong sensation of emptiness. These feelings usually resolve completely within about twenty minutes of eating something.

Satisfaction (Satiety) Cues

If that's how a balanced system tells you when to eat, how does it tell you when to *stop* eating? Those signals are a little subtler, and most of us have to be very tuned in or we'll miss them. At a certain point in the meal, your body will start to send you gentle cues that you are close to having eaten enough. The first sign is often a slight change in the intensity of the flavor of the food. That's right, when you have eaten enough at one sitting, the food will actually stop tasting as good to you.

Ever notice how, when you are really hungry, the first bites of whatever you eat taste especially good? That is part of the *hunger* cuing system. If you pay attention, however, you will notice that in the middle of your meal, the food no longer tastes as delicious. That is your body cuing you that it is becoming *satisfied*. And if you overeat (which is easy to do if you are very hungry or eating quickly), the final bites of the meal have the least flavor impact. You can actually eat to the point where it is hard to taste the food much at all.

Another subtle satisfaction signal is feeling a sense of weight or expansion in your stomach. The hollow feeling of being hungry is replaced by a sense of gentle pressure below your ribs. This is a very comfortable and relaxing sensation, different from the I-can't-breathe-until-I-loosen-my-belt feeling that comes from eating too much. Even if you can't feel these specific, subtle physical sensations, you might feel an overall sense of peace or relaxation.

It actually takes about twenty minutes for your brain to get the satiety signal from your stomach and to produce those pleasant feelings. Twenty minutes is a pretty long time where eating is concerned. Some of us can put away a whole cake in twenty minutes! If you are a fast or gulping eater, chances are that you are putting too much food inside your body before your system has time to indicate that you are satisfied. You are probably eating more than you need, or is good for you, at your meals.

Satiety versus Fullness

We'd like to make a distinction here between satiety and fullness. When we talk about satiety, or feeling "satisfied," we are using that as the body's measure of a healthy portion at one sitting. Feeling satisfied does not indicate that you are "full." Full is when your stomach is actually filled up, and that means you've had too much food.

You may have noticed that after eating a particularly large meal, such as at a restaurant or a holiday meal, you not only feel uncomfortable in your belly but also a little drowsy. You may even be tempted to lie down for a nap. Part of this reaction is your body borrowing your living energy to digest all that food. Even your blood supply must be diverted to the center of your body when you are digesting.

A healthy stopping place is about three-quarters full, leaving a little bit of room in your stomach. The average stomach is about the size of two closed fists put together. Close your hands loosely, then put them together and look: that's around the most chewed food your stomach can hold at one sitting. (For some of you that may look small. You certainly can't fit an Applebee's ribs plate into that amount of space!) If you don't fill your stomach completely,

Bringing Up Baby

Babies who are breastfed experience one of the most natural forms of portion control. A mother's breast milk production and baby's appetite have a wonderful synchronicity developed through delayed supply and demand. A new mother's mammary glands initially produce a small quantity of milk that more or less matches the baby's stomach capacity. As the baby grows, he will need more milk and will consequently keep sucking on the nipples, which will stimulate the glands to increase milk production over time. As the baby moves on to solid foods and needs less milk, his mother's breasts will feel overloaded for a day or two, but will then begin to produce less. This system is so well designed that the glands of working moms can be trained to produce much less milk from 9 to 5, and fill them for a regular feeding time of 5:30 P.M.!

Milk flows slowly out of a human nipple, forcing the baby to slow down and giving her brain time to receive the satiety signal. A satisfied baby gets a little blissed out: flushed cheeks, soft eyes, and a peaceful, relaxed demeanor. That's her body telling her that she can stop eating now. However, with a bottle, there is a faster running stream that can encourage the baby to eat too quickly, and therefore feed beyond her need.

If the baby is allowed to eat on demand, rather than put on a strict schedule right away, he will naturally heed his own internal cues and ask to eat, usually with "rooting" for the breast or mild fussing, when his stomach is empty. As the baby grows, however, external cues begin to affect his eating behaviors. Once a toddler is eating solid food from a bowl or a plate, he will receive visual cues. He will start to recognize certain foods that he likes, and will begin visually registering portion sizes. He is learning many things by modeling (copying the behaviors he sees in others around him), and with eating it is no different: he sees the size of your plate and how much food you eat, as well as how much is on his plate.

By about the age of three, a toddler is probably receiving as many external cues as internal cues. If she is being raised in the SAD Lifestyle, then those external cues and imbalanced sugar and other cravings will likely control her desired portion sizes, rather than the sensations of hunger and satiety.

This behavior can actually be reversed fairly easily at this stage, preventing the child from routinely overeating. One way is to offer toddlers small portions. If they start with a small amount on their plate, they are less likely to ask for more unless they are actually still feeling hungry. If, however, you offer bigger portions at first, they will be more likely to overeat, even if they feel a gentle satiety signal.

To get a sense of roughly how much chewed food will fit in your child's stomach at a sitting, use the hand guide: close his fists and put them together. Also remember to help your very young child cultivate the habit of eating slowly and chewing her food.

it will have an easier time shifting and rolling the food around to mix it with the digestive acids and enzymes. It will also take less energy to digest, leaving more energy for the activities of your life.

Eating to satisfaction and not to complete fullness also acts as natural weight control. If you are a SAD Eater, achieving a balanced weight is difficult simply because you find it challenging to feel your own sensations of hunger and satiety. You may rarely if ever feel actual hunger. This is most likely because you eat based on other cues—cravings, habits, visual images of available food, etc.—rather than actual physiological hunger. If you use the actual size and sensations of your stomach as a guide, you will not overeat. This is easier said than done, we know, but with a little practice, it is a real possibility for most of us.

The Importance of Chewing

To begin tuning in to your satiety signals, you need to learn to eat slowly enough to hear them before you are done with your meal. In this country, most of us eat like snakes: we break up the food enough to get it down our throats without choking, and then swallow it. Sometimes the food is still practically whole. The next time you are in a public eating area, notice how many times people chew a bite. Watch someone talking and trying to get an unchewed piece of meat down—you might see them using the same motions as an owl swallowing a mouse whole! Most people chew one bite between four and seven times, depending on what the food is—most of the time that is just not enough chewing.

The act of chewing is a crucial part of the digestive process, especially for carbohydrates, and it plays a vital role in the hunger/satiety cuing system. This point was brought home to Jeannette very clearly while watching a cool IMAX movie about the workings of the human body. As you probably know, the screens for IMAX movies are many stories high, so watching is a visually intense experience.

In an early sequence in the film, a woman is eating a pasta salad. In a fascinating shot from a camera placed inside her body, we see the pasta salad falling down her esophagus (throat), and splashing down into her stomach. Watching barely chewed Volkswagen Bug–sized cherry tomatoes and gigantic pieces of fusilli crash down into her stomach really brought home how much work the body has to do to break down whole chunks of food into the tiny particles that can fuel our bodies.

Okay, we're not swallowing Volkswagens here, obviously, but we are giving the body a real challenge every time we don't chew enough. The task of digestion is to break your food into small enough pieces that the nutrients can be easily absorbed. If you don't chew your vegetables, grains, and beans, chances are that they will travel through your digestive system and pass out the other side fairly intact (you can probably imagine an eleven-year-old boy's joke about corn here). It is much harder for the body to extract the phytonutrients from a whole piece of food than from a mash of tiny particles mixed with saliva.

CHEWING AND CARBOHYDRATES

As we've discussed, carbohydrates provide critical fuel and nutrients to your body, and chewing them well is a crucial stage in their digestion. Saliva contains the most important digestive enzymes for breaking down carbohydrates. The enzymes begin to convert carbohydrates into sugar right in your mouth. Next time you are having rice or a cracker, chew one bite until it's almost water and notice how sweet it becomes—right in your mouth! Chewing your carbohydrates thoroughly may actually reduce sweet cravings because your body will be receiving a deeper level of sweetness from the healthy complex carbohydrates you are already eating.

If you don't chew your carbohydrates and mix them with saliva, they are not going to digest well, and:

- Your body will have a harder time realizing that it has eaten them, so your brain won't send you that peaceful sense of satiety.
- Your body will have to work twice as hard to break down that food, so you won't absorb all the available nutrients.
- The large pieces will ferment in your digestive tract, causing bad breath, gas, and bloating.
- You will be more likely to become constipated.

Part of the benefit of eating complex carbohydrates is that they provide a "broom" of fiber to sweep out your intestines. Insoluble fiber is the tough, indigestible part of plants. But you must break down those fibers first by grinding them with your teeth. Also, some of the best nutrients in plants are inside the hulls of the plant: you need to crush the tough cellulose walls to get to the nourishing centers.

It's less important digestively (and much harder) to chew your proteins so thoroughly because the acids for breaking down proteins are released inside the stomach and further down the digestive tract, not in the mouth. It's also a lot less pleasant to chew, say, a bite of egg twenty times than it is a mouthful of brown rice. Again, this is by design, to encourage you to chew your carbohydrates!

CHEWING AND THE CEPHALIC PHASE DIGESTIVE RESPONSE

Chewing well is crucial to getting your body to recognize the fact that it's eating at all. Your brain won't tell you when to stop if your body isn't really "getting it" that you're eating in the first place. In his phenomenal book *The Slow Down Diet*, Marc David has written an elegant description of an important part of digestion with a very complex name: the cephalic phase digestive response (CPDR). It is helpful to know about this so you can use it to your advantage to help you naturally control your portions.

CPDR is your body's response to the sensual cues of eating; it revs up the processes of digestion so that you can fully enjoy and absorb your food. CPDR kicks in before you even take a bite—it gets your saliva flowing and stomach working when you see, smell, and anticipate your meal. And while you are eating, the more you look at, savor, chew, and enjoy your food, the more effectively you will digest it and the less you will actually eat. CPDR helps turn on and improve the whole digestive process, fully engaging your brain and body to understand that you are nourishing yourself; this helps you know when you have eaten enough. Pretty neat, huh? It turns out that fully enjoying your food is good for you!

The converse is, unfortunately, also true: the less attention you pay to your food, and the more distracted you are (by television, driving, talking, etc.), the less you chew and the less effectively that food will be digested. If your body doesn't recognize that it has eaten, it may send you another imbalanced craving for food an hour after you've eaten, even if your belly still has food inside! It certainly will not be giving you those subtle satisfaction signals during the meal. Even if it does, if you aren't paying attention while you eat, you probably won't notice anyway.

Practical Natural Portion Control

The following are some of the ways you can harness chewing, the CPDR, and other techniques to boost the internal satiety cues of yourself and your family, thereby naturally beginning to control your portions, instead of relying on restriction or willpower:

1. Serve meals already plated, rather than having platters of food on the table for family members to serve themselves. This will help offset any visual cues from the amount of food on the platter, as well as provide a better model for portion sizes than those seen in restaurants.

2. Take a moment before meals for everyone to settle down a bit before they begin to eat. This can be as simple as lighting a candle and asking for everyone to remain quiet for a moment. Or you might encourage everyone to take two or three deep relaxing breaths together before eating. Or you might have a ritual of mealtime grace: a simple spoken or sung thank you and acknowledgment of the food and its source.

3. Encourage everyone to actually look at the food they are about to eat and take in its wonderful aromas. (Now we understand that you may want to skip right over this part if your fussy seven-year-old is already squirming in her chair because her chicken is touching "that green stuff" on her plate— so use your discretion with this exercise.)

4. Remind family members from time to time to taste and chew their food. You could even have a contest to see who can chew one bite the longest before swallowing.

5. Encourage your kids to take breaks between bites and put their forks down, and to check in periodically with their stomachs to see if they can feel themselves becoming satisfied.

6. Generally slow down the pace of the meal in any way you can. Don't rush yourself as you are eating. Spend a moment or two after you've eaten your last bite just sitting in your chair before you hop up for dessert or to clean the kitchen. Your own relaxed attitude will go a long way toward creating an environment of peace and relaxation at your family table.

7. Talk to your kids about hunger and satisfaction cues and help them become familiar with their own. For example, Jeannette's son now recognizes that he usually needs to eat some protein when he feels grumpy or frustrated in the evenings.

8. Try to minimize any extra stimulation at mealtime. For example, turn off the radio or

the TV, and don't allow talking on the phone or other frequent interruptions during meals. This will go a long way toward slowing and calming people's energy at mealtime.

9. One wonderful ritual to try, if your kids are old enough, is to occasionally have a meal in complete silence. This may be difficult, or feel awkward at first, but it can have tremendous benefits in becoming more present to the act of eating. You might think it's impossible with children, but in some progressive schools it's done routinely in classrooms even with very young children: they light a candle and don't speak until the candle is blown out at meal's end.

Portion Sizes for Stabilizing the SAD State

While you work on getting attuned to your internal cuing systems, you may also want to regulate your initial portion sizes externally using the hand guide. As we mentioned, the size of two closed fists is roughly the size of the stomach. To approximate balanced serving sizes for SAD Eaters, use the fist/palm/cupped hands guide in the Balanced Plate chart on page 54:

- A palm-size portion of protein
- A fist-size portion of sweet vegetable, grains, legumes, or fruit
- A cupped hands–size portion of high fiber, high water content veggies (especially the green leafies)

Because the hands and the belly grow at the same time, these guides work for people of all ages.

Remember, this is not a hard-and-fast rule, but rather a general guideline to give you a place to begin. Try not to get into food restriction with your kids—that can lead to further problems down the road. Honor their hungers, and instead help them learn to differentiate between the "mouth" hunger of SAD cravings and the "belly" hunger of a body that needs fueling. Help them feel inside when they need more food after a big day on the soccer field, or less on a lazy, hot summer day. A sense of playfulness and learning around this issue will take you a lot further than will pushing any restrictive "diet" mentality.

If your children are very SAD-imbalanced and chronic overeaters, you might find these recommendations challenging. You may just want to focus on upgrading their food quality for a while. It is your responsibility to offer them healthy choices, but it is ultimately their responsibility to choose what and how much they wish to eat. If, over time, you feel that your kids are eating a good balance of nutrients and yet their overeating is not naturally calming down, you might want to consult a nutritionist or even a psychologist who specializes in childhood overweight. There could be some other significant elements involved in their behaviors, such as sugar addiction, food sensitivities, or emotional issues.

Remember, your goal is to help your children get into a better relationship with their body and its internal cues—what you *don't* want is for them to get into a bad relationship with food and eating at a young age.

Top Takeaways

Internal Hunger Cues

- Hollow feeling near solar plexus
- Stomach "growling" above the belt line
- Light shakiness or mild lightheadedness
- An overall sense of emptiness or hunger

Internal Satiety (Satisfaction) Cues

- Gentle pressure or weight near solar plexus
- Reduction of food's taste appeal as the meal goes on
- Sense of peacefulness or relaxation
- Overall sense of being gently energized

Great Techniques for Natural Portion Control

- **Chewing:** Slow down and chew each mouthful of food, especially carbohydrates
- **Eating Awareness (CPDR):** Notice the colors and aromas of your food before you eat it. Pay attention to the food's flavors and textures and savor them as you eat.

FOR YOU

- Don't become the Portion Police—generally speaking, that's not helpful in creating lasting change and will likely be detrimental. You can offer initial plate portions at a reasonable size, but let your child decide how much he eats.
- Put emphasis on the *quality* and nutrient *balance* in the foods you offer rather than on the *quantities* consumed.
- Focus more on *how* everyone is eating rather than on *how much*.

- Practice tuning in to your own cues for hunger and satiety. You might wish to choose a time when you are eating something alone and really "listen" to your body as you eat. Can you chew each bite slowly and deliberately until it is nearly dissolved? How does it feel to eat that slowly?

FOR YOUR KIDS

- You are in charge of which foods you *offer* at meal- and snack times, but, as much as you can, let your children be in charge of which of those foods they *choose* to eat. This allows them to connect to their own hungers and cravings.
- If you don't want your children to eat a particular food, don't keep it in the house.
- Describe the list of possible activities under Practical, Natural Portion Control to your child and let her choose one or two practices for the family to try.

Fitting in the Food

By the time a food reaches your stomach, it has hopefully been well chewed, so it takes up less space than it did on the plate. Consider a lettuce salad: if you whipped that up in a blender it would only take up about 20 percent of its original size, right? That's what happens when you chew some foods well. (Steak, on the other hand, doesn't diminish all that much by being chewed.)

Classic Berry Smoothie (see page 185)

7

When and Where We Eat: Daily Routine

One of the simplest and most effective ways to improve your family's overall health and nutrition has nothing to do with food. It is something that was part of typical daily life until about twenty-five years ago, and only when it began to disintegrate did it become clear how vital it was to people's well-being. This simple practice prevented scores of "modern" problems that flummox today's parents: getting their children to go to sleep, to eat a variety of foods, to stop watching television, even to honor rules and respect others. What is this magical tool, this miraculous "cure-all"? It is routine.

The Magic of Daily Routine

In chapter 5 we talked a lot about the natural cycles of the seasons and your body's relationship to them. Just as there are broad seasonal cycles throughout the year, there are also shorter cycles throughout the day. These daily cycles are largely dependent on the sun, and so are impacted by the seasons as well. A winter's day on the East Coast is shorter and darker than a hot day in August. Simply by tuning in to the natural cycles of each day throughout the year, you will find a useful starting point for developing a daily routine for your family.

What elements of family life need routines? To answer that, think of your family as a small herd of animals. Consider what animals need on a daily basis: food, water, exercise, and sleep. If you look at animals who are very close anthropologically to humans, such as monkeys, you will find that they also need time each day to groom, work (to hunt and gather and build shelter), play, and enjoy companionship (or strengthen family bonds). These fundamental aspects of everyday life are common to most primates. Because we are animals too, we are programmed to spend time daily on these activities. Each day has a rhythm to it, with periods of time most natural for all these different elements of life.

FINDING THE RHYTHM

Daily rhythmic patterns of activity based on twenty-four-hour cycles are called *circadian* rhythms. All mammals, including people, have a "master circadian clock" located in the brain in an area called the suprachiasmatic nucleus (SCN).[1] The SCN communicates to the rest of the body when it is time to eat, stretch, sleep, etc. These functions are also influenced by the external, natural rhythms of light and dark. Activities such as movement, eating, focusing our minds, falling asleep, body temperature, and even going to the bathroom are governed by a combination of internal circadian cues and external cues from nature. Together these cues create natural "time zones" for your body. When you align your daily routines with these time zones, in which you were biologically designed to thrive, you can greatly support your health.

NOTEWORTHY NOURISHER

Quinoa

- 1 cup cooked contains 5 grams of fiber and 8 grams of protein and has 222 calories
- Is high in manganese; good source of magnesium and iron
- Is a light-textured, crunchy grain with a mild flavor similar to that of rice or couscous
- Contains the highest amount of protein of all the cereal grains; has eight essential amino acids and a lower glycemic load than that of most other grains
- Is versatile—can be used as a breakfast cereal with almonds and cranberries, as a side dish with vegetables, on a salad, or in soups or stews; try substituting for rice
- Is an ancient food of the Incas, and an important staple in South America
- See page 164 for more about quinoa

For instance, in the morning when you rise refreshed from a night of sleep, it is natural for your body to want to move and stretch. Biologically speaking, in the early part of the day people have the most energy available for *physical* endeavors. This is an optimum time for exercise; morning workouts tend to increase your metabolism more than those in the evening because your body is primed for movement.

As afternoon approaches, your biochemistry changes. You naturally enter a phase where you have less energy for physical activity and more for mental activity. The afternoon is a good time for working on creative projects or learning in school.

By the time the sun goes down, your body is less oriented toward action and thinking. It is also finishing up its food digestion and energy production for the day. In the evening your body begins to slow down, preparing for rest and the natural cleansing and renewing that will happen overnight while you are asleep.

When your daily routine is in alignment with these natural daily rhythms, energetically you are paddling *with* the current, as opposed to swimming upstream. This automatically makes all your daily activities easier—it is like going to the root of a problem instead of trying to "fix" each branch.

KEEPING THE BEAT

Another reason routines can make life easier for families is that our young ones thrive on clear, consistent structure. When your child's body "knows" food is coming (from having eaten at that same time every day for weeks), and when mealtime is at the ideal time of day, her digestion and assimilation of food will be easy. In the same way, when your child's body "knows" bedtime is coming, he will naturally begin to wind down.

If your young children eat and sleep at about the same times every day, you will hear their bellies grumbling right before dinner and see their eyelids drooping right before teeth-brushing time—with little to no protest on both counts. In other words, there will be maximum efficiency with minimum effort. It's a beautiful thing.

This practice was the norm in middle-class American families for decades. Regular family routines began to break down in the mid- to late seventies, when women began going to work in earnest. Prior to that time, a majority of mothers stayed home to raise their families, and working fathers' schedules were often very consistent. Bedtimes, bath times, wake times, school times, and mealtimes were very dependable. Of course, consistent routines weren't part of every household, but they were common. Today, the American family looks very different. More mothers are working now, and both parents work longer hours. Kids' after-school time is filled up with activities. Family members are going in different directions all day long, and their schedules may not align with one another's.

Although there are many exciting and beneficial things about living in a modern family, one thing that has gotten lost is a cohesive daily structure, which is extremely important for a family's overall health. Looking forward, our new American families need to regain a sense of healthy routine by working together in new ways. The kind of routine you create will probably look very different from the one you had growing up, or even from your next-door neighbor's, and that's fine. But it is important to create a consistent daily, or even weekly, schedule that works for you and your family.

A Word to the Supermoms

Many mothers try to "do it all" for their children. They choose their children's clothing and food each day, and cook and clean for them. On one level this might feel like a loving way to parent, but on another level it is not a very practical division of household labor in today's family, and it can actually sabotage a child's budding self-sufficiency.

In general, children are far more capable of regular household tasks than adults give them credit for. There is no physical or developmental reason why children should have everything done for them until they leave the home. Further, some tasks can be fun for kids.

Jeannette's daughter has a great love of cooking. She started making full dinners for the family at the age of eleven. Her pea soup is better than Jeannette's! Cooking is not one of her regular chores, but it's something she enjoys, so, with the exception of the "hot work" in the oven, she is allowed to take part in all aspects of daily cooking. This is just one example. Explore different ways to get your kids involved in caring for their home.

When they are in place, these routines will solve many parental dilemmas. A child whose family eats at the same time every day will naturally stop asking when dinner will happen. If the routine of the house is that dinner is from 5:30 to 6:15 and after that the kitchen is "closed" (this may not be your personal choice, we're just offering that as an example), then eventually your children will stop asking for after-dinner snacks. You might also notice a marked improvement in their dinner appetites when they understand that that's all there is to eat for the night. Similarly, once children have a relaxing bedtime routine, many of the challenges of falling asleep naturally fade away.

The magic of routine is that it removes the battle: an understanding of "how things are done" replaces the power struggle between parent and child. The discussion shifts from "*I want you to eat your dinner*" to "This is dinnertime and this is what is available to you now." Some power also shifts to the child in a positive way, as she is free to make choices *within the confines of a healthy routine* (rather than being strong-armed into something by the parent).

You may be thinking right now that your child will just challenge the routine instead of challenging you. It's been our experience, however, that this is not the case. If you try to change too much too fast, you will certainly face some rebellion from your family, but if you make changes gradually, children will usually accept that this is "how things are done"—that their schedule is not really set by you but by the natural cycles of the day. We encourage you to try this out for yourself and see what happens. You may find, as have many of our clients, that the magic of routine is the missing link to your family's balance and well-being.

Suggestions for Effective Daily Routines

Here are some suggestions about basic family routines that will give you the most bang for your buck. In chapter 8 we'll provide a helpful timeline for implementing the most important of these routines. Again, we have found that most often it is best to make changes slowly and gently over time.

1. EAT YOUR MEALS AT THE SAME TIMES EVERY DAY

Eating at consistent times each day will greatly enhance everyone's digestion and help naturally regulate appetites. You won't be able to make this happen all at once, though, so here are some places to start:

MAKE EATING BREAKFAST A PRIORITY

As we discussed extensively in chapter 4, breakfast is a crucial part of overall nutritional health, and vital for rebalancing the SAD state. This is especially true for children. There are countless studies demonstrating the connection between a good breakfast and good performance. Kids have more energy and mental clarity and just plain feel better when they have a healthy breakfast. If you help them by making their breakfast or, if they are older, providing options they can make themselves, they will be much more likely to eat. If you sit down and eat with your older children, the likelihood that they will eat is much stronger. See the Mix and Match section on breakfasts for many quick and healthy breakfast ideas.

HELP YOUR KIDS WAKE EARLY ENOUGH FOR BREAKFAST

Consistency at breakfast is fairly easy for those of us with school-age children to achieve, because there is a very specific block of time available in the morning before they have to get out the door. *Just make sure they are awake early enough to have the time to sit down and eat.*

PACK LUNCHES INSTEAD OF BUYING AT SCHOOL

Getting a healthy lunch can be tough for school-age children. The school lunch period has shrunk down to almost nothing. Many high school students have just seventeen minutes to buy (or unpack) and eat their meals. Sometimes they have to walk a long way to get to the lunchroom as well, which bites into their already scant mealtime. Most public school cafeterias are also loud and full of social stressors, which make them not very conducive to healthy, relaxed eating. With the three strikes of being rushed, being stressed, and the generally poor quality of cafeteria food, the average American kids' lunchtimes "strike out" when it comes to nutritional health. Creating quick, healthy lunchtime meals at home can help your child offset this special challenge.

OFFER "MINI-MEALS" TO YOUR KIDS AFTER SCHOOL

This idea comes from John Douillard, an Ayurvedic (the ancient Indian "Science of Life") practitioner and author of *The 3-Season Diet*. It can radically improve the latter half of the day for everyone in your family: better energy, less complaining, fewer meltdowns, lighter eating at dinner, etc. A mini-meal is something in between a snack and a lunch, and it usually includes a complex carbohydrate and a good-quality protein or fat. After school is an essential snack time for kids: they have been going all day with few breaks and not enough to eat. They are energy depleted and need food. Their impulse may be to reach for something sweet—that's their body looking for fast energy—but this craving will fade in time if they consistently have a solid mini-meal right after school. See chapters 13 and 14 for some good lunch and snack ideas that can work for this "extra" kid meal.

EAT DINNER EARLY AND, WHENEVER POSSIBLE, TOGETHER

Eating dinner early at a consistent time, between 5 and 6 P.M., is great for children. The body does not need heavy calories in the evening: the active period is over and the resting cycle will be starting in a few hours. If you can't eat early, it helps to prepare "lighter" fare for dinner, so you aren't giving everyone's bodies a heavy load right before bed.

We know consistent early meals can be almost impossible if you have children in after-school activities or sports. A good alternative is having consistent dinnertimes for each *day* of the week. For example, in Jeannette's house they work around the kids' karate and voice classes and Jeannette's hospital teaching schedule. Every Monday night they eat at 5:30 because everyone is available; every Tuesday night at 5:00 because karate is later; and every Wednesday is late healthy pizza night because everyone is busy earlier. Although this is a challenge, they do their best to hold consistent *weekly* routines. Once you achieve a daily or weekly schedule that works for you, it's helpful to stay as consistent as possible on weekends too, even though everything feels a little more relaxed.

Regular mealtimes have the most benefit if your whole family can dine together. Research on families who eat most of their dinners together is broad and compelling: kids from those families are much less likely to partake in dangerous behaviors such as smoking, drinking, and drug use, and they are more likely to use good table manners and eat more nutritious foods. Youths from families who eat meals together at least five to seven times per week report less stress in their families and the ability to go to a parent with a problem.[2]

2. HELP EVERYONE IN YOUR FAMILY GET FROM EIGHT TO NINE HOURS OF SLEEP EACH NIGHT

There are no nocturnal humans. For people, nights are primarily for sleeping. This is even truer for children. Sleep is as important a vital nutrient as water or minerals or protein. According to the National Institutes of Health's National Center for Sleep Disorders Research, all school-age children and teenagers need at least nine hours of sleep per night. According to the National Sleep Foundation, only about 20 percent of American children get the minimum recommended amount of sleep. Twenty percent! There is a growing body of evidence that suggests that a chronic lack of sleep increases the risk for heart disease, diabetes, and infection. Here's how to make some changes for your family:

PUT THEM TO BED BETWEEN 7:30 AND 10 P.M. DEPENDING ON THEIR AGE

Many of our kids simply stay up too late to get the full night's sleep they need. The best-quality sleep occurs between 10 P.M. and 6 A.M. Most school-age children need to go to sleep between 7:30 P.M. and 10 P.M. (yes, even your high school senior!) to get enough rest.

Sleeping in does not rest the body as much as going to bed earlier. You may have noticed that if you sleep in to the later morning hours, you wake feeling a little heavy and sluggish. That is because your body has passed out of its natural resting cycle and into the waking one, a time when you are meant to be active. Sleeping during the late morning is like eating in the middle of the night: it is certainly possible, but you are "swimming against the current" of the natural cycle, and it negatively impacts your body.

SET CONSISTENT WAKING TIMES

If you or your child is staying up too late, for whatever reason, the first step to remedy that is to wake everyone up a little earlier and keep that time consistent. Between 6 and 8 A.M. is the best window for school-age children. The earlier waking time will make you feel a little more tired when you are trying to go to sleep earlier at night. In time, after getting enough hours of sleep during the night and waking at a consistent time each morning, you will begin to wake up automatically, with no alarm or other help. This can even happen for heavy sleepers.

REDUCE STIMULATION AT BEDTIME

To get yourself or your child to sleep at a good time of night, the first step is to quiet the stimulation of the day. Many families have televisions in every bedroom; it's common practice for many to watch TV late at night and even to fall asleep with it on. On a sensory level, all sorts of things are being stimulated: your brain is processing vast amounts

Making Up Sleep

When you (or your children) have stayed up late at night, or are particularly exhausted for any reason, go to sleep *earlier* the next night rather than trying to catch up by sleeping in the morning—you will recover more quickly!

SIMPLE FOOD FOR BUSY FAMILIES

of visual data, including hundreds of quick camera changes, patterns, colors, and movement, as well as aural data, including noises that aren't normally part of the end of a day at home (guns firing, people screaming, rock music . . . you get the picture).

According to the National Institutes of Health's National Center for Sleep Disorders Research, 97 percent of American children have at least one electronic gadget in their bedroom. Adolescents with four or more electronic items in their rooms are more likely to be sleep-deprived than children with fewer. And these "plugged-in" kids are more than twice as likely to fall asleep during school.

Watching TV and playing video games or loud music before bed are not very restful practices, especially for anyone in your family with sleep challenges. The senses are being stimulated (or overstimulated) at a time when the natural world is calming them with dark and quiet. We think it is a healthier practice to create times and spaces in the home where there is little or no electronic (or other noisy and bright) stimulation. Our clients have seen their children's sleep habits improve by stopping after-dinner TV watching or giving their children a couple of TV-free hours before bedtime. At the very least, making the effort to calm and quiet your children's sleeping spaces at night will pay you and your child back in restful rewards.

CREATE A REGULAR, RELAXING BEDTIME ROUTINE

If your child goes to sleep easily, often the simple routine of teeth brushing and changing into pajamas is enough to start her yawning. If she resists bedtime or can't seem to relax at night, then you might try adding some soothing steps to help her transition to sleep time.

Are You Overstimulated?

In modern life we are exposed to a lot of stimuli—bright lights, loud engines, sights and sounds from TV and computer screens. Most people will eventually adapt to whatever stimulation they are given on a regular basis. However, some people have a harder time coping with high levels of or particular kinds of stimulation. Although we haven't seen any official studies, it's been our experience that our clients who have the most difficulty falling asleep (and the "night owls" who don't even try) tend to be very sensitive to levels of light, noise, and sound in their environment.

Dr. Elaine Aron, a research psychologist who has made an extensive study of this genetically inherited trait, calls it being "highly sensitive." If you are one of the 20 percent or so of the population who has a highly sensitive nature, there is nothing wrong with you! You are just in the minority. If you think you or your child is "highly sensitive," you might benefit from reading Dr. Aron's books, *The Highly Sensitive Person* and *The Highly Sensitive Child*. They contain life-changing information.

In general, very active physical play should be kept to a minimum after about 7 P.M., but you can do other more calming activities before bedtime with your child. A very restful way to end the day is with reading time. Children of all ages enjoy reading. Reading stories together will not only help children relax and sit quietly, it will also connect you in a very sweet way and improve their reading skills. Try it even with your teens—it's more fun than you think! You might invite everyone to be cozy together for a "family" read, snuggled with blankets in the living room, or piled onto the "big bed" in your room. (If you're too exhausted to read aloud to your kids, get some books on tape from the library and let a professional do the reading for you—the *Harry Potter* reader, Jim Dale, is fantastic!) Older children might be perfectly content to lie in their rooms reading alone or listening to soft music with the lights on low.

Our number one favorite bedtime ritual is the warm bath. Water is soothing and calming to jangled nerves. Immersing in it can help a body balance and integrate all kinds of stimulation. It has the added bonus of washing away all the germs picked up at school that day. You can then encourage your child to brush his teeth and hair and climb into some soft, comfy pajamas. Keeping the light low in his bedroom in the evenings will help as well.

Whichever rituals you put into your children's bedtime routine, consistency will heighten their effectiveness: doing the same things in the same order each night will "train" your child's body to rest and relax in preparation for sleep.

3. SET ROUTINES FOR SIMPLE GROOMING TASKS

Having routines for grooming cuts down on arguments and teaches good self-care habits. The types of grooming you assist with depend, obviously, on your child's age. Although children definitely become more independent with each passing year, they often need you to check in with their budding grooming efforts as they grow older. (The bath of a sixth-grade boy, for example, can become unfortunately rare without the strong "encouragement" of a regular routine.) We would like to make special mention of the following key tasks:

HAND WASHING

Hand washing after using the bathroom and before eating is a lost art in this country. Although many schools are making some efforts to teach this habit, the responsibility really lies with you, the parents and guardians. Cultivate the routine early and it will become a lifelong habit, preventing numerous bouts with illness and other, even less pleasant experiences (pinworms are something you don't want to have to deal with!). By encouraging this simple routine, you will also help others by slowing the spread of disease.

BRUSHING AND FLOSSING

Jeannette's ninety-year-old grandmother taught her, with words and experience, to take extra special care of her teeth. They do wear out in time, with very expensive and unpleasant consequences. After your kids' baby teeth fall out, they only have one set to last them a lifetime!

DAILY BOWEL MOVEMENTS

Although this may not fall exactly into the grooming category, and you may not want to address it at all, it is important for you to be aware of your child's bowel movements (BMs). Most parents are delighted to say good-bye to that particular awareness on the happy day when they throw away the very last diaper, but for your child's overall wellness, that would be a mistake.

Most children tend to go to the bathroom as little as possible during the school day, and may in fact work very hard *not* to have a bowel movement while at school. (And who can blame them?) This continual "holding" pattern can lead to a little backing up. Children who are already prone to constipation from eating the Standard American Diet might find it even more difficult to maintain regularity once they have started attending full-day school.

Just check in with your children every once in a while to see how often they are moving their bowels. It doesn't have to be an invasive inspection or anything—you want to respect their privacy—but you can teach them that it is a natural part of supporting their health, like eating well and sleeping enough. If they are not eliminating at least once a day, you might consider some gentle home remedies to get things moving. If increasing fluids and fiber doesn't work, consult your doctor.

4. MAKE MORNING PREPARATION FOR WORK/ SCHOOL A RELAXING TIME

Most people have fixed school and work schedules already. All too often, however, they end up waiting until the last possible moment to get started in the morning. The frantic rushing that inevitably ensues sets a tone of stress for the entire day. Here are some ideas for easing morning preparation for work and school:

PREPARE WHAT YOU CAN THE NIGHT BEFORE

Have everyone lay out the next day's clothes (in the wintertime, your kids can put them on the radiator so they are nice and toasty on a cold morning), and put together the "dry" ingredients for lunch. (Items such as cold pasta and crackers and fruit can be assembled and popped into the fridge the night before; things such as peanut butter and jelly sandwiches will get soggy if prepared too early, so leave those until the morning.)

How Often Is Enough?

According to Traditional Chinese Medicine (TCM), anyone who has fewer than two bowel movements a day is considered constipated. Based on the reports we hear, that would make just about all of America constipated! While appreciating the TCM focus on frequency and regularity, we feel it is satisfactory if your child has one good bowel movement per day—especially if it is in the morning.

The body is programmed for elimination after the digestive "janitorial" cycle has run its course in the night during sleep. If you or your child goes longer than one day without eliminating, then the waste can actually start to ferment in the bowels, causing gas, bloating, and other various discomforts. Plus, it isn't good for clarity of mind to be carrying around a big bellyful of waste. Efficient digestion and elimination are crucial elements of good health, so getting things moving is a priority.

SOME SAFE WAYS TO GET THINGS MOVING

- Drinking a glass or two of room temperature water upon waking
- Drinking hot water with lemon upon waking or before breakfast
- Drinking extra water throughout the day
- Drinking a small amount of heated orange juice
- Taking homeopathic remedies (they can cause no harm and have no side effects)
- Stretching in the morning, especially gentle twists
- Increasing the balance of high-fiber vegetables and fruits in the diet
- Taking 1 to 2 teaspoons of flaxseed oil before bedtime (flaxseed oil doesn't taste terrific to most kids, so try blending it into a little juice so they can drink it straight)

WAKE UP EARLIER

Give you and your children at least one full hour to get the day started in the morning—once you are used to the new wake-up time, you will be amazed at how pleasant the morning can be when you are all able to wash up and have breakfast without rushing.

TEACH YOUR CHILDREN TO PICK UP AFTER THEMSELVES

This simple routine can save parents a remarkable amount of time each day, especially in the morning. If your kids have hung up their coats, put their clean clothes away, and kept up with any dishes used throughout the day, your morning will not be bogged down with searching for misplaced items and clearing the kitchen to make room for breakfast.

You can introduce these routines very simply, starting with bed-making: even a four-year-old child can pull his or her blankets up to the pillow. Next, whenever anyone uses a dish to eat a meal or snack, let him be responsible for scraping it and putting it in the dishwasher (or stacking it neatly for hand-washing). Also, start the "one-cup-a-day" rule, which will cut down on dirty glasses: each person chooses a cup in the morning and sticks to that one all day long. Then help each child get into the habit of hanging up her coat and putting her hat and gloves into a nearby basket each time she comes home; then, when it's time to go back out in the morning, everything she needs is right by the door.

5. ENCOURAGE ACTIVE PLAY AND LIMIT TV AND COMPUTER TIME

Most children need at least a couple of hours a day of active play. But with the full schedules, fast pace, and abundance of electronic entertainment available to our modern families, children's active playtime is disappearing. At school, recess period and even physical education classes have been getting shorter and shorter due to academic performance pressures. Fewer children walk to school. Our neighborhoods are changing, too; they are no longer considered safe havens where children can play freely and without concern out of doors.

You might find that your child prefers to stay indoors watching television or playing on the computer. There are many games online now that feel "social" in nature: a group of friends can log on after school as different characters, talking to one another inside the game. They can fight battles, build a village, or go on safari. They might feel like they are connected with a group and being active. In a way they are, but they are also sitting relatively motionless in a chair with their eyes glued to a screen.

A child's active playtime is his equivalent of exercise. If he is limited in playtime or play space at school, he is probably not getting enough healthy

> ### Scary Statistic
>
> According to the TV Turn-Off Network, the average child spends more time each year in front of the television set than in the classroom: more than 1,000 hours![3]

exercise. Childhood obesity research points strongly to a link between the amounts of time children spend in front of a screen and their weight. Depending on the study you read, each extra hour your child watches TV corresponds to a weight increase of between 2 and 6 percent![4]

We believe that to increase the amount of movement and unstructured outdoor play in your child's day, it is essential to put some limits on her screen time. If the child is not allowed to watch TV or play on the computer every day after school, her boredom and restlessness might be effective motivators to "go out and play." Again, we can't stress enough that gradual change is the least likely to meet with open revolt. If your children aren't getting enough playtime, try these ideas for making it part of their routines:

SCHEDULE ACTIVE PLAY IN YOUR CALENDAR

Create several blocks of time throughout the week for the kids to just play. Book these times the way you would a lesson or team practice and honor them as just as important. If weather permits, getting the kids outside for these times is even better.

GRADUALLY REDUCE TOTAL TELEVISION AND MOVIE TIME

Our clients who have tried this have had good success implementing a "No TV on Schooldays" policy. TV and movies become a weekend treat and are appreciated much more. This leaves a lot more time during the week to play in a more active way.

KEEP A DAILY "LOG" OF TIME SPENT ON THE COMPUTER

Write up a weekly computer-use log and have your kids "sign on and off" when they use it. This will give you a rough idea of how much time they are actually spending in front of it. If it works for your family, you might try implementing a daily limit, such as one hour, and asking them to "budget" their on-screen time accordingly. You can even use a kitchen timer to help them keep track.

6. HAVE REGULAR FAMILY NIGHTS

It's easy for weeks to just fly by without families finding time to connect in a significant way. One way to build in nourishing together time is to have routines for certain nights of the week. Here are some ideas:

GAME NIGHT

Have a good collection of different games and let everyone take turns choosing which to play. Some of our favorites are Cranium (or Cadoo, the younger version), Rumikub, Guesstures, Pictionary, Monopoly, Twister, Operation, Chess, Sorry, Clue, Crazy 8s, and Penny Poker. The possibilities are endless!

HEALTHY PIZZA NIGHT

You can buy high-quality, premade whole grain dough and have children add their own toppings, or just order out and add a lot of extra veggies and a great salad.

DESSERT NIGHT

If you are struggling with too much sugar in your family's diet, save dessert for certain nights, maybe every other, or on Tuesdays and Saturdays, and make it special. Offer some do-it-yourself options, such as frozen yogurt sundaes, or bake healthy cookies together.

FAMILY MOVIE NIGHT

Take turns choosing the movie and have everyone bundle up together with blankets and popcorn for the film. Younger children enjoy movies more when the whole family watches together.

It may seem daunting to think about implementing a lot of new routines in your household, but don't get overwhelmed with trying to do everything at once. Start slowly, with one thing that is a challenge in your home, such as bedtime. The more consistent you are with your one new routine, the less work you will eventually have to do to make it stick.

Think of regular schedules and routines as another nutrient of Whole Life Nutrition. It will support your family members' efforts to improve their dietary health and their overall well-being. Remember, how people live and what they feel affects what they choose to eat; in the same way, what they eat affects how they live and how they feel. Anywhere along this cycle that you can make a positive change will help in all the other areas.

Top Takeaways

- The human body is naturally designed to function according to cycles and routines.
- Instituting routines around important elements of daily life will help your family thrive.
- Routines can reduce power struggles with your children and ease your transition to a healthier lifestyle.
- Key routines might encompass mealtimes, sleep times, grooming times, work and playtimes, and screen times.

FOR YOU

- What is the most stressful time of day for you and your family right now? In the morning, when you are getting ready for work and school? Around 5 P.M., when you are getting home from work and everyone is hungry and cranky? Bedtime?
- What is one thing each person could do to make things go more smoothly at that time?
- Design a new routine for that time of day that everyone can easily follow. Talk it over with your family and ask for ideas on each family member's tasks and responsibilities.
- Write out the new routine on a card or paper and hang it on the wall. Refer to it each day when that time rolls around until you all begin to do your parts automatically.

FOR YOUR KIDS

- Ask your kids to tell you what they most like to do together as a family and build that into your regular weekly (or monthly) routine.
- Go on a tour of their rooms, asking them to "scout" for electronics. Brainstorm ways to make their rooms more peaceful havens for resting.
- Give your children a list of the daily and weekly chores that you regularly perform. Ask them to choose something from the list as their job for that week or month. Consider having some kind of reward system, such as stars on a chart, every time they do their chore without being asked. When they get a certain number of stars, give them a prize.
- If the children are older, consider increasing their allowance periodically, like little raises, as a show of support for their increased contributions around the house.
- Are any of your children old enough to prepare meals? If so, consider "apprenticing" them while you experiment with the Mix and Match formulas later in this book. This will teach them how to make soups, stews, and other meals. When they are ready, you can put them on a schedule to cook a few times per month. Kids love having the power of deciding what the family will eat for dinner.

Simple Succotash (see page 174)

8

Putting It All Together: Whole Life Nutrition for Your Family

It is possible for your family to let go of the SAD Lifestyle and have a more nourishing, natural rhythm of eating, working, playing, and relaxing. By improving the overall quality of your food, balancing your nutrients and your portion sizes, eating more seasonal foods, and incorporating some healthy routines into your days, you can support your family to move out of the SAD state and become more Natural Eaters.

Implementing a high-quality, Whole Life Nutrition lifestyle is much more of an ongoing practice than a specific, one-time act. The final results will be quite individualized because you will personalize the suggestions to suit the needs of your family. We will offer guidelines for a chronological schedule, with encouragement to give yourself time goals for each one— not because it has to be done that way, but because we've noticed that things tend to actually *get* done only when you make a specific goal and set a deadline for it!

We have broken down our suggestions into two sections:

- Section 1: Power Steps for Creating a Whole Life Nutrition Foundation
- Section 2: Power Goals for Balancing the SAD State

Following the steps in section 1 will help you build a solid base for better family health. It will also give you a good foundation from which you can more easily work on the additional goals in section 2. If your family is relatively healthy and just needs a little boost to get on track to great health, section 1 may be enough for you. If, however, you have a family of chronic SAD Eaters, then you may want to go on to section 2. These Power Goals are more advanced steps that will help rebalance the SAD state.

We've presented all these steps in the order that is usually most effective for our clients. But if any of the suggestions make more sense to you arranged in a different order, then by all means, switch things around to perfectly fit your family. The point is to choose and implement changes that will actually work for you.

Taking It Easy

We advocate bringing in some of these changes under the radar. It's probably best not to announce to everyone that you have seen the light and will be throwing out all the sugar! Too many changes made too quickly could create a mutiny under your roof, and you don't want your kids to run away screaming when you say things such as "good for you" or "healthier lifestyle."

Here are some guiding principles for avoiding the pitfalls brought on by your zeal for change:

- Make changes one at a time.
- Add new things before taking away the old and familiar. It's always easier to try

something novel than to say good-bye to an old habit. For example, offer small tastes of vegetables before cutting back on the french fries and rolls. Eventually, when you find some vegetables your family likes, it won't be as big a deal when those rolls get replaced.

- Avoid telling people they are "wrong" for their current behaviors—that can separate you and alienate them. Instead, overpraise any small steps they make in a healthy direction. For example, if your child tastes something and doesn't like it, you might say, "Nice job, you gave that cabbage a real taste, good work!" versus "You never like anything new, what's the matter with you?"
- Do your best to frame everything in the positive—for instance, "We're trying to get more sleep tonight so we'll feel really good tomorrow," versus "You can't stay up late tonight because you'll be exhausted when you wake up." See how the first version might be easier to hear?

Section 1: Power Steps for Creating a Whole Life Nutrition Foundation

Read through the seven Power Steps. Choose one to start with. Set aside one to two weeks to practice that step or "focus point" with your family. After you've mastered that step, move on to any other of the seven steps and practice for one to three weeks. Repeat until you've tried all seven steps.

If you try a Power Step and it just isn't clicking with your family after two or three weeks, that's fine; move on to a different step. You can always come back and try again later. Your family may need some other changes in place first. Feel free to skip, add, or mix and match to your heart's content: make it your own process. If something doesn't work, ditch it. If you really like something a lot, make it a permanent change. You know your family better than anyone, so just dive in and start experimenting.

After trying each of the seven Power Steps, if you want to work on antidoting one or more of the SAD imbalances, then move on to the Power Goals.

STEP 1: GET ENOUGH SLEEP

Aim for 8 to 9½ hours per night; implement helpful bedtime and morning routines.

Principles: Routine, seasonality
Time frame to implement: 3 weeks or longer

- Set a consistent bedtime based on the cycle of the season and school year (later in the summer, earlier in the fall and winter) and stick to it, especially on weekdays.
- Create a regular, relaxing bedtime ritual.
- Wake your children at a consistent time each morning.

The first routine to tweak when trying to improve everyone's overall nutrition and health is sleep. Making other changes, especially nutritional ones, will be much easier if everyone is well rested and therefore has good energy. For school-age children, as we've mentioned, this means getting them to bed early enough to get at least eight and preferably nine or more hours of sleep, and waking them early enough to have a relaxed breakfast and prepare for school in the morning.

If falling asleep is difficult for your kids, gradually set up a regular, more restful evening routine. If they watch a lot of TV or use the computer after dinner, try offering to play a game (not a video or computer game) or read with them during what would be their "screen time." The goal is to get them to reduce, or even eliminate, TV watching. After game or playtime, suggest that they have a warm bath or shower and brush their teeth.

Set a "lights out" time and stick to it. Remember to wake your children earlier in the mornings while you are trying to do this, so they are tired at night. For further discussion about sleep routines, see chapter 7.

STEP 2: DRINK PLENTY OF WATER

Aim for 5 to 8 glasses of fresh water daily. Use routines and tricks to encourage drinking more water.

Principles: Routine, balance
Time frame to implement: 1 to 2 weeks

- Begin to offer water to drink at regular times throughout the day, such as first thing in the morning, after school, and after exercise or hard play.
- Leave water around in conspicuous places in fun cups and water bottles to make it more likely that your children will remember to hydrate.
- As you increase their water intake, begin watering down or reducing any other sweet drinks they drink throughout the day, especially soda and fruit juice.

The body is usually a little dehydrated in the morning, so offer your child a drink first thing when he or she wakes up. Encourage older kids to get into the habit of filling a fresh glass for themselves each night and leaving it on their nightstand for the morning. There are some fun water bottles with caps that are cups; these are safe to leave on a bedside table for a young child.

Let your children see you drinking lots of water when you are thirsty, and offer them water at times when you think they may be thirsty, such as when they walk through the door from school, from playing, or from exercise.

Offer your kids plain water or milk instead of juice or soda at mealtimes. If your kids are hooked on sweet drinks, water down their drinks very gradually over a long period of time until there is very little sugar in them. Commercial soda is easily replaced with real juice and plain seltzer, or even fruity (noncaffeinated) herbal tea and seltzer. You can also encourage your children to drink some water first, and then their regular sweet drink after—they might drink less of the latter.

STEP 3: INCREASE MOVEMENT OR EXERCISE

Aim for a minimum of 1 to 2 hours of physical activity daily; double that when they are on summer vacation from school.

Principles: Routine, balance
Time frame to implement: 1 to 3 weeks

- Let your kids walk, skate, or ride their bikes. Can they walk or ride to school in good weather?
- Try parking farther from any destination and have races to the door. They can be fast or slow races, funny walk races, backward walk races, or whatever you can think up.
- Engage them in yard work. Grow a garden and put your kids in charge of weeding and watering. Sometimes a little extra allowance money can sweeten this offer.
- Find ways to make your TV time less passive. Encourage standing up and moving during commercials—this will have the added bonus of reducing the number of advertisements your kids see!
- A ten-minute walk around the neighborhood after dinner is a great way to relax, improve digestion, and get some extra movement in.
- Put on your favorite music (even if your kids consider it out of date) and dance around to it. This might appall your older kids at first, but even your middle-school-age children may eventually join in if it looks like enough fun! The important thing is to model for them that movement and exercise are fun.
- Remember Twister? Try this or one of the charades-style games, such as Guesstures, to get everyone up, moving, and laughing hysterically.
- Help your older child find an active job, such as a paper route, shoveling snow, walking dogs, or babysitting.
- Encourage your children to join an after-school or intramural team or exercise class, such as soccer, tennis, yoga, or karate. Helping them find a physical activity or sport they love can be the key to a lifetime of good exercise.

School-age children need physical play and movement for at least one to two hours every day. How can you get every member of your family to move more? Where are the opportunities for increasing movement in a fun way? Model exercise for your children; let them see you involved in adult physical activities, sports, games, or dance or exercise programs. Talk together as a family to come up with ideas for more family movement.

STEP 4: IMPLEMENT REGULAR EATING ROUTINES

Aim for consistency in mealtimes each day, especially at dinner.

> **Principles:** Routine, quantity
> **Time frame to implement:** 1 to 3 weeks

- Organize in the evening so in the morning there is time for breakfast: have your kids bathe and lay out clothes at night; wake them up one hour before they have to leave the house; teach them to make a healthy simple breakfast themselves.
- Pack a healthy school lunch for your children: assemble the dry components the night before, use dinnertime leftovers, and see chapter 13 for great lunch box ideas.
- Serve a regular after-school mini-meal: this can be the second half of their lunch or even the first part of dinner.
- Stick to a family dinnertime: set the family suppertime and keep it consistent; after cleaning up, you can "close the kitchen" except for water and hot drinks until the next morning.
- Keep a weekend schedule: even if you allow things to be looser on the weekends, try to keep dinner at a consistent time.

Having a family dinner develops or improves family intimacy. As children age, it can become harder to get them to share what's going on in their daily lives. If you raise them with a lively family dinner, however, communicating at dinnertime becomes a regular habit. Eating on the early side is generally better for both digestion and quality of sleep. See chapter 7 for some specific suggestions about creating regular mealtimes within a busy family schedule.

STEP 5: UPGRADE THE QUALITY OF YOUR STAPLE FOODS

Investigate your pantry and gradually bring in healthier versions of familiar foods.

> **Principles:** Quality, balance
> **Time frame to implement:** 3 weeks or longer

- Venture into the "natural foods" sections of your regular grocery store and take a tour of your local health food store.
- Begin switching out your processed foods for less refined, more intact versions with a higher nutrient profile.
- Trade prepared foods with a lot of ingredients you don't recognize for the corresponding product from the store's "natural" line, such as Stop and Shop's "Nature's Promise" products.
- Also investigate organic brands for higher quality versions of the same foods you usually buy.
- Purchase whole wheat or whole spelt pastry flour. The next time you need to use flour, use half white, half whole wheat or spelt.
- Introduce your family to a lower glycemic load healthy sweetener, such as agave nectar; try serving it over waffles instead of syrup.
- Upgrade the ingredients of your standard family recipes; see if you can reduce the

amount of sweetener, increase the amount of fiber, and reduce fat or replace the fat with a higher quality fat.

This step is about transforming your pantry. Take inventory of the foods you regularly stock at home, make a list of poor-quality foods to wean from, and replace these with higher quality versions. Also make a list of any new foods you'd like to try. As staples run out and need to be replaced, upgrade to higher quality versions. Consult the Core Pantry Ingredients list in chapter 9 for healthy, basic whole-food staples. When investigating the labels on the processed foods you buy (crackers, snack bars, bread, etc.), take note of the following:

- How many ingredients are listed? Do you recognize them all as food? What is the number one ingredient?
- Are the grain ingredients whole or highly refined?
- What is the content of the salt? The sugar? Twenty percent or more means the food has a "high fat" or "high sugar" content. Five percent or less is "low."
- What is the fat content? What type of fat is it? Are there trans fats or hydrogenated oils in the ingredients?

STEP 6: DO MORE OF YOUR OWN COOKING

Move from restaurant food to home-cooked food to ensure higher quality.

Principles: Quality, quantity, balance, seasonality

Time frame to implement: 3 weeks or longer

- Experiment with one new fresh whole food each week: choose an unfamiliar vegetable, grain, or bean and look it up in chapter 11 or 12 of this book or on the Internet. Learn what it is and some ways to prepare it. Try using it in a Mix and Match recipe from chapter 13.
- Replace some of your standard foods with organic versions, especially dairy, internationally imported fruits and vegetables, and meats.
- Upgrade your kitchen tools: make a basic equipment wish list of items you'll need for preparing home-cooked meals.
- Cook at least one more meal from scratch per week. Try regularly making a basic food, such as a pot of quinoa or a roasted chicken, and use it in several meals over a few days.

There are some things to consider when you decide to make the move from having restaurant food to home-cooked food. Is your kitchen ready? Take an inventory of your equipment and make a wish list of any items you'd like to purchase. Keep it handy and, when the money is available or when Aunt Sally needs a Christmas present idea for you, get something from the list. If you have the time, look at garage sales and flea markets for inexpensive, basic cooking tools.

Begin looking for whole, organic versions of the fresh foods that you already eat. If you belong to any bulk buying clubs such as Sam's Club or BJ's, check to see whether they have organic choices. Organic or "natural" meats in particular can be quite a bit cheaper if you buy in bulk and freeze what you won't use right away. (The term "natural" refers to processing only, not how it is produced: minimal processing with no artificial ingredients, but it may have been raised in conventional feedlots. "Natural" meat may contain growth hormones or antibiotics, so look for meats that say "natural—no growth hormones or antibiotics used.")

Also start thinking seasonally. What are some of the foods of the season right now? An added bonus of buying seasonal produce is that it's often the cheapest option because it is plentifully available at that time. Try adding a few seasonal foods to your cart each time you shop.

If you are not already a confident cook, read through part 2 of this book to familiarize yourself with basic whole foods, spices, and cooking techniques. Begin to experiment with the Mix and Match formulas for meals. Choose one main dish, such as stew; learn the formula, choose the ingredients you'd like to use, and try it out. For more great suggestions for how to become a great everyday cook, see chapters 9 and 13.

STEP 7: SLOW DOWN AND CHEW

Make chewing a core practice to help your family slow things down.

Principles: Routine, quantity
Time frame to implement: 1 to 2 weeks

- Pause and give thanks before eating.
- Remember to breathe while you eat.
- Model being calm at mealtimes, even if there's a cyclone of activity around you.
- Practice chewing with the help of fun games and reminders.
- Experiment with having a silent meal, and note the difference in how everyone feels afterward.

It's hard to notice what you're eating, let alone pay attention to how you chew it, when the dinner table is chaotic with TV noise, with bickering or complaining, or with people coming and going to answer their cell phones. It is possible to create an oasis from the chaos, but it takes a determined effort. Today's families have to work at creating calm and making it part of daily life.

The family dinner is a perfect time to shift out of stress mode and enjoy a slower, gentler pace. People who are distracted and still moving about don't digest food well. By paying attention to what you eat, chewing more, and taking some slow, deep breaths during the meal, you can start to relax a little bit and begin settling in toward evening and bedtime. When things are quieter you will be better able to hear what your children are telling you, with and without their words. You will notice more about how your body is feeling and about what your family needs.

To get started, first find the ability to relax within yourself. Learn to take a few slow breaths and notice the food under your nose, *regardless of what is going on around you,* and it will be easier for your children to follow. If you wait until everyone else is calm and quiet before you relax, it may never happen! Start with leading by example, and then you can gradually introduce others at your table to the concept of slowing down and enjoying their food as well. For more suggestions about slowing down and chewing, see chapter 6.

Section 2: Power Goals for Balancing the SAD State

If you or your family has been living the SAD Lifestyle for a number of years, then you are probably suffering from one or more of the SAD imbalances discussed in chapter 4: the SAD Blood Sugar Cycle, the Overfed and Undernourished State, or the Flawed Fats Imbalance. This section introduces five Power Goals specifically designed to improve the overall health and nutritional balance of SAD Eaters with these issues.

Each of the Power Goals has its own column filled with suggestions. Choose one goal that feels the most important or the easiest to achieve. Select a suggestion from that column and incorporate it into your life over a period of one to two weeks.

When you have incorporated that suggestion, move on to another *from the same column* until you've completed them all to your satisfaction.

When you feel you've mastered that particular goal, move on to another one, and so on, until you have thoroughly explored the goals that feel most valuable for your family. As always, if a particular suggestion doesn't seem to work well, move on to the next. You might revisit it later, or just decide that one doesn't fit.

SECTION 2: POWER GOALS

GOAL 1: Increase High-Quality Vegetables	GOAL 2: Increase High-Quality Protein
Invisible vegetables: Shred or dice vegetables: carrot, zucchini, pepper, squash, radish, sweet potato, cabbage, onion, broccoli stem, etc. Add to meatloaf, soup, meatballs, tacos, salad, spaghetti, sandwiches, etc.	**Add protein to breakfast:** Use plain, low-fat yogurt, low-fat cottage and other cheeses, soy sausages, Canadian bacon, whey protein powder, beans, nut butters, leftover dinner meats, eggs (keep some hard-boiled in the fridge), etc.
Have vegetables at breakfast: Have sweet root veggies and greens with miso, or spinach with eggs, etc.	**Convert carbohydrate snacks to mini-meals:** Add part-skim mozzarella sticks or other low-fat cheeses, organic cold-cut roll-ups, bean dip, nuts and seeds or nut butters, etc.
Repeat offerings: Get kids used to new vegetables by offering small amounts up to 15 times.	**Experiment with vegetarian protein options:** Combine grains with nuts or seeds, beans with grains, or beans with nuts or seeds; taste-test different vegetarian "meats," such as tofu nuggets, ground "beef" crumbles, Tofurkey, etc.
Vary cooking techniques and presentation: For example, roast Brussels sprouts, asparagus, or root vegetables, making them sweet and chewy.	
Drink low- or no-salt vegetable juices: Fresh is best, but bottled organic is okay, too.	**Increase the quality of your animal proteins**: Choose organic or certified natural meats whenever possible; minimize nitrate-heavy meats such as conventional hot dogs and cold cuts; look for products from "free range" animals raised "on pasture" or "grass fed." Choose organic eggs from chickens that are "cage free" and fed with omega-3s.
Have fun with food: Have tasting "parties"— let kids do vegetable prep or help grow vegetable gardens.	
Offer dips for veggies: Try hummus, salad dressing, nut butters, guacamole, bean dip, etc.	

FOR BALANCING THE SAD STATE

GOAL 3:
Upgrade Simple Carbs and Flawed Fats

Gradually replace some white foods (white potatoes, rice, breads, and pastas) with higher quality sweet carbohydrates: instead use sweet potatoes, quinoa, sprouted grain breads, whole grain pasta, etc.

Introduce new grains and beans: Try one new item at a time; make it plain (cooked fresh or canned/jarred beans) and add it to different meals all week: soup, stew, salad, sandwiches, etc.; prepare grains in a rice cooker to make it easier.

Choose lean meat cuts and trim all visible fat and skin: Look for 97% lean ground beef or ground turkey for your ground meat meals; choose nonnitrate cold cuts with a lower fat content, such as turkey or chicken breast.

Replace fried foods with baked or steamed options.

Try switching butter for olive oil as a vegetable topper, for cooking your eggs, or even drizzled over potatoes.

Add omega-rich foods: Try omega-3 eggs and "clean" young cold-water fish; put ground flaxseed on your salad and cereal, etc.

GOAL 4:
Balance Portions and Proportions

Serve food on individual plates versus serving platters at the table.

Invest in smaller-size dish sets.

Offer a glass of water first when a child asks for a sweet snack before a meal.

Limit sweet drinks throughout the day, especially within two hours of a meal.

If portions are too big, try reducing by 5–10% per week: Or do this even more slowly until the amount on the plate roughly matches the hand guide.

Close the kitchen at night: Do not allow snacks after the dinner meal.

Gradually adjust servings until nutrients are better balanced in each meal: Use cupped hands to determine portions of core veggies, a closed fist for sweet carbs, a palm for protein, and a thumb for healthy fats.

GOAL 5:
Trade Screen Time for Family Time

Gradually reduce total TV hours: Wean by turning TV off when no one is actively watching; make it a rule to turn it off by dinnertime.

Alternate TV nights: Allow TV use every other day; then sometimes switch to books on tape or music on TV night, and then alternate nights with nothing in the background.

Restrict TV watching to one room: Remove TVs from the bedrooms—replace with a radio, CD player, or an MP3 player for music only.

Experiment with weaning off cable TV: Look into Netflix or Blockbuster versus cable; consider slowly implementing a TV-free school week, with watching limited to weekends only.

Write up a schedule for computer use: Set a daily limit and have kids sign in and out, perhaps with a timer.

Create special family nights: TV night, pizza night, game night, Friday night at the movies, walk night, etc.

Consider taking a regular after-dinner walk as a family when weather permits.

In Conclusion

In the Whole Life Nutrition Principles, we've provided you with many ideas for helping your family, but none of them is a "magic pill." Although we wish it were different, the most truly stunning transformations take place very slowly over a long period of time. If you feel overwhelmed by all these suggestions, don't give up: just remember that you don't have to do it all. *Any* small step you take toward improving your family's health—even just reading through this book and gaining some new insights—is positive and significant. It means that you are truly dedicated to doing the best for yourself and your family. Simply changing your basic ideas about food can change the direction in which you and are your family are headed. Nourishing your body and your life affects everything you do, everything you think. The impact of even a small change toward health and balance cannot be underestimated.

DID YOU KNOW?

Holiday Nutrition

The major holiday season typically begins with Halloween (and a sugar binge) and rolls through Thanksgiving (the biggest meal of the year) right on into Christmas (cookie time with all the trimmings), Hanukkah (eight nights in a row of sweets and treats), or other food-filled December celebrations. Many of us emerge in early January, blinking, loosening our belt buckles, and wondering what happened to our healthy routines. As you create a better lifestyle for your family, you may wonder what will happen at holiday time. Will all your healthy habits go out the window? Will your healthful choices make the holidays "no fun"? On the contrary . . .

A great way to maintain the Whole Life Nutrition Lifestyle year-round is to make the holidays about something more than food. Although we know intellectually that holidays are about much more than eating, most of us have a deeply ingrained habit of putting food, rather than one another, at the center of our celebrations. We can find better balance during the holidays by creating and focusing on some wonderful traditions that aren't food related, and by avoiding "empty" eating. Here are some strategies:

1. Offer "tricks" instead of "treats" at Halloween. There are many stores and catalogs that sell inexpensive toys in bulk. Kids really love to dig into a grab bag for things such as small yo-yos, Halloween pencils, balloons, tattoo stickers, jacks, and bubble pipes. If you avoid giving candy away, you'll also remove the temptation to buy more than you need and eat what you don't give away.

2. To celebrate your December holiday, instead of just preparing and eating a meal, include an annual reading of a favorite book, such as *Mr. Willowby's Christmas Tree* by Bob Barry; *Festival of Lights: The Story of Hanukkah* by Maida Silverman; or *Seven Spools of Thread: A Kwanzaa Story* by Angela Shelf Medearis.

3. Spend quality time on activities other than baking. Instead of making holiday cookies for yourselves and others, make ornaments or decorate picture frames with found objects in nature and give those away. Make the decorating more important than dessert. Use the time you might normally spend making fudge to volunteer some hours as a family at your local animal shelter.

4. Invent a family-oriented New Year's Eve tradition. Jeannette's family spends every New Year's Eve watching family videos taken throughout the course of that year. Inevitably, the kids want to go all the way back to their earliest days and admire themselves as beautiful babies. At the end of the night, they videotape a message to themselves, to be watched the following year.

Enlist your kids to help come up with ideas for new and unusual ways to celebrate the holidays. Adapt your traditions as the children grow and their abilities and interests change. The possibilities need only be limited by your imagination.

As you create fun and meaningful holiday rituals, you may find that your need for sweets and empty calories decreases—having fun is much more satisfying than cramming sugar! Not that we are against indulging now and then. It is wonderful to make and eat special foods on special occasions. But that's a very different thing than giving yourself carte blanche to eat candy out of every holiday bowl you see at the bank, at your neighbor's house, at Barnes and Noble . . . you get the picture.

While you reduce mindless eating, also experiment with converting recipes for your favorite holiday dishes into higher quality versions. It is easy to simply remove one-quarter of the sugar from nearly any recipe without much effect, and to switch the fats from unhealthy to healthier choices. If you simply must have your grandmother's gorgeous pumpkin pie with the perfect crust, switch the Crisco for a nonhydrogenated shortening, use organic canned pumpkin, and change the sugar to agave nectar. The effects of the changes will be minor to the palate, but more nourishing for the body.

Top Takeaways

Power Steps for Creating a Whole Life Nutrition Foundation

1. Get enough sleep. Aim for 8 to 9 1/2 hours per night.
2. Drink plenty of water. Aim for 5 to 8 glasses of fresh water daily.
3. Increase movement or exercise. Aim for a minimum of 1 to 2 hours of daily physical activity for kids.
4. Implement regular eating routines. Aim for consistency in mealtimes each day, especially at dinner.
5. Upgrade the quality of your staple foods. Gradually bring in healthier versions of familiar foods.
6. Do more of your own cooking. Move from restaurant food to home-cooked food.
7. Slow down and chew. Make chewing a core practice to help your family slow things down.

Power Goals for Balancing the SAD State

Goal 1: Increase high-quality vegetables.
Goal 2: Increase high-quality protein.
Goal 3: Upgrade simple carbs and flawed fats.
Goal 4: Balance portions and proportions.
Goal 5: Trade screen time for family time.

FOR YOU

- Remember, this is a marathon, not a sprint. Take it slow, but stay committed over time.
- Try focusing on the easiest changes first: success breeds success.
- Don't take it on alone. Educate your family about how and why living a healthier lifestyle will benefit everyone and enlist their involvement wherever you can.

FOR YOUR KIDS

- If, while you're implementing some of the more challenging changes, you sense that your kids need a break, occasionally offer them a "freebie." For a younger child, this could mean letting him take a pass one night on setting the table.
- For an older child, give her a couple of "coupons" for things such as an "anything goes" dessert or "no bedtime" on a sleepover night—something empowering for times when she needs a little extra freedom.

PART II Everyday Cooking: Keeping It Real

Whole Life Nutrition Kitchen

Everyday healthy cooking is possible for everyone. It doesn't have to take up a lot of time or involve complicated recipes. If you haven't done a lot of cooking before now, you probably suffer from a lack of confidence in the kitchen. Don't worry! Everyday cooking is very forgiving—it's not like baking, where if you forget one little ingredient the whole thing can die an awful death, or like holiday meals where you want everything to look perfect. Your goal is to get simple, clean, tasty meals onto the family table, quickly and efficiently, over and over again, week after week. All it takes to become confident in your cooking is a little knowledge and the willingness to get some pans dirty.

The work of becoming a better family cook involves first becoming familiar with basic foods and cooking techniques, and then building your skills with practice. We will give you all the information you need to know.

In this chapter, we provide a comprehensive list of core staples for your pantry, plus basic kitchen equipment and foundational cooking techniques. Chapter 10 will give you a better understanding of herbs and spices and how to put them together skillfully to add flavor and extra health benefits to your meals. In chapters 11 and 12, we give you a guide to the basic greens, roots, grains, and beans, so you'll know how to find them in the store and how to prepare them at home.

Chapters 13 and 14 comprise our Mix and Match cooking instructions. This innovative "recipe" section provides standard formulas for putting together many simple, everyday dishes and charts of ingredients that you can "mix and match" to create countless variations of those dishes. Working from formulas and choosing your own ingredients, rather than mimicking a recipe, will help you understand how simple meals are constructed. It will build your confidence, and eventually your intuition, around how to select ingredients and combine foods in a way that matches your family's tastes and nutritional needs.

Cooking this way is a lot like learning to play a musical instrument (only faster and easier!): preparing plain whole foods such as grains and vegetables gives you the "notes." Combining them in different ways in a soup formula, for instance, is like playing the "scales." As you get the hang of this everyday cooking method, eventually you'll be able to play your own "tunes," and you'll become less reliant on recipes. The key to being able to play your own songs is practice! As Joshua Rosenthal, founder of the Institute for Integrative Nutrition, likes to say, "You've got to burn the rice a few times to learn how to cook it."

Becoming an everyday cook is an experiential, hands-on process, so after you read these chapters, pick a dish that interests you and try it out. Remember, don't be afraid to make mistakes—that really is how we get better at new skills. As you become more confident in your cooking, your children will notice and start to learn from you. Then one day, when they strike out on their own, they'll be able to cook for *their* families, too. By restarting the tradition of cooking, you may be setting your family on a path to better health that will last for generations.

To be a good everyday cook, you must have the proper tools and equipment and know how to use them. With the following guide as a starting point, you will be on your way to creating your own Whole Life Nutrition Kitchen.

NOTEWORTHY NOURISHER

Avocado

- 1 cup has 16 grams of fiber
- Has a sweet flavor
- Comes in many varieties; most common one is California Haas with pebbly, black-green skin
- Is high in fiber, vitamin K, lecithin, folic acid, and oleic acid, a monounsaturated fat
- Has a high amount of copper, which helps in red blood cell formation
- Is a good food for the brain and the skin
- Is great as a spread for sandwiches, or used in guacamole, dressings, and smoothies; great as a healthy base for raw chocolate mousse or as a thickener for raw vegetable soups
- Add to stews, soups, and sauces at the end of cooking to thicken
- Turns brown easily; after cutting, leave the pit inside the avocado and wrap entire avocado airtight. Adding an acidic ingredient also prevents browning; lime is a popular choice
- Enhance ripening by putting avocado in a paper bag with a banana; the banana will emit ethylene, which speeds the ripening process. Ripen at room temperature

Guide to Kitchen Tools

This guide is broken down into two sections: Everyday Cooking Tools and Now-and-Then Equipment. Although you don't need everything on these lists, once you start experimenting with cooking on a regular basis, you will quickly figure out what your kitchen is missing and what equipment would make your life easier. Use this section as a purchasing guide to help you build a set of kitchen tools that suits your needs. The safest cookware options are stainless steel, cast iron, and enameled cast iron. Avoid Teflon-coated pans, as their emissions may be toxic.

EVERYDAY COOKING TOOLS

Here are some basic cooking tools you'll need.

BAKEWARE

Foods absorb more heat and bake more quickly in a dark metal or glass pan than in a shiny metal one. It is helpful to reduce the oven temperature by 25°F to make up for this faster baking time and to avoid burning. Baked goods also brown more in glass or dark metal pans. If you prefer lighter baked items, use a shiny metal pan.

Loaf pan: 9 × 5-inch pan, for meatloaf and quick breads.

Pie plate: Round pan with sloping sides for Naked Quiche (page 187), fruit cobblers (page 214), pies, and other baking. A 9 × 1½-inch pie plate holds about 5 cups; an 8 × 1½-inch pie plate holds about 4 cups.

Sheet pans or cookie sheets: For cookies, toasted nuts, and other baking. Sheet pans have ½-inch sides. Cookie sheets are completely flat except for one raised edge. Purchase pans or sheets that are 2-inch narrower on each side than the inside of the oven. This promotes even heat circulation.

BLENDER OR IMMERSION BLENDER

For puréeing ingredients for soups or smoothies. Glass blenders are sturdier than plastic ones. An immersion blender is a hand-held blender wand used directly in a pot or bowl to purée soups, froth drinks, or blend smoothies.

COLANDER

Sturdy, bowl-shaped container with holes for draining water from cooked pasta or boiled greens.

CUTTING BOARDS

There are many different kinds to choose from, each with some benefits and some disadvantages. Hardwood boards are easier on your knife blade, but can retain odors such as garlic and onion. Bamboo is the hardest and has natural antibacterial properties. Plastic boards are lightweight and the easiest to clean (can be put in the dishwasher). They also have antibacterial properties, but can wear down knife blades and do groove with use. Wooden cutting boards should be wiped down with soap and water after each use. All boards should be wiped down with a solution of 1 teaspoon of chlorine bleach to 1 quart of water at least once a week to clean and sterilize.

Large cutting boards, any material: one medium board for garlic and onion (to keep their strong odors away from your other foods); one for raw meat, poultry, and seafood; and one for everything else. Give yourself plenty of room to work; a small cutting board makes your cutting motions difficult.

GRATERS

Nut and cheese grater: Small hand held grater, great for using at the dinner table. Each family member can grate the amount of cheese he or she would like. Also helpful for grating spices, such as nutmeg.

Box grater: Four-sided grater with different blades for finely or coarsely grated cheese, fruits, or vegetables.

KNIVES

Working with a good knife can make all the difference. When purchasing chef knives, look for three rivets in the handle, and a blade running through the handle as well ("full tang"). Stainless steel knives are popular because the blades don't rust and don't react chemically with foods. Carbon steel knives slice well and sharpen easily, but they can stain food and need to be washed and wiped dry immediately after each use. Ceramic knives are very sharp and thin, great for fine cutting work, but are expensive and brittle. You only need three or four knives for regular use. Choose from these types:

Paring knife: Small and inexpensive, for peeling fruits and vegetables.

6-inch chef's knife: Small enough for paring, as well as some slicing and chopping.

10-inch chef's knife: For chopping and slicing.

Heavy cleaver: For cutting thick winter vegetables.

Small serrated knife: Inexpensive, useful for slicing tomatoes.

Large serrated knife: For slicing bread.

Stay Sharp!

It is important to learn how to use a knife properly when cooking, especially when working with vegetables, because you will chop, slice, trim, and pare on a regular basis. Keep your knives sharp: sharp blades are easier to work with, and if you cut yourself it will heal more quickly and won't hurt as much. Use a steel or magnetic knife sharpener once a week to keep the blades honed. Whetstones are used with running water or oil to sharpen knives. Diamond steel is used to hone the sharpened edge of a knife and keep it sharp during food preparation.

MEASURING CUPS AND SPOONS

Glass cup for liquids: 2- to 4-cup capacity. Has a pouring spout, calibrations, and extra uncalibrated space at the top so you can carry wet ingredients without spilling them. For accuracy, should be read at eye level.

Measuring cups for dry ingredients: They are calibrated at the rim to make it easier when measuring flour so you can shake off excess. These are important for baking. Choose stainless steel, linked together on a ring for convenience.

Measuring spoons: Choose stainless steel, linked together on a ring for convenience. Level off the spoon with a knife when measuring dry ingredients such as baking soda.

MIXING BOWLS

Stacking bowls in different sizes made of glass or stainless steel. Stainless steel bowls adapt well to temperature changes, so they can be used to give ice baths to cool foods such as hard-boiled eggs or can be placed in a heated saucepan and used as a double boiler.

PEPPER AND SPICE MILLS

For freshly ground pepper and coarse sea salt.

POTS, PANS, AND SKILLETS

6- to 12-quart soup/stock pot: Not just for soups and stocks, it is useful to prepare large quantities of tomato sauce, corn, stews, and more, as well as to braise meats. We prefer a 12-quart pot, but you can get one as large as 20 quarts, which is quite large for everyday cooking.

10- or 12-inch sauté pan: Cooks many meals for four to six people. Sauté pans with sloping sides are light, versatile, and popular with restaurant cooks. French sauté pans have straight sides and are heavier, not meant to be picked up.

4-, 5-, or 6-quart sauté pan with lid: Most have straight sides and a second handle for lifting—choose a model that isn't overly heavy. Nothing better for cooking down large batches of greens.

6- or 7-inch skillet: Helpful for toasting nuts, cooking eggs, and making ghee (clarified butter). Choose one with a cover for slow-cooking dishes in which moisture should be retained.

2-quart saucepan and/or 3½-quart saucier pan: Good for sautéing vegetables, cooking grains, and heating sauces.

SALAD SPINNER

For drying greens and herbs after washing. Some drain right into the sink and others drain into a bowl attachment. Look for a model with sturdy parts—cheaper versions have handles or string attachments that can break easily.

SPOONS AND SPATULAS

Spoons: We like wooden spoons. They are cool in your hand; don't clang when they come into contact with metal bowls, pots, and pans; and are inexpensive, so you can have several varieties. You'll want some slotted spoons, some solid mixing spoons, and a flat-bottomed spoon for stirring sauces. They can harbor bacteria, especially if cracked or soft, so replace them periodically.

Spatulas: A straight-edge rubber spatula for spreading, scraping, and leveling off; a flat metal spatula to flip pancakes and lift cookies; and a flexible metal pie spatula with a triangular shaped blade to fit under slices of pie, pizza, or quiche.

SLOW COOKER

Reasonably priced, convenient, and worth the investment. Create delicious, easy meals while you're busy working, shopping, at your child's sporting event, etc. Many sizes available; choose a model large enough to feed your family (and make extra to freeze) with a timer and variable heat settings (high, low, and high/low).

STEAMING BASKET

Collapsible metal basket that fits into most pots. Inexpensive, makes steaming vegetables easy.

STRAINER

Fine-mesh strainer, 7 or 9 inches across, for rinsing grains, beans, and other small items. Choose one with a handle on one end and a hook on the other so it can rest over a bowl or pan for convenience.

THERMOMETER

For meat and poultry. Reliable way to ensure that food is thoroughly cooked.

TONGS

We recommend spring-loaded tongs—longer ones for cooking over a grill and shorter ones for working in the kitchen. Useful for turning things in a pan and picking up foods that won't balance on a spatula.

VEGETABLE PEELER

Important staple as you increase your vegetable intake. Oxo brand is a favorite.

NOW-AND-THEN EQUIPMENT

APPLE CORER/SLICER

Circular-shaped tool for coring and slicing apples easily. Even kids can use it. Very handy for making quick apple cobblers and applesauce.

CLAY POT COOKER

Glazed clay, two-piece roaster that produces juicy, healthy meats and perfect browned vegetables without the addition of fats and oils. Meals can be prepped ahead in the clay pot cooker, placed in the refrigerator, and cooked when you're ready.

COFFEE GRINDER

Small, electric, for grinding spices or flaxseed only. Keep a separate one for your coffee. Grinding some of your spices fresh will lend an extra level of flavor to all your meals.

DOUBLE BOILER

Great for making sauces, melting chocolate, and reheating food. Boil water in the bottom and place food items in the top for gentle heating—quick, healthier alternative to the microwave for reheating almost any food.

DUTCH OVEN

For slow-cooking meats and simmering soups and stews. Great for browning meat before baking or stewing: can go from stovetop to oven to table.

ELECTRIC MIXER

A heavy-duty mixer with a dough hook, paddle, and wire whip is expensive but worth the investment. Great for whipping foods and for making batters and doughs. Comes with other attachments for different kinds of food prep.

Lunch and Travel Containers

Here are our favorite products for taking healthy food on the go. Most of these items are available from Fit & Fresh (www.fit-fresh.com), the Container Store (www.containerstore.com), or the manufacturers' websites. We recommend avoiding Teflon-coated containers. There is some evidence that a chemical used in the manufacture of Teflon could cause tumors.[1]

Today, there are many questions about the safety of Bisphenol A (BPA) in polycarbonate plastic containers and bottles. The amount of BPA released by polycarbonate plastics is low, but you should avoid heating plastic containers in the microwave or dishwasher, and not use any container if the plastic is scratched. The Environmental Working Group states that plastics with recycling codes #1, #2, and #4 on the bottom of plastics are safer choices and do not contain BPA. Studies have shown that BPA might interfere with human hormone functions.

- Fit & Fresh Snack Carrier, Lunch on the Go
- FUNtainer Food Jars
- Glacier Insulated Containers
- Salad Blasters
- Salad Blaster Bowls
- Sandwich Plus Lunch Containers
- Snack & Dips
- Thermos Food Jars
- Thermos Snack Jars
- Thermos Translucent Food Bottles
- Zojirushi Mr. Bento Stainless Lunch Jar

FOOD MILL

Inexpensive item, used to grind and purée foods by hand, sometimes called a ricer. Great for purée-ing foods such as tomatoes for sauces or soups.

FOOD PROCESSOR

Makes chopping, slicing, and shredding fast and easy. Lets you chop onions without tearing eyes. Useful for speed, but chopping by hand is more therapeutic if you have the time. It does take up counter and storage space. Great for making dips and other purées—easier to work with than the blender for some processing jobs.

GARLIC PRESS

Good alternative to chopping garlic by hand. Preferably one that lets you leave the skin on the cloves; try Pampered Chef brand.

MORTAR AND PESTLE

For pounding fresh spices. Comes in handy when you have a very small amount of spice to crush and don't want to use the electric grinder.

PRESSURE COOKER

Completely sealed pot that cooks foods at high temperatures up to 70 percent faster than stovetop cooking. More vitamin and minerals are retained than with conventional cooking methods.

RICE COOKER

Convenient and versatile, it can be used for a variety of grains, not just rice. Can cook foods ahead of time—automatically turns off to a warm setting after cooking. Many can double as steamers or warmers for vegetables and other food. Be sure to choose a model that can handle brown rice vari-eties; many are built for white rice only.

Basic Cooking Techniques

Following are simple descriptions of basic cook-ing techniques that you can use to prepare healthy everyday meals. We've also included helpful hints and recommendations for which types of food are best suited to which cooking method.

BAKING

Great for: whole chickens, fish, root vegetables, breads, cookies.

1. Preheat oven for 10–15 minutes (unless indi-cated otherwise).
2. Place foods on center oven rack and cook until desired doneness.
3. Important: do not crowd the oven, as it will prevent the air from circulating and cause uneven baking.
4. A convection oven provides the most even results; it contains a fan that circulates air within the oven and cooks the food faster.

BLANCHING

Great for: loosening the skins of nuts and toma-toes, enhancing the color of vegetables before sau-téing, killing microorganisms, making raw foods such as crudités more digestible, and mellowing strong flavors.

1. Drop food carefully into a pot of boiling water and cook for 2–3 minutes.
2. Remove food carefully from the pot and plunge into a bowl of cold water or ice to halt the cooking process.

BRAISING

Great for: tougher cuts of meat such as top blade roast or chuck eye roast, tough hardy vegetables such as turnip or parsnip.

1. Heat a healthy fat in a heavy pot, such as a Dutch oven, over a medium-high burner.
2. Brown the food on all sides in the fat.
3. Add a small amount of an acidic cooking liquid, such as wine or diced tomatoes.
4. Cover food with a tight-fitting lid and cook slowly, over low heat or in a low-heat oven, until it is tender when poked with a fork.

BROILING

Great for: most medium to thin cuts of meat, fish, chicken parts.

1. Slide oven rack directly under broiler.
2. Preheat oven to desired broil temperature (most ovens have a setting for broil, high broil, or low broil).
3. Place food on a broiling pan and place on top rack.
4. Leave 5–8 inches of space between the heat source and the top of the food.
5. Cook food under intense heat of broiler until lightly brown and heated to desired doneness.
6. You may need to flip thicker cuts of meat halfway through cooking time to avoid burning.

DOUBLE BOILING

Great for: melting waxy foods such as chocolate or coconut oil, cooking delicate sauces and other foods that can't tolerate direct heat.

If you don't have a double boiler, use a heat-resistant bowl that fits on top of a saucepan. Leave 2–3 inches between the bottom of the bowl and the bottom of the pan.

1. Add 2–3 inches of water to bottom pot of the double boiler.
2. Heat the water to a gentle simmer.
3. Add foods to the top pot and melt or warm to desired doneness.

DRY SKILLET COOKING

Great for: fatty meats, such as ground beef, dark-meat poultry, 1–1½-inch cuts of fish.

A ridged bottom pan or griddle will allow the fat to drip into the ridges, helping to keep it separate from the food.

1. Dry heat a cast-iron skillet or griddle—no oil or other liquid.
2. When hot, add the food to the pan.
3. Gently turn or flip the food in the pan during cooking to ensure even browning until heated to desired doneness.
4. If fat accumulates, drain it off periodically so it is not absorbed back into the food.

GRILLING

Great for: shrimp; scallops; chicken; thick cuts of fish such as tuna or salmon; lean cuts of meat; thick-cut hearty vegetables such as red peppers, summer squash, or corn on the cob; summer fruits such as chunks of peach or thick pineapple slices; or hardy leafy greens such as whole kale or collard leaves. Kabob smaller chunks of food on a skewer to meld flavors of fruits or vegetables and meats, and to prevent food from falling through.

Whole Foods for Daily Living

Here are some special tips for streamlining whole foods cooking and bringing it into your daily life.

PREP ON THE WEEKENDS
- On Saturdays plan three or four main meals for the week; write your shopping list and purchase all the ingredients you will need.
- Rinse and soak beans or grains on Saturday night. Cook them on Sunday.
- On Sunday wash and chop less perishable salad vegetables. Assemble a base of leafy greens for salads during the week. Get fresh crudités-style vegetables ready for snacking.
- Prepare a protein dish or purchase one that is precooked, such as a rotisserie chicken.

COOK ONCE, EAT THRICE
- Use the protein dish for Sunday dinner and then quick, easy snacks and lunches for the next couple of days.
- Use the beans and/or grains cooked the first night throughout the week by adding them to salad, soup (fresh or canned), or stew, or mash and reheat as patties. Or reheat, sweeten, and serve for breakfast.

MAKE A MIDWEEK PIT STOP
- If you have time on Wednesdays, prepare a new salad and grain base or make a soup to last you until the weekend.

USE SLOW COOKER OPTIONS
- In the cooler seasons, save time by preparing food in advance with a slow cooker or clay pot cooker at least once per week. See chapter 12 for details.

REDUCE CHOPPING TIME
- Many fresh vegetables can be purchased prewashed and chopped or shredded or diced. Look for bagged salad greens, prewashed spinach, broccoli and cauliflower florets, kale, diced butternut squash, green beans, sugar snap peas, shredded carrots or cabbage, bean sprouts, etc.

FIND YOUR RHYTHM
- Cook one new meal each week to build your skills and repertoire.
- Vary your vegetables from week to week, month to month and season to season to prevent boredom and increase nutrition.
- For good health, serve an omega-3-rich fish or seafood a few times per month.

Covering the grill speeds cooking time by circulating heat around the food.

1. Preheat indoor or outdoor grill as directed, either gas or charcoal.
2. Scour hot grill rack to remove any residual detritus.
3. Lay foods gently on rack, carefully placing them across the bars to prevent any thin pieces from falling through.

4. Cook until a light sear-crust is formed on the outside, and the inside is heated to desired doneness.
5. Turn the food at least once during cooking to allow sear-crust to form on both sides.

SAUTÉING

Great for: peppers, mushrooms, zucchini, yellow squash, onions, shredded carrots, greens (hardier ones such as kale benefit from being steamed or briefly boiled first to soften them).

If using onions, add first and sauté for a few minutes to caramelize and release aroma and best flavor. If using fresh garlic, add later in the cooking time to avoid a bitter or burnt flavor.

1. Heat a small amount of healthy oil in a sauté pan over low-medium heat.
2. Increase the heat to medium-low and add foods to the pan.
3. Move the ingredients from side to side in the pan for even cooking.

STEAMING

Great for: medium-bodied vegetables such as broccoli or green beans, medium-bodied greens such as chard or bok choy; also a great reheating method.

1. Place a steamer basket in a cooking pot.
2. Add a small amount of water to a level just below the steaming basket.
3. Bring water to a boil over high heat.
4. Add vegetables and cover.
5. Cook until vegetables are bright and just tender, usually 2–8 minutes, depending on their hardness.
6. The remaining nutrient-dense liquid can be saved to use in soups and water sautéing.

Core Pantry Ingredients

Flexible everyday cooking requires that you keep your pantry well supplied with high-quality basics. Following is a list of foods you will want to stock on a regular basis. How well does your current pantry stack up? Copy this list and take it with you to grocery and natural food stores. It will guide you in building a good base of staples for your Whole Life Nutrition Kitchen. As you use the Mix and Match charts in the following chapters, you will discover which ingredients are the most useful staples for you. You may also come across new, unusual ingredients that you want to experiment with. You can learn more about those in appendix B at the back of this book.

DRY GOODS PANTRY

- Beans, dried or canned (salt-free, organic): black, kidney, garbanzo, navy, adzuki, split pea, lentils, etc.
- Broth, organic: free-range chicken broth, vegetable broth, beef broth
- Capers, jarred
- Cereal, cold: oat bran, low-fat and low-sugar granola, raw muesli
- Cereal, hot: steel-cut oats, amaranth, millet
- Flour: cornmeal, spelt, whole wheat pastry
- Fish, canned: tuna in water, skinless and boneless salmon in water
- Fruit, dried: cranberries, cherries, blueberries, raisins

- Millet
- Nuts: walnuts, almonds
- Oils: extra-virgin olive, grapeseed, avocado, walnut, sesame, chili, flaxseed, sunflower
- Olives, jarred
- Pasta: soba noodles, whole spelt, whole wheat, brown rice pasta (try Tinkyada brand)
- Quinoa
- Rice: Arborio, brown basmati rice, brown rice
- Salt and salt substitutes: Celtic sea salt, Bragg Liquid Aminos, gomasio (combination of sea salt and ground sesame seeds)
- Sea vegetables: dulse flakes (as a condiment), kelp, kombu, nori, wakame
- Seeds, raw: sunflower, pumpkin, sesame
- Soy sauce: shoyu (traditional soy sauce made with wheat and soy), low-sodium tamari (wheat-free soy sauce)
- Spices: cardamom, cayenne, cinnamon, cumin, fennel, ginger, nutmeg, paprika, turmeric (see chapter 10)
- Sweeteners: agave nectar, 100% maple syrup, rice syrup, stevia extract, xylitol, blackstrap molasses, raw honey (but not for young children)
- Tea: green tea, herbal teas, kukicha "twig" tea (roasted flavor, lightly caffeinated)
- Tomatoes: canned, paste, sun-dried
- Vinegars: apple cider, balsamic, red wine, white wine, Japanese umeboshi plum (salty and sour, lightly citric flavor)
- Wine: sherry, cooking wine

PERISHABLE PANTRY BASICS

- Breads: sprouted, whole grain, rye, whole wheat pita, sprouted corn tortillas, sprouted wheat tortillas (also frozen breads to store in freezer for future use as needed)
- Eggs: organic or free-range, cage-free, preferably with omega-3s
- Fish: wild Alaskan salmon, farmed bay scallops, farmed blue mussels, sardines, tilapia
- Fruits (seasonal): apples, berries, cherries, lemons, melon, pears, etc. (low glycemic load)
- Fruit spreads: unsweetened apple butter, fruit spreads without added sugar
- Herbs: basil, mint, cilantro, parsley, rosemary (see chapter 10)
- Horseradish, prepared
- Meats: chicken, turkey, very lean beef (organic or free-range, antibiotic-free, hormone-free)
- Milk: organic cow's milk (low-fat), unsweetened soymilk, oat milk, rice milk, or almond milk
- Miso paste
- Mustard, natural: brown spicy mustard, Dijon mustard, honey mustard
- Nut butters, natural, organic: almond, cashew, peanut
- Sauerkraut, organic
- Spreads and dips: hummus, tahini, baba ghanoush, olive paste, salsa
- Vegetables (seasonal): beets, broccoli, carrots, cauliflower, celery, eggplant, garlic, ginger, greens, onions, tomatoes, squash, sweet potatoes

10

The Spice Rack

Demystifying Herbs and Spices

Herbs and spices can add a tremendous amount of variety to whole foods. They bring extra nutritional value and medicinal properties to your meals, as well as providing wonderful flavors to satisfy the taste buds.

What is the difference between an herb and a spice? An herb is any leaf, flower, or stem of a plant used for seasoning food or for medicinal purposes. Spices are seeds, seedpods, barks, roots, or rhizomes (underground stems such as ginger) prepared into aromatic food seasonings.

We will provide you with a "Starter Spice Rack" for your Whole Life Nutrition Kitchen, which includes both herbs and spices. These are some basic seasonings you should have on hand to get your everyday cooking off to a delicious start. We include plenty of information on how to store, work with, and combine everything in your new Spice Rack.

ABOUT HERBS

Fresh summer herbs should be chopped or torn, then tossed into your dish at the last minute so they cook only lightly and taste very fresh in the dish. Some great examples are basil, oregano, parsley, cilantro, tarragon, mint, and chives. When using fresh herbs, you really have to play with the quantity to see what tastes best to you. Start with less and taste it. You can always add more.

In general, we prefer fresh herbs to dried, but dried herbs are definitely essential if fresh herbs are not accessible. When cooking with dried herbs, you always need about half the amount you would when using fresh herbs. When substituting in recipes, a general rule of thumb is ¼ teaspoon of ground herb or 1 teaspoon of dried herb leaves equals 1 tablespoon of finely chopped fresh herb.

Winter herbs are more effective when dried. They lend themselves to heartier dishes such as stews and soups. They add depth and aromatic flavors, which become more pronounced with longer methods of cooking such as braising and slow cooking. These herbs include bay leaves, rosemary, thyme, and marjoram. They shouldn't be used raw; cooking mellows their intense flavors and aromas.

Organic herbs, whether dried or fresh, are often more flavorful than conventional herbs because they are harvested in smaller quantities, and prepared and sent to market more quickly.

ABOUT SPICES

Spices are usually dried, either whole or ground. If you will not use certain spices often, it's a good idea to buy them whole and grind or grate them when needed.

The seeds last longer and impart an intense flavor if you buy them whole and grind them as needed in a coffee grinder that you designate for spices only, no coffee beans. (This is also a cost-effective strategy; your whole spices will stay fresh longer.) You can also intensify their flavor by toasting spice seeds: shake them for a couple of minutes in a dry skillet until you smell their aroma, being careful not to burn them.

NOTEWORTHY NOURISHER

Ginger

- Has a pungent taste
- Gingerol and zingerone give ginger its pungency and have antioxidant and anti-inflammatory effects[1]
- May help prevent cancer, and help relieve osteoarthritis of the knee
- Relieves nausea, motion sickness, and other digestive ailments
- Ginger tea can be made from slices of fresh ginger or candied ginger steeped in hot water
- See page 128 for more about ginger

If these techniques seem like too much work, simply buy small quantities of your spices already ground. They will still be quite flavorful.

HOW TO STORE

Fresh herbs are quite perishable. They need to be stored properly once cut from their original plants. Store bunched herbs in the refrigerator with the stems in water. For loose leaves and flowers, pack them loosely and store in perforated plastic bags in the refrigerator crisper. If there is extra moisture on the leaves, pat them dry and put a crumpled paper towel on the bottom of the bag. Place the leaves on top. A bit of moisture is good to help keep leaves fresh, but too much will make them spoil sooner. This storage technique also works well for spices such as whole gingerroot that need to be kept fresh.

There are many herbs available fresh in most grocery stores today. Some stores also carry herbs frozen in small containers. A great economical alternative to buying herbs every week is keeping a small window herb garden. Pick your favorite herbs that you will cook with most often. Herbs growing in your kitchen window will be accessible during meal preparation and leave a great fragrance in the kitchen. Also, you won't have to bother with storage.

Dried herbs and spices should be packed in tightly closed glass jars and kept in a cool, dry, dark place. The refrigerator is ideal but not practical for most people. Glass keeps aromas in and out best. Most herbs become stale quickly (some more than others), and stale herbs do not enhance the flavor of food. For freshness, it is best to buy small quantities and check expiration dates. If your herbs go stale, it's best to throw them out.

Using Herbs and Spices for Health: The Six Tastes

Think back to your middle school science class when you learned about the four distinct tastes—sweet, sour, salty, bitter—that can be experienced on the tongue. Each food, herb, and spice you eat has a dominant taste that has an impact, not only on how your meal tastes, but also on how your meal makes you feel. In this book, we will discuss six primary tastes, or flavors:

- sweet
- sour
- pungent (spicy, hot)
- bitter
- salty
- astringent (drying)

Some ancient systems of health have a deep understanding of how these tastes impact the body. For example, in Ayurveda, the ancient traditional health-care practice of India, practitioners prescribe herbs for health and balance, taken internally and externally, and individualized dietary guidelines, along with breathing exercises and yoga. Ayurveda teaches that it is important to include all six of these primary flavors in every meal to keep the body in balance and to heal health problems. Traditional Chinese Medicine (TCM), an extensive system of health used in China for thousands of years, holds a similar philosophy. Both TCM and Ayurveda emphasize that the taste of each thing you eat has an effect on the body and the mind.

Even without going deeply into these Asian philosophies, it's easy to see the benefits of meals that are well rounded in all six flavors. You can find complete meals like this at most ethnic restaurants, such as Korean, Chinese, Japanese, Italian, Mexican, Mediterranean, and Middle Eastern. For example, at a traditional Japanese restaurant, you might start with miso soup (salty) and then a small amount of protein such as tofu, fish, chicken, or seafood (sweet or, salty). This would be followed by rice (sweet), ginger or wasabi (pungent), and sautéed vegetables (bitter), preferably in sesame oil and soy sauce (salty). With your meal, you would drink green tea (bitter and astringent) and end with fruit such as an orange (sweet and sour). This Asian meal is healthy, light, and satisfying; stimulates digestion; and pleases the taste buds.

Compare this to a typical SAD dinner of grilled chicken breast (bland or salty), iceberg salad (bland or sour), and french fries (very salty). This meal is missing many flavors and does not stimulate the digestive system. It may be filling, but it is not healthy, light, or satisfying. Afterward, you will almost certainly crave a rich dessert.

Herbs and spices are a great way to start expanding the number of tastes in your meals. In fact, with very little effort you can start using the six flavors to improve your family's health, help them attune to the seasons, and calm extreme cravings brought on by SAD imbalances. Below is a description of the benefits of each of the different flavors, as well as suggestions on where to find them and when to eat them. The Spice Rack below also includes information on tastes so you can keep their balancing effects in mind as you add them to your meals.

SWEET

Sweet tastes are calming, relaxing, and moist to the tongue. They're "anabolic," which means they help build tissue; in excess, they will increase body weight. Sweet foods are best to eat in the summer, autumn, and winter.

Sweet herbs and spices: cinnamon, cardamom, poppy seed, aniseed, dill, fennel seed, tarragon, nutmeg, ginger

Sweet foods: sugar, honey, maple syrup, butter, cream, milk, ricotta cheese, tofu, wheat, barley, almonds, sesame seeds, meats, sweet fruits, dried fruits, carrots, beets, sweet potatoes, winter squashes, fennel, cucumbers, avocados

SOUR

Sour tastes stimulate the digestive system and appetite, increase metabolism, and help relieve gas. They also help add tissue and increase body weight. Decrease sour foods, especially yogurt and some cheeses, in the spring and summer. Winter and autumn are particularly good seasons to eat sour foods.

Sour herbs: cilantro, lemongrass, lemon thyme, lemon verbena

Sour foods: yogurt, sour cream, kefir, lemons, limes and other citrus fruits, plums, strawberries, raspberries, tomatoes, fermented cheeses, vinegar, pickles

SALTY

Salty tastes are warming, soothing, and drying. In small quantities, they can help speed digestion and increase appetite. However, too much salty food can stimulate water retention. This taste also increases tissue and body weight if eaten in excess. Celtic sea salt contains all of the trace minerals from the ocean but doesn't have water retention properties or raise blood pressure the way processed iodized table salt can. We recommend reducing your intake of salty foods in the spring and summer, as you look to lose weight and stay hydrated, and then increase them in the autumn and winter to help you stay warm and digest heavier foods.

Salty spices: celery seed. (You can also purchase premixed herbal "salt substitutes" such as Vegit or lower salt herbal combos such as Herbamare.)

Salty foods: sea salt, iodized table salt, sea vegetables (kelp, nori, dulse, etc.), soy sauce, tamari, Bragg Liquid Aminos, celery, deli meats, smoked meat or fish, baking soda, baking powder, prepared condiments such as ketchup, mustard and chutneys, brined foods such as pickles, olives, and sauerkraut. (Note: Many poor-quality SAD processed foods have a strong salty taste because they are high in added salt: snack foods such as chips or pretzels, processed cheeses, instant soups, frozen foods, fast and other restaurant foods.)

PUNGENT

Pungent tastes are what we think of as spicy. They boost metabolism, digestion, and circulation, and they can be drying. They are "catabolic," which means they help burn fat. They can be helpful in lowering body fat. Spring is a good time to indulge in spicy foods. Summer is a time to avoid pungent, spicy foods because too much of them may overheat you, which can be uncomfortable in the hot and humid weather.

Pungent herbs and spices: basil, chili powder, cumin, curry, ginger, cloves, peppermint, spearmint, fennel, aniseed, cayenne pepper, black pepper, Hungarian hot paprika, mustard seeds and powder, dried horseradish, cinnamon, rosemary, nutmeg, turmeric, garlic

Pungent foods: hot peppers or chiles of all kinds, mustard, chili oil, hot sauces, horseradish, mustard greens, radish, radish sprouts, onion, ginger, garlic, dill

BITTER

Bitter tastes often have a sharp flavor, which is pleasant once the taste buds become accustomed to it. They are drying and cooling. Small amounts help stimulate digestion, and because they're catabolic they can help reduce body fat. Spring and summer are great seasons in which to embrace bitter foods. Reduce your consumption of them in the autumn and winter.

Bitter spices: turmeric, fenugreek, cumin seeds, cinnamon, parsley, oregano

Bitter foods: eggplant, rhubarb, green tea, coffee, tonic water, dark chocolate, licorice, lemon and orange peel, dark green leafy vegetables such as kale, collard greens, beet greens, chard, spinach, dandelion greens

ASTRINGENT

Astringent tastes are drying, cooling, and catabolic, so they can help reduce body fat. They are best eaten in late spring and summer, and less useful in the autumn and winter.

Astringent herbs and spices: nutmeg, bay leaf, basil, tarragon, turmeric, rosemary, sage, cumin, cinnamon

Astringent foods: pomegranate, green apples, pears, rhubarb, green grapes, citrus peels, chard, cabbage, spinach, lentils, most beans, aloe vera juice, avocado

Guide to Herbs and Spices

Below is a detailed guide to stocking your spice rack, with information about what to buy, uses, benefits (including medicinal properties), cautions, and tastes. We recommend experimenting with this set of seasonings to see what appeals to you and your family. When you are ready to experiment with more elaborate spice combinations or add more to your repertoire, check out appendix C.

Starter Spice Rack

Here is a simple collection of eighteen staple herbs and spices we recommend for starter cooks.

basil
bay "laurel" leaf
cardamom
cayenne pepper
cilantro
cinnamon
cumin
dill
fennel
garlic
ginger
mint
nutmeg
oregano
paprika
parsley
rosemary
turmeric

BASIL

Basil has green leaves and an aromatic smell when raw. When using fresh basil, rinse it with running cold water or with a damp cloth. It's best not to use a knife to cut it, as it turns the basil black and causes it to lose some of its vibrancy. If you don't want to use whole leaves, simply tear them gently into smaller pieces.

Taste: Pungent

Purchasing: Fresh basil is best. Growing your own is economical and allows you to pick it as needed. It's best to pick vibrant green leaves and not use the bruised, black leaves. Dried basil, while not as flavorful as fresh, can still be bought and stored easily.

Uses: Flavoring for meat, fish, chicken dishes; in vinegar, soups; with oil and garlic; with tomatoes. Flavor remains stronger when not cooked. Once basil is cooked in a stew, soup, or tomato sauce, the flavor diminishes. Add it at the end of cooking, just before serving. Basil's aromatic properties lighten up dark beans and heavy sauces. It is a main ingredient in pesto sauce, which can be made in the summer and frozen for the winter.

Benefits: Warming and calming. Possesses anti-inflammatory and antimicrobial properties.

BAY "LAUREL" LEAF

The bay leaf is the leaf of the laurel tree. It is firm, long, and narrow, and has a smoky flavor. Whole bay leaves in a tightly closed glass jar in a cool cupboard keep indefinitely. Wipe each bay leaf lightly with a damp cloth before using. If you have a garden or window garden, you can plant California bay, a sturdy perennial that grows quickly to provide a long supply of leaves for the kitchen. This bay leaf is sweet, lemony, and spicy, with a slight clove flavor.

Taste: Astringent, pungent

Purchasing: Imported Mediterranean bay leaves are particularly aromatic.

Uses: In soups, pasta sauces, stews, and marinades. Requires long, slow cooking for the full flavor to develop. Usually removed before serving.

Benefits: Warming and soothing. Antioxidant properties.

CARDAMOM

These are small green and large black pods from India. They are highly aromatic with a spicy scent. When crushed, black cardamom pods have a powerful woody and a smoky aroma; they are milder than the green pods. Mortar and pestle works well to grind the seeds as needed. Ground cardamom has a milder flavor than whole cardamom does.

Taste: Sweet, slightly astringent, slightly pungent

Purchasing: You can buy the whole pod, which needs to be steamed or blanched for a while to soften, or just the seeds, whole or ground.

Uses: To make chai (Indian tea), in sweet baked desserts, with sweet grains (such as rice or oatmeal), in poultry dishes.

Benefits: Considered a great digestive spice. Relieves gas and calms the nervous system. Chewing green pods freshens the breath. Balances out the negative effects of caffeine—one reason it's used in chai.

CAYENNE PEPPER

Cayenne is a member of the capsicum family of chile peppers. Use it to add a kick of spicy flavor to your food.

Taste: Pungent

Purchasing: Powdered form, in a tightly sealed glass jar.

Uses: In meats and vegetable dishes, salad dressings, soups, chili, marinades, and even with hot lemonade as a warming winter treat.

Benefits: Heats your body, stimulates digestion, and provides quick energy. Antioxidant, anti-inflammatory, antimicrobial, and congestion-relieving properties; stimulating to metabolism.

Caution: Too much cayenne pepper could be painful to young mouths or irritate the digestive tract.

CILANTRO

These greens of the coriander plant have a delightful, fragrant aroma.

Taste: Sour, slightly sweet (citruslike)

Purchasing: Buy fresh. Dried or frozen cilantro is not particularly flavorful, is highly perishable, and is prone to wilting. Trim, wash, and spread to dry on a kitchen or paper towel. Wrap lightly in a paper towel and put in a zip-closure plastic bag.

Uses: In salads, salad dressings, soups, chili, curries, hummus, salsa, with beans.

Benefits: Fresh and uplifting. Very strong antibacterial properties, especially against salmonella.

CINNAMON

Cinnamon adds a pleasant fragrance to food. See also Noteworthy Nourisher, page 40.

Taste: Sweet, astringent, bitter

Purchasing: Ground form or stick (rolled bark) form. Store cinnamon sticks in a tightly closed container; will keep for a year.

Uses: In desserts of all kinds; in hot drinks such as tea, cider, and cocoa; in Mexican savory dishes; with root vegetables, such as sweet potatoes.

Benefits: Aids overall digestion and other stomach ailments such as nausea and gas. Produces warmth in the body. Powerful antimicrobial properties. May help those with diabetes balance blood sugar. Using cinnamon on foods that are high in carbohydrates will reduce blood sugar increases.

CUMIN

This spice has thin, small brown seeds. Heat cumin seeds in a dry skillet before using whole, or grind into a powder for a stronger flavor.

Taste: Pungent, astringent, bitter

Purchasing: Dried or ground seeds in a tightly closed glass jar.

Uses: In soups, stews, chili, curries, yogurt sauces; add to ground beef, chicken, turkey.

Benefits: Reduces gas, aids digestion, helps relieve colic, promotes energy circulation, and increases metabolic rate. Has a cooling effect on the body. High in iron.

Caution: Eating excessive amounts may inflame the stomach.

DILL

Dill has thin, green feathery leaves.

Taste: Sweet

Purchasing: Fresh dill, packed loosely in a perforated plastic bag; dried dill sold as dillweed in a sealed glass jar; or dill seeds, which have a similar flavor to fresh dill. Store in a cool pantry.

Uses: In salads; with cucumbers, beets, or potatoes; in carrot soup, chicken soup, yogurt dressings; with salmon, lamb, chicken, eggs; in breads, muffins.

Benefits: Warming and calming effect on the body. High in iron and calcium.

FENNEL

The bulb, stalks, and seeds can all be used. Fresh fennel can be prepared as a vegetable or used in smaller quantities as a seasoning.

Taste: Sweet, pungent

Purchasing: Fresh stalks or bulbs; or seeds, whole or ground, sealed tightly in a glass jar.

Uses: In fish soups or with fish on the grill. A few fennel seeds or thin slices of the bulb under an oily fish help eliminate its fishy taste. Slice a bulb into thin strips, plunge into ice water until crisp, then serve with lemon juice and salt—a refreshing snack for kids.

Benefits: Cooling effect on the body; helps aid digestion and reduces gas symptoms.

GARLIC

The bulb has a papery covering. Separate the bulb into individual cloves and peel. To achieve maximum health benefits, cloves must be crushed or chopped, not used whole.

Taste: Pungent

Purchasing: Raw garlic bulbs, crushed garlic in refrigerated glass bottles, peeled garlic cloves in plastic containers, garlic powder in tightly sealed glass bottles.

Uses: Sautéed with oil as a flavor base for greens, soups, or stews; in sauces, spreads, or dips (raw or cooked); on toast; roasted in the oven with olive oil.

Benefits: Aids in eliminating toxins from the body, aids digestion, promotes cardiovascular health, helps the body fight off winter ailments. High in phytonutrients and antioxidant properties. Very high in vitamin C. Helpful with supporting a healthy immune system.

GINGER

Ginger is a beige, shiny, bumpy root (rhizome). The root must be peeled and finely chopped before it is added to dishes. Also available as ground ginger, crystallized ginger, pickled ginger, and preserved ginger (all should be refrigerated). See also Noteworthy Nourisher, page 122.

Taste: Pungent, sweet

Purchasing: Large, plump shiny root. Avoid roots with any shriveling dryness or mold on the edge. As powder tightly sealed in glass jars.

Uses: In tea, stir-fries, soups, stews, salad dressings, marinades, desserts.

Benefits: Stimulant to digestive and circulatory systems. Beneficial for nausea, fever, muscle aches and pains, and respiratory disorders. Helps relieve gas, colic, indigestion, vomiting, morning sickness, and travel sickness. Ground ginger has a heating effect on the body. Anti-inflammatory properties.

MINT

This herb is popular worldwide, with about forty different varieties. The fresh leaves have a strong aroma. It is great to grow in a window box or herb garden.

Taste: Pungent

Purchasing: Fresh peppermint or spearmint.

Uses: In salads, salad dressings, marinades, tabbouleh, desserts, teas, smoothies and other drinks (cold or hot); with fresh fruit.

Benefits: Appetite stimulant, calms the nervous system, helps indigestion and stomach issues, natural antiseptic, freshens breath.

NUTMEG

This is the wrinkled, brown, oval-shaped nut inside the brittle, shiny shell of a nutmeg seed. It has a warm, citruslike fragrance that balances the bittersweet flavor.

Taste: Sweet, pungent, astringent

Purchasing: Whole nutmeg (to grate yourself) or ground nutmeg sealed tightly in a glass jar.

Uses: In baked goods, puddings, shakes, smoothies, tea, hot milk, eggnog; on root vegetables.

Benefits: Heating effect on the body; calms the nervous system, relieves gas.

OREGANO

A close relative of marjoram, oregano has small green, somewhat heart-shaped leaves. It changes color and aroma as it gets stale and has a short shelf life.

Taste: Bitter, slightly pungent

Purchasing: Preferably dried oregano; it is more pungent than fresh. Store in a tightly closed glass bottle in a cupboard.

Uses: On pizza, in soups, in Italian sauces, with eggplant, beans, or salads; in sauce for fish steak, such as tuna.

Benefits: Softly warming. High in phytonutrients and antioxidant properties. Outstanding antimicrobial properties—oregano essential oil is quite popular during cold and flu season, and as protection against food-borne illnesses.

PAPRIKA

Sweet paprika (from India) is a beautiful red powder made from mild red chiles and is primarily used for its color. It has a sweet chili aroma and bitter aftertaste, but mellows with cooking. Hungarian hot and smoked paprikas are pungent varieties.

Taste: Pungent, slightly sweet

Purchasing: Ground Indian, Hungarian, and smoked paprika sealed tightly in glass containers or metal tins.

Uses: To top white fish of all varieties; with salt and pepper as part of a flour-based coating for chicken or stew meat; in egg, ham, or chicken salad. Use smoked paprika as an alternative to liquid smoke in pea soup and casseroles.

Benefits: Member of the capsicum family—capsicum spices and peppers aid in pain reduction and have cardiovascular benefits. High in vitamin C. Soothing.

PARSLEY

Parsley has flat-leafed or curly green leaves. Flat-leaf parsley has a more complex, pungent flavor than curly parsley does. Parsley brings out other flavors in a dish. Chewing the leaves will help remove the smell of onion or garlic on your breath.

Taste: Bitter, slightly pungent

Purchasing: Fresh, vibrant, green, flat-leaf parsley. Dried parsley flakes are dull and flavorless.

Uses: In soups and salads, and for garnish. Parsley stems are used in white stocks and sauces because they do not color the sauce but do add a rich flavor. Great juiced in small amounts with vegetables such as carrots and celery.

Benefits: Improves digestion and prevents bad breath. Diuretic; could help with bloating and PMS. High in vitamins C and A, antioxidants, and flavonoids, which work like antioxidants. Slight warming effect on the body.

ROSEMARY

Rosemary's gray-green leaves look like pine needles on a thin stem. It grows easily in a garden or window garden. Indoors, it likes a sun-warmed spot. It produces pretty violet, pink, or white flowers twice a year. Snip off the tips of the younger, more fragrant branches to use in cooking.

Taste: Pungent, slightly sweet

Purchasing: Fresh rosemary. Dried whole rosemary leaves are acceptable if there is no access to fresh.

Uses: In sauces and roasts: beef, lamb, chicken, potatoes; tossed with sweet root vegetables; in stuffings. Rosemary should be chopped finely so more of the flavor is released.

Benefits: Warming and clarifying. Possesses anti-inflammatory properties; especially helpful for asthma sufferers. Boosts immune system.

TURMERIC

 This is a bright yellow-orange powder. The form we use in the West is the boiled, peeled, sun-dried rhizome of a tropical plant in the ginger family. It has a warm, peppery aroma, similar to that of ginger, and a strong, bitter taste that mellows with cooking.

Taste: Bitter, astringent, pungent

Purchasing: Ground turmeric sealed tightly in a glass bottle.

Uses: In poultry, meat, tofu, rice dishes; as an alternative to curry; or used for its color.

Benefits: Anti-inflammatory, aids in stabilizing blood sugar, natural antiseptic, blood purifier.

11

Vegetable Basics: The Missing Link

Vegetables provide a treasure trove of health benefits for human bodies: they nourish, protect, heal, and energize us. They supply crucial micronutrients, purify the body of toxins, and replenish the blood. Vegetables, especially leafy greens, are the key food group most missing from the Standard American Diet.

Many adults are simply not comfortable with vegetables—their look or texture may be unfamiliar. Some of us have never eaten vegetables prepared in a tasty or satisfying way. American adults aren't in the habit of preparing lots of vegetables at home or ordering them when they go out. If they do, they often choose the same ones over and over again—those they are familiar with, such as carrots, potatoes, or frozen corn. With this anti-veg attitude and behavior, is it any wonder that our kids aren't eating them? Children are very aware; they pick up on their parents' likes and dislikes and model their eating habits on those of the adults around them.

Making vegetables a regular, central part of your meals is vital to getting your family off the Standard American Diet. When cooked properly, vegetables are so delicious that even kids like them. They are not difficult to prepare, and there are endless ways to make them enticing. You are sure to find many flavor combinations that your family will enjoy.

Greens

You may not be in the habit of eating green leafy vegetables—they are often completely absent from American cooking. The following guide will assist you to begin adding greens to your daily diet and enjoying their delicious flavors. They are terrific in soups, stews, and sauces, or served as a simple side dish. They make great accompaniments to whole grain pastas, beans, rice, potatoes, eggs, and even pizza! At the end of this section, we will touch on more familiar green vegetables, including asparagus and broccoli.

The latest dietary guidelines suggest that adults eat at least three cups of dark green leafy vegetables each week, due to their numerous health benefits. Greens contain beta-carotene, as well as chlorophyll, an immune-system stimulant. They contain important antioxidants that have been linked with a lower risk of breast, lung, and skin cancers. Dark green leafy vegetables supply a significant amount of folic acid and certain phytochemicals that can help stop cancer before it begins. These phytochemicals block enzymes that activate carcinogens and increase enzymes that detoxify them. Eating them regularly also just plain makes you feel better. With so many health benefits associated with these vegetables, you have good reason to try them. Once you get the hang of working with greens, incorporating them into your daily diet will be a snap.

NOTEWORTHY NOURISHER

Kombu

- Is a sea vegetable harvested from the ocean
- Is green in color; sold as long, large leaves, folded up or cut into small pieces
- Is rich in iodine, calcium, folic acid, and magnesium
- Is a great source of vitamins A, B, C, E, and K
- Add to beans to tenderize them; the minerals increase beans' digestibility
- Do not wash because flavor is near the surface; wipe with a damp cloth before using
- Is nutritionally dense; use in small doses
- Is best to buy organic to ensure there are no heavy metals or other toxins from the sea
- Is a gentle chelation agent; aids in ridding the body of heavy metals

LEAFY GREEN BASICS

Spinach, chard, beet greens, bok choy, and many Asian greens have delicate, mellow flavors and cook very quickly. Broccoli rabe and collard, mustard, dandelion, and turnip greens are more intense in flavor and require longer cooking time. Kale is right in the middle. You can use the same selection, washing, storage, and preparation methods for most greens.

Purchasing: Look for greens with vibrant, fresh, colorful leaves. When greens have a yellow tinge, droopy leaves, or a sharp bitter smell, this is an indication of age and loss of quality. The same variety of green may look somewhat different from season to season, depending on its growing cycle. Small leaves indicate that they will be quite tasty and delicate. Larger leaves will require slightly longer cooking to make them sweet and tender.

Portions: All greens decrease tremendously in volume when cooked. For two substantial portions, use approximately 1 pound of greens. Check the weight of greens at the market—many stores package them in 1-pound bunches.

Storage: Ideally, greens should be cooked right after purchasing or picking. However, they may be purchased ahead of time and refrigerated for 2 or 3 days. Store in plastic bags or perforated plastic vegetable bags. The whole vegetable should be covered, but not tightly sealed in. This will ensure freshness. If you buy frozen greens, choose organic—they are usually flash-frozen, so the nutrients remain intact.

Cleaning: Greens are often grown in sandy soil, and water splashed from rain and irrigation can make them gritty. All greens need to be washed carefully. Submerge them in a large bowl of cold water or a full sink, agitate gently, then remove and put them in a colander. If there is sand on the bottom of the sink or bowl, discard the water, refill the bowl, and repeat the process up to three times. Make sure all sand is removed, because grit can ruin your vegetable dish. If your greens are a little wilted, add 1 tablespoon of white vinegar to your rinse water to plump them slightly. If you are working with nonorganic greens, use a safe vegetable wash or spray on greens before submerging.

Homemade produce wash: Although there are many commercial varieties of terrific fruit and vegetable washes, you can make your own inexpensive version by combining ⅓ cup of distilled white vinegar with 3 cups of water in a spray bottle.

Preparation: Most greens can be cut off at the stem. Kale and collards have tough stems and midribs you can remove before cooking. Those ribs are high in nutrients, however, so you may want to dice the tender, upper sections into small rounds and cook them in your dish. Discard the tough ends.

Cooking methods/uses: Most greens are cooked on the stovetop using water for steaming, boiling, or blanching, or oil for sautéing or wilting. Water dilutes the flavor of greens, so water-based cooking is best for strongly flavored greens such as broccoli rabe, collards, and mustard greens. Milder greens such as beet greens, chard, and spinach can

be cooked in water, but wilting or sautéing them in a skillet will better preserve their flavor. Other interesting ways to prepare greens include grilling, braising, and roasting.

Simplest Preparation Technique: Blanched Greens

1. Boil about 2 cups water (or vegetable or chicken broth) in a large skillet with a tight-fitting lid.
2. Add 1 lb greens, washed and chopped.
3. Cook in boiling water until tender (3 minutes for delicate greens, up to 5 minutes for tougher greens).
4. Drain greens in a colander and dress to taste.
5. Optional: The cooking water contains many nutrients from the greens. Reserve some to drink as tea, or reuse it as cooking water for rice or whole grain pasta.

GUIDE TO LEAFY GREENS

In the sections that follow, you will see different types of information listed about each food. **Taste** generally refers to the one or two tastes most present in the food: sweet, sour, salty, pungent (spicy, hot), bitter, or astringent (drying). For more information about these six tastes, see chapter 10. **Benefits** describes nutrient information or special health properties. **When to eat** tells you when that food is best eaten as a seasonal antidote, as described in chapter 5. For instance, chile peppers are listed as a winter food because their pungent, warming qualities help balance out the chill of that season. **Varieties** lists the different types of that food available. **Storage** and **Preparation** tell you how to keep the food at its best and prepare it for cooking and eating. **Accompaniments** lists complementary flavors or foods. **Cooking methods/uses** provides some simple and delicious ways to cook and eat each food.

ARUGULA

A delicate, peppery versatile green, arugula works well as a salad accent or cooked into dishes.

Taste: Pungent

Benefits: Cruciferous vegetable with cancer-fighting properties. High in vitamin C; higher in calcium than kale or collards.

When to eat: Spring, summer, fall

Varieties: Wild, with small leaves (stronger flavor), or cultivated, with wide leaves (milder flavor).

Storage: Best to use immediately. Can be stored for 1–2 days in a plastic bag.

Preparation: If the leaves are large or tough, cut off the stems at the bottom of the leaves, then wash. If leaves are small, leave whole. Otherwise, gently cut leaves with a knife or scissors (they bruise easily).

Accompaniments: Mild lettuce, avocado, berries, citrus fruits, eggplant, potatoes, tomatoes, walnuts, balsamic vinegar, and cheddar, boursin, goat, and fontina cheeses.

Cooking methods/uses: Great as a salad green; sautéed with other vegetables; added to soups, pasta, or grains; as a pizza topping; in sandwiches: try rolled up in a pita with a filling of boursin cheese or hummus and shredded carrot.

Basic Recipe: Arugula Salad

5 C arugula
3 hard-boiled eggs
2 T chopped black olives
1–2 T finely chopped red onion
3 T balsamic dressing

1. Wash, dry, and tear large leaves into bite-size portions.
2. Separate and chop egg whites.
3. Mix together arugula, egg whites, olives, and onion.

4. Dress with balsamic and toss lightly.
5. Crumble yolks over salad.

BEET GREENS

Buying whole beet stems provides two types of vegetables: the greens and the beetroots. (See Roots and Winter Squashes in the next section for more information on beetroots.)

Taste: Astringent, pungent, slightly sweet

Benefits: High in vitamin C, calcium, and iron.

When to eat: Fall, winter, spring, summer

Varieties: From any type of beet, such as red or golden.

Storage: May be stored for 2–3 days in refrigerator, with beetroots attached or separate, in a loose-fitting plastic bag.

Preparation: Separate leaves by cutting or squeezing them off where they attach to the stalk. Stack the leaves on top of each other and cut into ½-inch ribbons.

Accompaniments: Olive oil, garlic, Vidalia onion, lemon juice, balsamic vinegar, sherry, dill, cinnamon, nutmeg, apples, toasted walnuts, carrots, cabbage, oranges, white beans.

Cooking methods/uses: Sauté, braise, or add to soups.

Basic Recipe: Sautéed Beet Greens

2 T olive oil
1 clove garlic, thinly sliced
1 lb beet greens, washed and cut into thin ribbons
Salt
Lemon wedge or vinegar (red wine or apple cider are good choices; optional)

1. Heat olive oil in a large skillet with a tight-fitting lid over medium heat.
2. Add garlic and sauté for 30 seconds.

3. Add beet greens and a few tablespoons water.
4. Toss to coat with oil and garlic.
5. Cover and cook for 8–10 minutes, until greens are tender. Stir once or twice while cooking, adding additional water if necessary.
6. Season with salt and serve hot with a lemon wedge or a little vinegar.

BOK CHOY

Green and white Asian cabbage found in many Chinese dishes. Leaves are long and dark green, with a white, edible stem.

Taste: Astringent, sweet

Benefits: Contains sulforaphane, an enzyme that protects against cancer. Very high in vitamins A and C.

When to eat: Spring, summer

Varieties: Matured or baby bok choy, also called pac choi.

Storage: Keeps in the refrigerator for 4–7 days, tightly wrapped in a large plastic bag.

Preparation: Chop the base of the cabbage off to separate the stalks. Rinse each stalk and leaf under water to remove the sand. The leaf and stalk are both edible. The stalk will take a minute or two longer to cook.

Accompaniments: Garlic, ginger, peanuts, peanut oil, soy sauce, red pepper flakes, toasted sesame oil, chili oil, cilantro.

Cooking methods/uses: Stir-fry, or add to a cabbage salad, soups, and one-pot dishes.

Basic Recipe: Stir-Fried Bok Choy

1½–2 lbs bok choy, washed
1 T sesame, peanut, or grapeseed oil
2–3 nickel-size slices peeled ginger
1 t toasted sesame oil

2 t soy sauce
1 T black or white sesame seeds (toasted, optional)

1. Cut stalks into ½-inch pieces and set aside.
2. Stack leaves, roll them, and slice into ½-inch strips.
3. Heat a large wok or heavy skillet over medium-high heat.
4. Add sesame oil and swirl to coat all sides.
5. Add ginger and bok choy and toss to coat with oil.
6. Cover for 30–40 seconds.
7. Stir frequently for about 2 minutes, until the cabbage looks bright green, is tender, and is still slightly crunchy.
8. Add 1–2 tablespoons water to prevent sticking, if necessary.
9. When greens are cooked, add toasted sesame oil and soy sauce, tossing to coat.
10. Garnish with sesame seeds.

BROCCOLI RABE

Broccoli rabe, despite its name, isn't actually related to broccoli—it's a member of the Brassica genus (along with Brussels sprouts and cabbage). Rabe is bitter and becomes more so as it ages, so it's best eaten very fresh with complementary accompaniments.

Taste: Bitter, pungent

Benefits: Rich in phytochemicals, which are proven to protect against cancer. High in vitamins A and C.

When to eat: Early spring, fall

Varieties: Broccolini is a close relative of broccoli rabe, but it's not as bitter.

Storage: In a loose plastic bag in the refrigerator for 3–4 days.

Preparation: Wash and chop off about 1 inch from the stalks and discard. Slice stalks into 1-inch pieces. Chop remaining leaves and florets into bite-size pieces.

Accompaniments: Olive oil, garlic, onions, capers, red pepper flakes, pasta, rice, grains, beans, vinegar (raspberry, balsamic, or ume plum are great choices).

Cooking methods/uses: Blanch, then sauté, for milder flavor. Sauté only for stronger, slightly more bitter flavor.

Basic Recipe: Broccoli Rabe with Udon Noodles and Beans

1 (8-oz) package udon noodles
1 lb broccoli rabe, stems and leaves separated and coarsely chopped
1 t plus 2 T olive oil
1 (15-oz) can cannellini beans, drained and rinsed
2 cloves garlic, minced
2 T soy sauce
3 T water or broth
1 T miso (mellow white)

1. Bring 4-5 cups water to a boil in a saucier pan.
2. Add udon noodles and simmer uncovered for 5 minutes.
3. Submerge the broccoli stems in the water and cook for 2 minutes.
4. Add the leaves and cook for 1 minute.
5. When pasta is al dente (firm), drain and rinse pasta and greens well.
6. Add 1 teaspoon olive oil, toss, and set aside.
7. Pour 2 tablespoons olive oil into stockpot over medium heat.
8. Add cannellini beans and garlic, and sauté for 1 minute.
9. Add soy sauce, water, and miso, stirring gently to combine.
10. Turn heat off, add pasta and broccoli rabe, and toss to coat.

CHARD

Hearty green. Easy to prepare and usually available year-round. Both stalks and greens are delicious.

Taste: Bitter, sweet

Benefits: Rich in vitamins A, C, E, and K. High in magnesium, potassium, manganese, iron, and fiber.

When to eat: Fall, winter, spring, summer

Varieties: Swiss chard has shiny green leaves with white ribs or stalks. Red or rhubarb chard has red veining in the leaf and could turn sauce a reddish color.

Storage: Whole bunch of chard in a large plastic bag in the refrigerator for 2–3 days.

Preparation: If stalks are only 1 inch wide or narrower, they don't need to be removed. If they are wider than 1 inch, run a small knife along either side of the stalk and remove. Coarsely chop leaves or tear into bite-size pieces. To make thin shreds, pile the leaves on top of one another, roll into a cigar shape, and thinly slice. To cook stalks, chop into ½-inch pieces or slice into 3-inch-long matchsticks.

Accompaniments: Olive oil, ghee, garlic, red pepper flakes, basil, cilantro, lemon, red wine vinegar, tomatoes, potatoes, pasta, chickpeas, onion.

Cooking methods/uses: Sauté with olive oil, shallot or garlic, and red pepper flakes. Or steam for 5 minutes and dress with olive oil, lemon, and sea salt. Stems take longer to cook, so add them to pan 3–4 minutes before leaves.

Basic Recipe: Sautéed Chard

1½–2 lbs red or Swiss chard, washed
1 T olive oil
1 shallot or clove garlic, thinly sliced
⅛ t red pepper flakes (optional)
3 T water
½ lemon
Salt and pepper

1. Chop chard into bite-size pieces.
2. Heat oil over medium heat in a large pan with a lid.
3. Add shallot and sauté for 2–3 minutes.
4. Add greens and red pepper flakes, and stir gently to coat with oil.
5. Add water, cover, and cook until greens are wilted and soft, 5–6 minutes.
6. Check greens to make sure they are tender; turn heat off.
7. Squeeze lemon over all just before serving (lemon makes greens darker), then season to taste with salt and pepper.

CHINESE OR NAPA CABBAGE

Asian cabbage with pale green and white overlapping leaves and a wide leaf stalk.

Taste: Sweet

Benefits: Decreases inflammation and reduces constipation. High in vitamin A, folate, vitamin B6, and manganese. Calcium content is higher in the outer leaves.

When to eat: Spring, summer

Varieties: Chinese, savoy, and napa.

Storage: Store unbagged in a salad crisper. The nutritional value decreases the longer it's stored. If any leaves wilt, remove them before cooking.

Preparation: Wash and use whole leaves as a wrapper for stuffing, or cut into quarters and core. Chop quarters into ribbon-size strips.

Accompaniments: Olive oil, ghee, sesame oil, rice vinegar, apple cider vinegar, lemon juice, tamari, garlic, ginger, mustard, horseradish, freshly ground black pepper, curry spices, soba noodles.

Cooking methods/uses: Stir-fries, salads, soups, stuffed leaves. Slice thin and use raw in a crunchy Asian salad with a dressing of sesame oil, rice vinegar, and tamari. Stir-fry with garlic, ginger, tamari, and sesame oil. Shred leaves and add to soup. Cook for only a short amount of time to maintain flavor; do not boil.

Basic Recipe: Napa Cabbage and Carrot Stir-Fry

1 T peanut or grapeseed oil
2 cloves garlic, minced
½-inch piece fresh ginger, peeled and minced
2 large carrots, cut on diagonal into ¼-inch-thick pieces
1 napa cabbage, washed and sliced into ribbons
2 T soy sauce
1 t toasted sesame oil
¼ t red pepper flakes (optional)
½ t miso paste (optional)

1. Heat a wok or large skillet over high heat. Add oil and swirl to coat pan.
2. Add garlic and ginger and cook for 1–2 minutes; don't brown garlic.
3. Add carrots and stir for 3 minutes.
4. Add cabbage and stir for 3 minutes.
5. Add soy sauce, toasted sesame oil, pepper flakes, and miso.
6. Stir gently to combine.

COLLARD GREENS

Possesses one of the highest nutritional values of all vegetables. See Noteworthy Nourisher on page 14 for more information.

Taste: Astringent, sweet

Benefits: Cruciferous, cancer-fighting vegetable; helps prevent cardiovascular disease. High in calcium, fiber, beta-carotene, vitamin C, B vitamins, pro-vitamin A, and alpha-linoleic acid.

When to eat: Spring, summer, fall

Varieties: No significant varieties.

Storage: Plastic vegetable bags in vegetable bin in the refrigerator.

Preparation: Use a knife to slice leaves away from the thick midribs, or fold each leaf in half and pull the ribs away from the leaves. To shred, stack 4–5 leaves on top of each other and roll into a fat cigar shape. Using a large knife, slice crosswise into ¼-inch strips.

Accompaniments: Tamari, soy sauce, toasted sesame oil, orange or lemon juice, onion, garlic, shallot, leeks, flavored vinegars, toasted sesame seeds, pine nuts, walnuts, pecans, tahini, eggs, daikon radish, white beans, dried cranberries, raisins, natural Worcestershire sauce.

Cooking methods/uses: Blanche, sauté, or grill. Steamed collard greens are chewy and don't taste great. Do not undercook collard greens, as they will have a grassy flavor.

Basic Recipe: Collards and Leeks

1 small leek
3 T olive oil
1 large bunch collard greens, washed
2–3 dashes Bragg Liquid Aminos

1. Remove tough green stalk and roots from leek.
2. Slice in half lengthwise and chop into 1-inch sections.
3. Separate and submerge in sink of water to rinse off all grit. Drain well.
4. Remove ribs and slice leaves into ribbons as described above.
5. Chop ribs into small rounds.
6. Heat oil in large skillet over medium heat.
7. Add leeks and sauté for 2 minutes.
8. Add greens with 3 tablespoons water and sauté for 8–10 minutes, until both leeks and greens are thoroughly wilted.
9. Add liquid aminos and stir gently to combine.

DUTCH HEAD CABBAGE

 Common cruciferous vegetable used for coleslaw or boiled or stuffed cabbage dishes. Choose cabbage heads with a firm, vibrant look.

Taste: Sweet, pungent

Benefits: Good source of sulfur, iodine, vitamins E and C; high in phytonutrients.

When to eat: Spring, summer, winter

Varieties: Green or purple.

Storage: Keep in a plastic bag in a salad crisper. Will keep for weeks without going bad, but the nutritional value will decrease over time. Cover cut cabbage tightly to slow nutrient loss.

Preparation: Use whole leaves as a wrapper for stuffing, or cut head in half or quarters and core, shred, or chop.

Accompaniments: Olive oil, apple cider vinegar, lemon juice, horseradish, mustard, dill, marjoram, sage, freshly ground black pepper, lemon pepper, slaw dressing, cilantro, fresh parsley.

Cooking methods/uses: Stir-fry or steam lightly to enhance sweetness. Add to soups and stews to enhance richness. Whole leaves can be stuffed with fish, vegetables, or ground beef. If boiling, do so for only a short time to avoid sulfurous odor.

Basic Recipe: Simple Cabbage Sauté

2 T olive oil
1 small head green cabbage, washed and cut into ribbons
3 carrots, peeled and shredded
Salt
2 T water
Freshly ground black pepper

1. Heat oil in large sauté pan over medium heat.
2. Add cabbage and carrots, sprinkle with salt and water.
3. Cover and steam-sauté for 3 minutes.
4. Remove cover, add pepper, and stir gently.
5. Re-cover and continue to cook for 4–5 minutes longer, or until cabbage has reduced in volume, softened, and become translucent.

ESCAROLE

Part of the chicory family (bitter greens), along with endive. Often used as a salad green, escarole is also delicious cooked.

Taste: Slightly bitter

Benefits: Rich in vitamin C, folic acid, and potassium.

When to eat: Winter, spring, summer

Varieties: No significant varieties.

Storage: Keep in a plastic bag like salad greens. Best used within 1 week of purchase.

Preparation: If using in salad, wash and dry with salad spinner. Cut greens carefully.

Accompaniments: Olive oil, garlic, onions, tomatoes, basil, parsley, rice, pasta, pine nuts, Parmesan cheese, lemon, dried basil, dried oregano.

Cooking methods/uses: Braise; steam-sauté; add to salads (raw or cooked) or soups; serve with grains, pasta, or beans.

Basic Recipe: Escarole, Bean, and Rice Soup

2 T olive oil
2 medium onions, chopped
2 cloves garlic
6 C chicken broth
1 medium head escarole, washed and chopped
2 (15-oz) cans navy beans, rinsed and drained
1 bay leaf
1/2 t salt
1/4 t cayenne pepper (optional)
1 C cooked brown rice

1. Heat oil in a large stockpot over medium heat.
2. Add onions; sauté for 4 minutes.
3. Add garlic; sauté for 1 minute.
4. Add broth, escarole, beans, bay leaf, salt, and cayenne pepper.
5. Increase heat to bring soup to a boil.
6. Lower heat to a simmer, add rice, and cook for 5–10 minutes, until escarole has wilted and darkened.

KALE

A greens staple, kale is an absolute powerhouse of nutrition, containing one of the most potent combinations of antioxidants, minerals, vitamins, and phytochemicals of all the leafy greens.

Taste: Astringent

Benefits: Extremely high in calcium and iron. One cup meets RDA's requirements for vitamins A and C. High source of chlorophyll, beta-carotene, vitamin E, and sulforaphane, which stimulates the body to produce cancer-fighting enzymes.

When to eat: Winter (flavor is particularly sweet after frost), spring, summer

Varieties: Dinosaur kale with thin, crinkled leaves; Italian kale with crinkled, blue-green leaves; red Russian kale with flat, purple-blue leaves.

Storage: Store unwashed in a plastic bag in the crisper drawer of the refrigerator for 3–4 days.

Preparation: Remove stalks from kale by stripping leaves by hand. Avoid overcooking, as this takes away some of the minerals and vitamin C. Save the water to drink or use in preparing pasta or rice.

Accompaniments: Olive oil, ghee, sesame oil, garlic, ginger, lemon, white wine vinegar, basil, cayenne, paprika, pine nuts, sesame seeds, walnuts, tahini, raisins, sweet bell peppers.

Cooking methods/uses: In soups; blanched or baked and then used in salads; sauté or stir-fry. Can also wash, dry, and freeze for 3 hours and up to 1 month in freezer bag, then use in sautés: freezing breaks fibers down without boiling. To bake, remove ribs, tear leaves into bite-size pieces, and toss lightly with olive oil. Spread evenly over cookie sheet and bake at 375°F for about 15 minutes, until desired crispness.

Basic Recipe: Quick-Boiled Kale

1 red bell pepper
2 C chicken broth
1 lb kale, washed and chopped
2 T oil-based dressing (Italian or balsamic work well)

1. Core the pepper and cut into 1/2-inch strips.
2. Bring broth to a boil over medium-high heat in large sauté pan with tight-fitting lid.
3. Add kale and peppers and simmer for 4–5 minutes; kale will spread out and cook quickly.
4. Boil until kale leaves are soft and wilted: test doneness with cooking tongs or a slotted spoon.

5. If you prefer softer greens, cook them a little longer. Make sure all of the liquid does not evaporate.
6. Drain in a colander, then toss gently with dressing.

MUSTARD GREENS

Very strong pungent flavor—works best as a salad accent or mixed with sweeter, less intensely flavored greens, such as kale and spinach. The seeds are used to make Dijon mustard.

Taste: Pungent

Benefits: The strong mustard pungency helps clear congestion and strengthens the lungs. High in vitamins A, C, K; folate; dietary fiber; and calcium.

When to eat: Spring

Varieties: No significant varieties.

Storage: Can dry out and yellow quickly; should be used within 1–2 days of purchase.

Preparation: Stack 4–5 leaves on top of each other and roll into a cylinder shape. Using a large knife, slice into strips crosswise.

Accompaniments: Lentils, beans, corn, sweet potatoes, leeks, Vidalia onions, olive oil, garlic, ginger, red peppers, nuts and seeds, coconut milk, all other greens.

Cooking methods/uses: Sauté, stir-fry, or add to stews, soups, or gumbos. Adding small amount of water creates steam to soften the greens. Add to sandwiches or use small amounts raw to give snap to green salads.

Basic Recipe: Sautéed Mustard Greens with Spinach

2 T olive oil
2 shallots or 1/2 sweet onion, minced
1 clove garlic, minced
1 lb mustard greens, washed

½ C water
1 lb spinach, washed
1 T balsamic vinegar

1. Heat oil in a large skillet or stockpot over medium heat.
2. Add shallots and sauté for 3 minutes.
3. Add garlic and sauté for 1 minute.
4. Add mustard greens.
5. Add water, cover, and cook for 2-3 minutes.
6. Add spinach and balsamic vinegar, cover, and cook for about 3 minutes more, until greens are thoroughly wilted, stirring to cook evenly.

SPINACH

The spinach *E. coli* crisis that occured in 2008 is yet another reason for buying locally grown produce. Buying from local providers you know and trust gives you more control over what you put in your body.

Taste: Sweet, astringent, pungent

Benefits: Rich in vitamins A, C, and E—antioxidant vitamins shown to reduce the risk of cancer. Fulfills the RDA requirement for folic acid and is very high in iron. Contains oxalic acid and high amounts of calcium. See page 44 for more information about oxalic acid.

When to eat: Spring

Varieties: Matured or baby leaves.

Storage: Wrap in a paper towel to absorb moisture, then place in plastic bag in the refrigerator. Keeps for 3–4 days, depending on how fresh greens were at time of purchase. Spinach bought in a bunch with stems is usually fresher than bags of loose-leaf spinach.

Preparation: Remove stems and wash leaves. Never cook spinach in an aluminum pan—its color and taste will change.

Accompaniments: Olive oil, ghee, sesame oil, basil, curry, dill, garlic, onions, mushrooms, chickpeas, pine nuts, toasted sesame seeds, lemon, eggs, dried cranberries, cheese, soy sauce, hot sauce.

Cooking methods/uses: Sauté or wilt spinach and add to salads (raw or cooked) with regular or warm dressings. Can also be used on pizza and in stuffings, soups, and pasta dishes.

Basic Recipe: Sautéed Spinach with Onion and Garlic

1 T olive oil
1 medium onion, quartered and sliced
1-2 cloves garlic, minced
2-4 T water
2-3 lbs spinach, washed and chopped
½ lemon

1. Heat 1 t oil in a large sauté pan over medium heat.
2. Add onion and sauté for 3 minutes.
3. Add garlic and sauté for 1 minute.
4. Add 2 T water and spinach.
5. Cover and cook for 2-4 minutes, until spinach is wilted, adding more water if necessary.
6. Add remaining 2 t olive oil and squeeze lemon to taste.

WATERCRESS

Vibrant green color. Can be picked in the wild by flowing streams.

Taste: Bitter

Benefits: High in calcium. Rich in magnesium; vitamins A, C, E, and K; and B vitamins. Cooling to the body.

When to eat: Spring, summer

Varieties: No significant varieties.

Storage: Extremely perishable. Look for vibrant green color in leaves. Do not eat if any of the leaves are yellow. It retains its freshness for 1–2 days in a glass of water in the refrigerator, covered loosely with a plastic bag.

Preparation: Wash and cut right before using. Wash leaves in a bowl of cool water, swirl around to remove any dirt, then dry in a salad spinner. Strip leaves from bottom stems by hand, if desired; thin stems are edible.

Accompaniments: Carrots, cucumbers, dried cranberries, raisins, jicama, endive, radicchio, wild mushrooms, Vidalia onions, pasta, black sesame seeds, garlic, ginger, tamari, peanut oil, sesame oil, red pepper flakes.

Cooking methods/uses: Use raw in salads. Sauté, stir-fry, or add to soups.

> ### Basic Recipe: Watercress, Tomato, Cucumber, and Quinoa Salad
>
> **1 bunch watercress (about 2 C), washed**
> **2 large tomatoes, diced**
> **1/2 C diced cucumber**
> **1 C cooked quinoa**
> **3 T Curry Lemon Salad Dressing (page 194)**
>
> 1. Mix watercress, tomatoes, cucumber, and quinoa gently in large bowl.
> 2. Toss gently with dressing to combine.
> 3. Serve at room temperature or chilled.

GUIDE TO OTHER GREEN VEGGIES

ASPARAGUS

 Reminds us that spring has arrived. In the winter, asparagus is grown in California or imported.

Taste: Sweet, bitter, astringent

Benefits: Provides more folic acid per serving than any other common food—60 percent of the RDA. High in vitamin C, vitamin K, and potassium, which helps muscles work properly. Also provides B vitamins and glutathione. A slight diuretic, it is cooling to the body. Its sulfur-containing compounds can make your urine smell funny, but that's a harmless side effect.

When to eat: Spring, summer

Varieties: Thin or thick, purple, green, or white. White asparagus is buried under the soil—it does not get sunlight, so is less nutritious due to the lack of chlorophyll. Green asparagus tastes slightly more bitter than does white, which is slightly sweeter.

Purchasing: Stalks should be deep green (or white or purple), firm, and smooth. Tips should be green or sprinkled with purple, dry, and close and compact like a flower bud. The entire stalk is edible. Kids generally like tips best, but buying tips only can be expensive.

Storage: Remove rubber bands or wires. Rinse with cold water to remove any sand stuck in tips. Place in tall container with an inch or two of cold water or store in a plastic bag in a crisper. Can be refrigerated for up to 3 days, but may last longer if you change the water a couple of times. Organic and garden-grown asparagus will perish more quickly than conventionally grown asparagus will.

Preparation: Trim by snapping off the bottoms of the stalks. Hold one end in each hand, with the tip end a few inches higher, and gently bend the asparagus. It should easily snap apart where the thick part and the tender part meet. Use the tender end only, or prepare the tough end by cutting off any discoloration and peeling with a potato peeler for smoothness.

Accompaniments: Olive oil, walnut oil, toasted sesame oil, balsamic vinegar, onions, shallots, garlic, lemon, basil, cilantro, tarragon, chervil, Parmesan cheese, berries, tomatoes, salad greens.

Cooking methods/uses: Grill, roast, steam, stir-fry, or sauté. Great in soups, soufflés, omelets, and salads. Serve hot, cold, or at room temperature. Choose stalks of similar size so they cook in the same amount of time.

Basic Recipe: Roasted Asparagus

1 bunch green asparagus, washed and trimmed
2 T olive oil
Salt
Freshly ground black pepper
1/2 head red leaf lettuce or 2 C arugula

1. Preheat oven to 375°F.
2. Lightly coat asparagus with olive oil, salt, and pepper.
3. Arrange evenly on a sheet pan or in a shallow roasting dish.
4. Bake for 15–20 minutes, or until tender when pierced with a fork and lightly caramelized.
5. Serve on a bed of lettuce.

BROCCOLI

Many kids call broccoli "little trees" and like to eat it with their fingers.

Taste: Sweet, astringent

Benefits: Higher in vitamin C than citrus fruit. High in B vitamins, vitamin K, iron, and sulfur. Good source of folate, fiber, carotenoids, and potassium.

When to eat: Fall, winter, spring, summer

Varieties: Green, purple, sprouted, and brocco-flower, which is a combination of cauliflower and broccoli.

Purchasing: Look for solid, thick stalks with tightly packed, bright green crowns. Leaves should look lively. Yellow signifies that the broccoli is old.

Storage: Refrigerate in a plastic bag or a plastic vegetable bag for up to 5 days in the vegetable bin.

Preparation: Clean crowns in a bowl of cold water to remove the sandy grit. Cut off woody stem. For flowers, cut high up on the stem so they separate easily into pieces. For stem, peel away fibrous, stringy outer skin with a paring knife and cut into rounds or matchsticks for efficient cooking. Raw broccoli contains sulfur, which can cause gas. When steaming or blanching, cover halfway to let sulfur content dissipate.

Accompaniments: Olive oil, walnut oil, dark sesame oil, ghee, sesame seeds, garlic, onion, shallots, ginger, red pepper flakes, lemon, mustard, olives, capers, parsley, dill, oregano, curry, cheddar, feta, Parmesan cheese.

Cooking methods/uses: Blanch, steam, sauté, stir-fry, or braise. Stems are great peeled and used in soups or cooked with root vegetables.

Basic Recipe: Steamed Broccoli

11/2 lbs broccoli
2 T olive oil
Juice of 1/2 lemon
1 T soy sauce

1. Place 1/2 inch of water in a 3-quart saucepan and bring to a boil.
2. Place prepared broccoli florets and stems in a steaming basket and cover halfway. Steam for 7–10 minutes, until bright green and stems are tender but firm.
3. Whisk together oil, lemon juice, and soy sauce.
4. Toss broccoli lightly with dressing to combine.

Although Brussels sprouts have the reputation of being hated by kids, we have found them to be quite popular when halved and roasted as opposed to cooked in a casserole.

Taste: Astringent, pungent

Benefits: High in vitamins C, K, A, B6; folic acid; potassium; and magnesium. Contains many nutrients that lower the risk of cancer. High sulfur content.

When to eat: Winter, spring

Varieties: No significant varieties.

Purchasing: Color should be dark green. At farmers' markets, fresh sprouts are found clinging to large stalks.

Storage: In a plastic bag in the refrigerator for a few days.

Preparation: Cut an X at the bottom of each sprout to cook the center quickly. Slice in half or slice thinly and they will absorb sauce well.

Accompaniments: Olive oil, ghee, butter, garlic, capers, lemon, onion, vinegar, cream soups.

Cooking methods/uses: Steam, boil, roast, braise, or bake in casseroles.

Basic Recipe: Brussels Sprouts with Garlic

1 lb Brussels sprouts
3 T olive oil
2 cloves garlic, crushed

1. Rinse Brussels sprouts, pat dry, and slice lengthwise.
2. Warm oil in a medium sauté pan over medium-low heat.
3. Add garlic to oil and sauté for about 3 minutes, until garlic browns lightly.
4. Remove garlic from pan with a slotted spoon.
5. Place Brussels sprouts in pan, cut side down.
6. Cover and cook over low heat until tender, 15–20 minutes.

Roots and Winter Squashes

Roots are a traditional staple food of many human cultures. They contain good-quality complex carbohydrates and a variety of micronutrients. The root vegetables you are probably most familiar with are potatoes and carrots, but there are many other tasty choices, such as parsnips, turnips, beets, and rutabagas.

Because they grow underground, roots are very hearty; in storage they last much longer than greens do. Root vegetables have aromatic flavors and are great for roasting, puréeing, and using in soups, stews, and salads. Cooking often brings out their sweetness, making them ideal for working sweet flavor into your meals, which can reduce cravings for dessert.

Winter squashes are another set of sweet and hearty vegetables. Native to the Northern Hemisphere, they come in beautiful colors and a variety of shapes and sizes. They have thick skins, which allow them to be stored throughout the winter. Most have sweet, yellow-orange flesh inside. Unlike so many other vegetables, some of these squashes are actually in season during the winter months, which is very helpful for those trying to eat seasonally.

Together roots and winter squashes are the "yang" to the "yin" of leafy greens. Greens are light, crunchy, and sharp tasting. Roots are dense, creamy, and sweet. In meals they balance each other well. Also, greens grow upward toward the sky, providing nutrients that develop from exposure to sunlight. Roots and squashes grow in or on the ground, providing nutrients that develop from being in the earth. For a complete vegetable nutrient profile, we recommend getting some of each kind into your regular diet.

ROOTS BASICS

Roots may look similar, but each type needs slightly different care in order to be served tasting its best. The following guide provides information on **Taste, Benefits, Season, Varieties, Purchasing, Portions, Storage, Preparation, Accompaniments,** and **Cooking methods/uses** for each type of root.

GUIDE TO ROOTS

BEETS

Buying whole beet stems provides two types of vegetables: the greens, covered in the Greens section of this chapter, and the roots, which are sweet and delicious. The juice of red beetroots runs and stains, which can make them tricky to work with.

Taste: Sweet

Benefits: Good source of folic acid, vitamins C and A. Helps with overall circulation.

When to eat: Fall, winter, small amounts in spring and summer

Varieties: Red, striped, white, or sweet golden beets. Golden beets don't ooze red juice, so they are nice to add to salads if you don't want your other veggies discolored.

Purchasing: If possible, buy with greens attached. The beetroot should be firm and the end relatively smooth. Two inches of red stem attached assists in keeping nutrients and color in the beet.

Storage: They will keep in the refrigerator crisper drawer, in a paper bag or perforated plastic vegetable bag, for weeks. If you buy them with the greens attached, see Beet Greens for storage instructions. Cooked beets can be kept in the refrigerator for 7–10 days.

Preparation: Wash, trim stem, and cut beets into segments. Peeling is optional. Skins are easier to peel after cooking, since the heat loosens the skin. If adding red beets to a salad, keep separate until ready to serve.

Accompaniments: Olive or walnut oil, balsamic or red wine vinegar, Greek yogurt, sour cream, freshly squeezed lemon or lime juice, orange sections, mandarin oranges, apples, sesame or poppy seeds, cilantro, dill, parsley, tarragon, onions, cumin, curry, horseradish, toasted walnuts, goat cheese.

Cooking methods/uses: Roast, pickle, steam, boil, bake, eat raw, use in soups such as borscht (a popular soup served hot or cold that is traditional in Eastern and Central European cultures).

Basic Recipe: Baked Beets

1. Preheat oven to 375°F.
2. Put unpeeled, uncut, scrubbed beets in a baking dish with about ¼ inch water in the dish, and cover. The steaming effect speeds up cooking time.
3. Bake large beets for about 40 minutes, and smaller beets for 25–30 minutes.

CARROTS

This is one vegetable most children enjoy. Raw carrots are very portable and easy to pack for school.

Taste: Sweet, a little pungent

Benefits: Great source of beta-carotene (pro-vitamin A) and contains a significant amount of silicon. Silicon reinforces connective tissue and benefits calcium metabolism. Carrots also aid in digestion, reducing excessive stomach acid. Good for the eyes.

When to eat: Winter, spring

Varieties: Red, yellow, and orange, different sizes and shapes. The tiny, 3-inch peeled organic baby carrots make popular snacks. There are also long, pointed carrots and thick hearty carrots that are great for soups and stews.

Purchasing: Carrots should have a nice, bright orange color and a firm texture. Carrots with cracks are fine for soups, stews, and stocks but not ideal for eating raw. When the green tops are attached, that assures freshness, but they can make the carrots a little rubbery, so remove greens promptly after purchasing.

Storage: Remove the greens and put carrots in a plastic vegetable bag or plastic bag in the vegetable bin in the refrigerator. They will be good for about 2 weeks. Carrots should not be stored with apples or pears; they emit a gas that spoils carrots.

Preparation: Carrots should be scrubbed well. Peeling is optional, but can reduce bitterness. Slice, dice, matchstick, shred, or chop, depending on the shape you want.

Accompaniments: Other root vegetables, cumin, dill, parsley, thyme, mint, tarragon. When braising, add apple cider vinegar, orange juice, flavored vinegar, apple-flavored brandy.

Cooking methods/uses: Raw in salads; raw as a snack with hummus, dressing, or nut butters; puréed; stir-fried; roasted or braised to intensify flavor. Using the whole carrot, including the top and stem, in soups and stews makes the meal more mineral-rich.

Basic Recipe: Cooked Carrots with Orange and Tarragon

2–3 C orange juice (optional)
1¹⁄₂ lbs carrots, scrubbed and peeled (optional), sliced on a diagonal
Salt
1 T chopped fresh tarragon or other fresh herbs

1. Fill saucepan to midline: half with cold water, half with orange juice.
2. Heat on high.
3. Add carrots and salt when liquid comes to a boil.
4. Cook until tender, about 10 minutes.
5. Remove from heat, strain, put in a serving bowl.
6. Toss lightly with chopped tarragon.

PARSNIPS

 In the same family as the carrot. Distinct sweet flavor. Parsnips picked after the frost are sweetest.
Taste: Sweet

Benefits: Good source of folate. Helpful to the stomach, pancreas, and spleen. Gentle diuretic.

When to eat: Fall, winter

Varieties: No significant varieties.

Purchasing: Select firm, ivory-colored roots.

Storage: Store in a plastic bag in the vegetable bin. Cold temperatures will continue to sweeten parsnips.

Preparation: Parsnips have an irregular shape, so they don't cook evenly unless they are cut into similar-size pieces. They have a noticeable core that does not have to be removed unless it feels very tough. Peel before cooking.

Accompaniments: Onions, apples, other root vegetables, ginger, curry, mustard, parsley, tarragon, thyme, honey, maple syrup, agave nectar.

Cooking methods/uses: Roast, bake, boil, braise, steam, sauté; add to soups, stews, or purées.

Basic Recipe: Braised Parsnips

1½ lbs parsnips
¾ C apple juice or cider, water, or broth
2 T olive oil
¼ t salt
½-inch piece fresh ginger, peeled and sliced
Freshly ground pepper

1. Preheat the oven to 375°F.
2. Peel and quarter parsnips lengthwise, removing cores if necessary.
3. In a shallow baking dish, combine parsnips, water, oil, salt, and ginger.
4. Cover and bake until tender, 30–40 minutes. Stir once or twice during cooking.
5. Remove cover and bake until parsnips are lightly browned, 10–15 minutes.
6. Season to taste with pepper.

SWEET POTATOES

 Sweet potatoes are the "candy" of the vegetable world. Baking them brings out extra sweetness—they make equally good side dishes, snacks, and desserts. See Noteworthy Nourisher on page 70.

Taste: Sweet

Benefits: High in vitamin A. Good source of fiber, vitamins C and D, manganese, copper, potassium, vitamin B6, and iron. High in antioxidants, which help eliminate free radicals from the body. Helpful for relieving diarrhea and eliminating toxins from the body. If you want to increase calcium absorption, eat sweet potatoes 2–3 hours after taking calcium supplements.

When to eat: Winter (best), fall, spring

Varieties: Garnet or jewel (small, red-orange skins), Louisiana (common), Jersey (tend to be dry, light colored), Japanese (light-colored skins with yellow flesh, dry, very sweet).

Purchasing: They should be firm, with pointed ends and without bruises. Quite perishable: if bruised, they will spoil soon after.

Storage: Use within 1 week of purchase. Store in a cool pantry or on the counter.

Preparation: Scrub the skin very well, especially if you want to eat it. While peeling, put peeled potatoes into a bowl of cold water to prevent browning. Best to have sweet potatoes of the same size for even cooking.

Accompaniments: Maple syrup, agave nectar, pecans, walnuts, cinnamon, ginger, nutmeg, chili powder, allspice, orange, dark sesame oil, roasted peanut oil, ume plum vinegar, dried fruit, ghee, miso paste.

Cooking methods/uses: Baked; baked french fries; roasted; puréed with cinnamon and agave nectar or other sweet accompaniments; steamed; in desserts: muffins, pies, cakes, pudding, bread.

Basic Recipe: Baked Sweet Potatoes

1. Preheat oven to 400°F.
2. Scrub potatoes well and wrap in aluminum foil to prevent seepage.
3. Bake until very tender when pierced, 45–60 minutes.
4. Slice down the middle and mash with a fork.
5. Season to taste (a few dashes of ume plum vinegar makes a delicious healthy substitute for the more traditional butter and salt).

TURNIPS AND RUTABAGAS

 These are closely related root vegetables, shaped like spinning tops. They are often interchangeable in recipes; however, rutabagas need to be cooked about 10 minutes longer than turnips.

Taste: Bitter, sweet

Benefits: Cancer-fighting, antioxidant properties. Turnips are a good source of sulfur, which aids in detoxification. They are also high in vitamin C, which is helpful in relieving congestion. Rutabagas have half the carbohydrate content of a potato and are high in fiber.

When to eat: Spring, fall, winter

Varieties: Turnips are smaller and thinner than rutabagas, with white skin, purple tops, and tender greens. Rutabagas look similar but are larger with sometimes waxy skin and drier flesh.

Purchasing: Avoid shriveled or cracked turnips or rutabagas. Avoid giant rutabagas.

Storage: Store in a plastic bag in the refrigerator, or in a cool, dry place. Rutabagas will keep for several weeks, fresh turnips only for a few days.

Preparation: Rutabagas and older turnips should be thickly peeled. Fresh garden turnips don't have to be peeled.

Accompaniments: Garlic, chives, leeks, tarragon, thyme, rosemary, parsley, other savory herbs.

Cooking methods/uses: Add to stews and soups; roast; steam; braise; mash with sweet or white potatoes; use raw in a crudité; or make rutabaga fries. Fresh garden turnips are great raw or lightly steamed in salads; the taste is similar to that of a very mild radish.

Basic Recipe: Rutabaga Fries

1 lb rutabagas, peeled and sliced into long, thin french fries
1 T grapeseed oil
Salt
1 T olive oil

1. Preheat oven to 400°F.
2. Toss rutabaga fries with grapeseed oil and a few pinches of salt to coat lightly.
3. Spread fries on a sheet pan and bake for 35–40 minutes, turning occasionally, until lightly brown and soft.
4. When cooked, brush fries lightly with olive oil and add an extra sprinkle of salt to taste.

Basic Recipe: Roasted Turnips

2 T olive oil
1 1/2 lbs turnips, peeled and cut into sixths or eighths
1 t dried rosemary or 2 rosemary sprigs
1 t dried thyme or 5 thyme sprigs

1. Preheat oven to 375°F.
2. Lightly oil a baking dish.
3. Place turnip chunks in baking dish and brush lightly with remaining oil.
4. Sprinkle herbs over oiled turnips and bake, uncovered, for about 35 minutes, until tender when pierced with a fork.

WINTER SQUASH BASICS

You will begin to see the winter squashes appearing on the market shelves in mid to late August (butternut squash is usually available year round). As their name indicates, they are cold-weather veggies and in many areas you can enjoy them straight through the winter. Experiment with different varieties and cooking methods throughout the season to find your family's favorites. Winter squashes tend to be popular with kids of all ages, and they make a great first solid food for babies when cooked and puréed well with a little breast milk or formula.

Benefits: High in vitamins A, C, K, B1, and B6, as well as potassium, fiber, folate, omega-3s, copper, niacin, and pantothenic acid. Also high in carotenoids, a group of antioxidants.

When to eat: Fall, winter

Purchasing: A fresh squash should be solid and heavy for its size. The heavier a squash is, the more moist and dense the flesh is inside. Rough patches on the skin are fine. Avoid soft, spongy spots, but you can cut them off at home if necessary.

Storage: Whole squash will keep for weeks if you put it in a cool dry place with a lot of ventilation. If you store it on your kitchen counter, use it within a week or two or it will dry out. Opened and cut squash will keep, wrapped and refrigerated, for a few days.

Preparation: Cutting a large squash can be difficult. You will need a strong, sharp, heavy knife or a cleaver. A rubber mallet can be useful for applying force to the knife handle. Wash squash before cutting to keep any external dirt away from the flesh. Set squash on a thick towel for balance. Start your cut next to the stem rather than trying to cut through the stem. Slowly strike the knife down and press gently on the top of the blade. Hammer gently with the mallet for more leverage, if needed. The knife should slowly pass through the squash. Some squashes have seeds inside; use a spoon to scrape and scoop them out, like you would when making a jack-o'-lantern from a pumpkin.

Once your squash is in two halves, you can move on to baking, or lay them flat and cut them into smaller segments. If a squash is too tough or large to cut raw, it is possible to bake it whole and cut it open after cooking has softened the skin. This method also works if you are puréeing and need to remove the skin entirely—you can bake it first so the skin is easier to remove. The easiest way to obtain peeled squash for a recipe is to buy it prepared; many stores sell squash already peeled and cut. Frozen organic squash is another option.

Accompaniments: Olive oil, sunflower seed oil, organic butter, ghee, maple syrup, agave nectar, honey, cinnamon, nutmeg, allspice, ginger, orange juice, soy sauce, sage, rosemary, garlic, red pepper flakes, cumin, lemongrass, lime, apple, pear, cherries, apple cider vinegar, onions, dried fruit; nuts and seeds; Gruyère, Parmesan, Romano, and fontina cheeses.

Cooking methods/uses: Bake, steam, roast, sauté; add to soups, stews, purées, or gratins; bake in pies, breads, and cakes. The seeds can be roasted and eaten.

Basic Recipe: Baked Squash

1. Preheat oven to 375°F.
2. Cut a squash in half, then scoop out seeds and fibers.
3. Brush squash flesh with a thin coating of oil and place cut side down on a sheet pan.
4. Bake until squash looks soft and crinkled and flesh is soft when pierced with a fork, usually 30–45 minutes.

Basic Recipe: Baked/Steamed Squash

1. Prepare squash as above.
2. Before baking, add 1/2 inch water to a shallow baking pan.
3. Bake squash until soft, about 30 minutes. The water evaporates, steaming squash to shorten cooking time, but note that this may discolor bottom of squash.

Basic Recipe: Roasted Squash

1. Choose an easy-to-peel squash, such as butternut. You could also use store-bought, prepared squash or frozen squash chunks.
2. Preheat oven to 400°F. *(continued)*

3. Peel, seed, and cut 2½–3 lbs of squash into pieces.
4. Toss squash with about 2 T of grapeseed or avocado oil. Season with salt and pepper, cinnamon, rosemary, or other herbs and spices.
5. Spread squash in large roasting pan.
6. Roast for 15 minutes, then turn pieces and cook for 25–30 minutes more, or until tender.

GUIDE TO WINTER SQUASHES

ACORN

Common, acorn-shaped squash. The flavor can be bland, so add a sweetener such as agave nectar or apple cider during cooking.

BUTTERCUP

Also called kabocha, green Hokkaido, or honey delight. Its sweet, dense, creamy flesh readily absorbs liquid. Good for baking.

BUTTERNUT

Buff-colored with a long, straight, solid neck and a round bottom that contains the seeds. Relatively easy to peel, it's ideal for gratins, purées, and baking. This is a great all-purpose winter squash that's easy to find already prepared in grocery stores.

DELICATA

Tube-shaped yellow, orange, or cream colored, with thin, dark green stripes running lengthwise along the grooves. Usually small, about 1 pound. Relatively easy to peel; they are full of seeds, so when seeded they have a lot of space for stuffing.

A Note about Pumpkins

Pumpkins are also a type of squash. You are probably most familiar with small sugar pumpkins and Connecticut field pumpkins. These are grown specifically for purées and pumpkin pie. Pumpkins are particularly good for making great fall and winter desserts, such as pies, quick breads, and custards.

HUBBARD

Orange, bluish, or gray; usually large and bumpy. Great flavor, works well in simple preparations.

MINI SQUASH AND MINI PUMPKINS

These tiny squash varieties can be stuffed, baked, or steamed and served one squash per person. Children love having their own.

SPAGHETTI SQUASH

Yellow skin and oval shape. The flesh is coarse and can be pulled into long strands that look similar to spaghetti. The flavor is watery and bland, so serve with tomato sauce or vinaigrette to give it a little snap. Spaghetti squash is extremely low in calories: 1 cup cooked has only 42!

TURBAN SQUASH

Bumpy, multicolored top with a thick, orange and green bottom ring. They look very cool, but are better for decorating than for eating.

SIMPLE FOOD FOR BUSY FAMILIES

Grains and Beans: Filling Fiber

As we discussed in part I, the Standard American Diet is loaded with stripped, highly processed carbohydrates that, when eaten to excess, can lead to the SAD imbalances. To regain nutritional balance, you need to include a wide variety of fresh vegetables in your family's daily diet. It's also important to upgrade those simple, highly refined carbs such as white hamburger buns and french fries to other high-quality, more intact carbohydrate foods, such as whole grains and beans.

Both whole grains and beans are higher in fiber and nutrients than their more refined counterparts: white flour products. Grains are naturally filling and provide a more nutrient-dense alternative to the rolls, white rice, or white potatoes so often used to fill out the American plate. But they need to be used sparingly, with care, because they are high in calories and most of them have a medium to high glycemic load, especially rice.

If you are trying to break the SAD blood sugar cycle, then quinoa (the highest protein "grain," which is really a seed, but more on that to come) and beans are better replacement options than the other grains. Beans are an ideal carbohydrate for many people recovering from the SAD state because they don't contain much sugar, and thus have a relatively low glycemic load and are a rich source of both fiber and protein.

If you begin to replace some of your animal proteins with beans and grains, you might notice your weekly grocery bills going down: they are some of the cheapest foods around, especially if you buy them in bulk. Experiment with different combinations of the two, and branch out to use seasoning combinations from other cultures: both Mexican and Indian recipes offer delightfully tasty options with spice combinations designed to improve their overall digestibility. See appendix C for some ideas to get you started.

Whole Grains

Whole grains have been a staple food for thousands of years for many cultures. They are inexpensive and provide a variety of nutrients. They are quite versatile and, when mixed with vibrant vegetables and colorful beans, make a satisfying meal.

When adding whole grains to your diet, start slowly and find a method that works for you. Start off with cornmeal, quinoa, or brown rice, which are soft, comforting grains, or mix your brown rice and white rice together. Add a handful of grain such as barley, quinoa, or brown rice to your soups. In Asian cultures, many families eat their meals around a central, shared rice bowl. Try this method at a family meal with any grain you like.

NOTEWORTHY NOURISHER

Adzuki Beans

- 1 cup contains 17 grams of fiber and has 294 calories
- Are hard, dark red beans rich in soluble fiber, which helps eliminate cholesterol from the body
- Are an excellent source of complex carbohydrates and protein
- Are high in niacin, manganese, folic acid, copper, phosphorous, and potassium
- Contain protease inhibitors, which help prevent the development of cancerous cells
- Are low in fat; great meat alternative
- Are popular in the Far East, especially Japan
- Are used in Asian sweet treats, such as pastry, candy, and even ice cream
- See page 169 for more about adzuki beans

WHOLE GRAIN BASICS

Whole grains are harvested and prepared in a variety of ways to make them ready for sale. Grains are sold on the market as groats (buckwheat, amaranth); pearled or polished grains (pearled barley, wheat berries, brown rice); grits (steel-cut oats, corn grits, bulgur); and flakes (rolled oats, rolled spelt).

Purchasing: Organically grown grains without pesticides are ideal. These grains are commonly found in supermarkets as well as natural food markets. It is best to buy grains in small packages and replace them as you use them; if grains are left unused they may deteriorate (go rancid; see below). Buying in bulk is fine as well—most bulk items turn over quickly, but check that your bulk grains look and smell fresh and have not gone rancid.

Portions: A serving is 4 to 8 ounces, depending on the grain, or the size of a closed fist.

Storage: Whole grains contain their germ layer, which has oil, so they go rancid faster than refined grains do. Store grains in tightly covered glass jars in a cool place for freshness. If there is room, your refrigerator is ideal. Whole grains can last for a few months when kept cool. Stone-ground cornmeal should be kept in the refrigerator or freezer to prevent mealy bugs. Cooked grains can be refrigerated for 4 to 5 days, or frozen for up to 6 months, in an airtight container. We recommend cooking plain, double portions of grains and storing them for meals throughout your week.

Soaking: Many whole grains cook more quickly and are digested more easily if soaked before cooking. Soaking removes phytic acid, which some grains contain. This acid can interfere with good digestion and micronutrient absorption. It's not necessary to soak rice and some other grains for more than two hours, but soaking overnight will soften them considerably, reducing cooking time. Soaking basmati rice lengthens and plumps the grains. See individual grains for more specific guidance.

Cooking methods/uses: *Stovetop:* A 2-quart saucepan with a tight-fitting lid is good for cooking 1 to 2 cups of grain. After the grains have cooked, let them stand for 5 to 10 minutes to continue absorbing the moisture. To produce fluffy, individual grains, after removing from heat put a clean towel under the pan lid and leave it. The towel, rather than the grain, will absorb the moisture.

Pressure cooker: A pressure cooker is a time-saver for long-cooking grains such as kamut, barley, whole oat groats, and wheat berries. When pressure cooking grains, there is no need to presoak. Cook grains for one-third less than the suggested time for stovetop cooking. If this is not enough, add 5 to 10 minutes. Fast-cooking smaller grains, such as quinoa and millet, are too delicate for a pressure cooker. Check your pressure cooker instructions for more specific guidelines.

Slow cooker: This is a great appliance for preparing groats or steel-cut oats the night before so you can wake up to a cooked whole grain. It can be used for cooking oat groats, barley, and wild rice—time-consuming grains to cook on the stovetop.

Rice cooker: Using a rice cooker is the easiest, most reliable way to cook rice quickly. Many rice cookers are versatile and allow you to steam vegetables as well. Be sure to check the brand carefully to make sure it can accommodate whole grains and not just white rice; not every machine is designed for the longer cooking grains.

Cooking tips: *Salting:* Grains need very little salt to bring out their flavor. Use salt in small amounts,

depending on how salt-sensitive you are. Add to bulkier grains, such as oat groats, during the last 30 minutes of cooking (as you would with beans).

Cooking liquid: You may substitute cooking broth or apple cider for all or part of your cooking water to give your grains added flavor and nutrients. Low-sodium varieties are usually best.

Combining: Some grains can be combined and cooked together. Make sure they have similar cooking times and liquid requirements before attempting. You may also add a small amount of nuts or seeds to your grains. To add before cooking, substitute part of the total grain measurement for additional grains, nuts, or seeds. For example, if you want to cook 1½ cups of grain, you could create a combination like this: 1 cup brown long-grain rice, ¼ cup wheat berries, ¼ cup sunflower seeds. Then cook as directed for the rice. You might also try ¾ cup millet with ¼ cup cornmeal. You may also add raw or roasted nuts or seeds to the cooked grain just before serving to add crunch.

To cook with other additions such as vegetables or dried fruits, use the basic cooking time as a guide for creating combinations. For instance, tough leafy greens work well with quinoa, a quick-cooking grain, but would disintegrate if you tried to cook them with barley, a long-cooking grain. Chunks of harder vegetables such as carrots can hold up well with millet or cornmeal. And dried fruit works well cooked with rice. Start with small amounts of the additional vegetables and fruits and increase the cooking liquid by the same volume: for example, if adding ⅓ cup of dried fruit, increase the liquid by an additional ⅓ cup.

Spotting True Whole Grains

The Whole Grains Council has created a stamp to help consumers identify legitimate whole grain products. The Whole Grain Stamp identifies products that contain a half-serving (8 g) or more of whole grains. The 100% Whole Grain Stamp identifies products that contain a full serving (16 g) or more of whole grains. These amounts conform to serving size standards set by the USDA's My Pyramid.

GUIDE TO WHOLE GRAINS

AMARANTH

 Significant food of the Aztecs. Very tiny brown, yellow, and black seeds. Becomes sticky when cooked and holds together like a thick pudding.

Taste: Sweet, bitter

Benefits: Extremely high nutritional value. High in protein, calcium, fiber, iron, magnesium, copper, vitamin C; unusually high in the amino acid lysine and a great source of manganese. Also contains magnesium and silicon. Calcium from amaranth is absorbed well; higher content than whole milk.

Varieties: No significant varieties.

Accompaniments: Miso paste, soy sauce, nuts and seeds, sea vegetables, broccoli, carrots, greens, sweet potatoes, fruit, dried fruit, cardamom, cinnamon, clove, ginger, mint, nutmeg.

Cooking methods/uses: Stovetop. Add to soups to thicken (amaranth has a slightly gelatinous quality); excellent to combine with other grains, such as bulgur wheat; serve as hot cereal; pop into "popcorn"; bake bread with flour form; include sprouted form in salads.

Basic Recipe: Amaranth

½ C amaranth
1½ C water
Pinch of salt

1. Do not soak amaranth, and no need to rinse.
2. Combine the grain, water, and salt in a small saucepan.
3. Bring to a boil, then reduce heat to a simmer.
4. Cover and cook over low heat until water is absorbed, about 25 minutes.

Yield: ½ C dry yields about 1½ C cooked

BARLEY

 Whole barley contains more nutrients than the commonly used pearl barley. Pearl barley has the husk and bran removed; it is more processed and not as nutritious. Scotch barley is not as processed as pearl—it takes about an hour to cook. It can be found in health food stores. Hato Mugi, also called Job's Tears, is a wonderful Japanese barley. It cooks up into a large, chewy grain and combines well with brown rice varieties (about ¾ rice to ¼ Hato Mugi to cook together). Look for it in high-quality natural food stores or Asian markets.

Taste: Sweet, salty

Benefits: Cooked whole barley is higher in fiber than pearl barley (13.6 g [whole] versus 6 g [pearl] per 1 cup). They both are a great source of manganese, and whole barley is also a good source of thiamin, copper, and selenium. Cooling effect and mild laxative properties. To decrease laxative effect, roast barley in a dry pan until it releases its aroma.

Varieties: Whole, pearl, Scotch, Hato Mugi.

Accompaniments: Mushrooms, lentils, nuts, seeds, red or white wine vinegar, rosemary, tarragon, parsley, cilantro, nut oils, ume plum vinegar.

Cooking methods/uses: Stovetop, pressure cooker, slow cooker. Add to soups, stews, pilaf, or risotto, or serve with vegetables.

Basic Recipe: Whole Barley

1 C whole barley
4 C water
1 t white vinegar (to prevent sticking and fluff grains)

1. Soak barley overnight to soften.
2. Rinse barley.
3. Bring water and vinegar to a boil in a saucepan.
4. Add grain, reduce heat to low and simmer, covered, for about 1 hour and 15 minutes, until water is absorbed.
5. Let stand for 10 minutes. Fluff with a fork.

Yield: 1 C dry yields 3¼ C cooked

Basic Recipe: Barley Salad

¼ C water
¼ C extra-virgin olive oil
1 T lime juice
3 T orange juice
1 T chopped cilantro
3½–4 cups cooked barley
2 avocados, diced
½ C dried cranberries
¼ C chopped scallion
1 C grated carrots
1 C diced cooked chicken (optional)

1. In a small bowl or measuring cup, whisk or blend together water, olive oil, lime juice, orange juice, and cilantro.
2. In a medium-size bowl, add barley, avocadoes, cranberries, scallion, carrots, and chicken. Pour the dressing over the salad and toss gently to combine.

Basic Recipe: Pearl Barley

1 C pearl barley
3 C water

1. Soak barley for 1 hour to soften.
2. Rinse barley.
3. Bring water to a boil in a saucepan.
4. Add pearled barley, reduce heat and simmer, covered, for 40 minutes until water is absorbed.
5. Let stand for 5 minutes before serving. Fluff with a fork.

Yield: 1 C dry yields 3½ C cooked

BUCKWHEAT

Buckwheat originally grew wild in Asia, then migrated north to Eastern Europe and Russia, where it is still popular. Buckwheat is one of the least allergenic grains. In the United States, it is most commonly eaten in the form of kasha, a grain dish made of toasted buckwheat groats, or soba noodles, a traditional Japanese noodle made with 100 percent buckwheat or a combination of buckwheat and wheat flour. Some soba noodle products contain herbs such as wild yam or mugwort, which provide additional flavor and nutrients. Cooked kasha has a "mushier" consistency than some of the other grains.

Taste: Sweet

Benefits: Very high in manganese and a good source of fiber and magnesium. Cleansing to the intestines. Can improve appetite. Contains bioflavonoids, which strengthen capillaries and blood vessels, reduce blood pressure, and increase circulation to hands and feet. Medium to low glycemic load.

Varieties: Raw or toasted (kasha)

Accompaniments: Soy sauce, nuts and seeds, raisins, dried cranberries, vegetables, mushrooms, onions, garlic, ginger, tahini.

Cooking methods/uses: Stovetop. Kasha can be used with noodles as *kasha varnishes* (a Jewish dish), as a pilaf with vegetables, as a stuffing, or as a hot cereal. Soba noodles can be used in any pasta dish, but are especially good with Asian flavors.

Basic Recipe: Kasha

2 C water
Pinch of salt
1 C kasha

1. Do not rinse kasha.
2. Bring water and salt to a boil.
3. Add grain to boiling water.
4. Cover pan, reduce heat, and let simmer for 15–20 minutes.

Yield: 1 C dry yields 2½–3 C cooked

BULGUR

This grain is very quick to prepare because it is precooked by a steaming method; the wheat is steamed whole, then dried and cracked into grits and packaged.

Taste: Sweet, salty

Benefits: Great source of fiber, high in manganese, and a good source of magnesium, which helps activate enzymes involved with glucose and insulin—may aid in reduction of symptoms of type 2 diabetes.

Varieties: Fine (for tabbouleh), medium, and coarse (for pilafs)

Accompaniments: Mint, cilantro, parsley, tarragon, dill, tomatoes, lemon juice, dried fruit, garlic, onion, carrots, cucumbers, parsley, zucchini, yellow squash, walnuts, almonds, pine nuts.

Cooking methods/uses: Stovetop. In tabbouleh, in pilaf, as a textured meat substitute in chili.

Basic Recipe: Bulgur Wheat

1 C fine or medium bulgur wheat
2½ C water
1 T olive oil or butter
Salt and pepper

1. Rinse bulgur wheat.
2. Boil 3 C water.
3. Combine 2½ C boiling water, pinch of salt, and grain in a heat-resistant bowl.
4. Cover and let stand: 15 minutes for fine bulgur, 25 minutes for medium bulgur.
5. If there is excess water, pour grain through a strainer.
6. Toss with olive oil.
7. Season to taste with salt, pepper, and garnishes of your choice.

Yield: 1 C dry yields about 2 C cooked

CORNMEAL

Cornmeal is dried, ground corn kernels. It has long been a dietary staple in South American, African, and Native American cultures. Fresh corn and dried corn have similar compositions. Grits are made from the endosperm, and polenta is made from coarsely ground kernels of corn.

Taste: Sweet

Benefits: Good source of thiamin and B vitamin pantothenic acid—helpful when under stress. Helps with digestion, strengthens teeth and gums, and can stimulate appetite.

Varieties: Yellow, white, or blue cornmeal

Accompaniments: Vegetables, dried cranberries or blueberries, raisins, nuts and seeds, cayenne pepper, chili powder, cumin, cinnamon, Parmesan cheese, Gruyère, mozzarella, tomato sauce (to top cooked polenta "cakes").

Cooking methods/uses: Stovetop, slow cooker, baked. As cakes in the oven, in layered casseroles, as hot cereal, as tortillas, baked as "crust" for pizza.

Basic Recipe: Polenta Cakes

5 C water or vegetable broth
2 t extra-virgin olive oil or butter
Pinch of salt
1 C polenta or corn grits
2–3 t Parmesan cheese (optional)

1. In a large saucepan bring water to a rapid boil with olive oil and salt.
2. Slowly add polenta, stirring continuously with a wire whisk. When mixture begins to sputter, reduce heat to low, cover, and let cook for 30–40 minutes, stirring occasionally.
3. Add cheese, herbs, or vegetables for flavor at this stage.
4. Lightly oil a pie pan or an 8" x 8" pan. Pour polenta into pan and smooth the top.
5. Cool for 5–10 minutes, slice, and serve.

Yield: 8 slices

COUSCOUS

Couscous is called a grain, but it's actually tiny pasta made from coarsely ground and steamed wheat. Usually it is made from refined wheat, although whole wheat couscous is becoming more readily available. Couscous sold in bulk, rather than in boxes, seems to be fresher.

Taste: Neutral

Benefits: High in fiber (whole wheat variety only), very good source of selenium, an antioxidant beneficial in reducing cancer risk.

Varieties: Refined, whole wheat, small and large

Accompaniments: Currants, dried cranberries, dried apricots, pine nuts, almonds, mint, parsley, thyme, marjoram, cayenne pepper, red pepper flakes, cumin, ginger, garlic, cinnamon, paprika, red and yellow bell peppers, peas, mushrooms, turnips, rutabaga, cauliflower, leeks, tomatoes, lemon, chickpeas, black beans.

Cooking methods/uses: Stovetop. Use in soups and stews, as an accompaniment for beans, or in a salad with added vegetables and dressing.

Basic Recipe: Couscous

1 C whole wheat couscous
Pinch of salt
1¾ C water
Flavored oil (olive, toasted sesame, almond, etc.)

1. Optional: For a nuttier flavor, toast couscous dry on low heat in a skillet first.
2. Bring water and salt to a boil.
3. Add couscous to the pot.
4. Cover and remove from heat. Let stand for 5–10 minutes.
5. Fluff with a fork before serving. Add a few drops of oil to avoid lumps.

Yield: 1 C dry yields 2½ C cooked

KAMUT

Large, chewy, yellow grain, resembling wheat berries. This is an ancient relative of durum wheat but is significantly less allergenic and higher in protein than wheat is. Many people with wheat intolerances or allergies may tolerate kamut. It is a very plain grain and works better as a dish when combined with another grain, such as brown rice.

Taste: Sweet, a little astringent
Benefits: High in protein, unsaturated fats, and minerals, particularly zinc and magnesium
Varieties: No significant varieties.
Accompaniments: Ginger, garlic, saffron, shallots, leeks, soy sauce, balsamic vinegar, sweeteners, dried cherries and cranberries, raisins, pesto, tomato sauce.

Cooking methods/uses: Stovetop, pressure cooker, slow cooker. Add to soups, mix with beans, mix with other grains such as brown rice for a pilaf, use ground as an alternative to wheat flour. Also available as store-bought cereal flakes and bread. Kamut may also be cooked overnight in a slow cooker on low or for 40 minutes in a pressure cooker.

Basic Recipe: Kamut

1 C kamut
1½ C water (if kamut is presoaked—if not presoaked, use 3 C water)
Salt

1. Soak kamut overnight, then rinse.
2. Bring water to a boil, add kamut and simmer, covered, for 1 hour, adding a couple of pinches of salt during last half hour.
3. Let stand for 3 minutes. Stir with a fork.

Yield: 1 C dry yields about 2½ C cooked

MILLET

A tiny, round, yellow grain, millet is a staple in Asia and Africa, but Americans often recognize it as birdseed. Its nutrients are enhanced when toasted in a dry skillet before cooking. Toasted millet is a popular Indian dish.

Taste: Sweet, salty
Benefits: High in B vitamins, protein, manganese, magnesium, phosphorus, and silicon. Has cooling properties. Low in allergens. People with weak digestion should avoid millet.
Varieties: No significant varieties.
Accompaniments: Salsa, tomatoes, onion, garlic, shallots, corn, sunflower seeds, pumpkin seeds, beans, cumin, basil, oregano, paprika, saffron, cilantro, parsley, cayenne pepper, chili powder, Parmesan cheese.

Cooking methods/uses: Stovetop, slow cooker. As cereal; in vegetable pilaf; in breads, beers, and malts.

Basic Recipe: Millet

1 C millet
2–3 C water
Pinch of salt

1. Rinse and drain millet. Repeat this process 2 or 3 times.
2. Optional: For a nuttier flavor, heat washed millet in a dry skillet, stirring constantly until it is toasted and gives off a nutty fragrance, about 5 minutes.
3. Transfer millet to cooking pot. Add water to millet. (Use 2 C water for a fluffy grain, 3 C for a creamier grain.)
4. Bring water, millet, and a pinch of salt to a boil.
5. Lower heat, cover, and simmer for 30–40 minutes, until all the water is absorbed.

Yield: 1 C dry yields 2½–3 C cooked

OATS

 Whole oat groats are unrefined and contain their bran, germ, and endosperm. Steel-cut oats are also unrefined—they are whole oats cut apart for easier cooking. Oat flakes are almost as nutritious as whole oat groats. They are lightly processed by steaming and rolling. Note that most packaged, presweetened oatmeal contains a lot of sugar or artificial sweeteners such as Splenda.

Taste: Sweet, slightly bitter
Benefits: High in manganese and a good source of fiber, phosphorus, thiamin, magnesium, and selenium. Known to decrease cholesterol and help cardiovascular functions. Oats have antioxidant properties and a significant amount of beta-glucan, which is helpful in strengthening the immune system.

Varieties: Oat groats, berries, steel-cut Irish, steel-cut Scottish, flattened rolled oats, presteamed rolled oats, oat flakes.

Accompaniments: Maple syrup, agave nectar, honey, cinnamon, ginger, cardamom, berries (frozen work well), banana, apples, dried fruit, vanilla.

Cooking methods/uses: Stovetop, slow cooker, pressure cooker (whole or steel-cut groats only). Hot cereal, cold cereal, soup thickener, bread, muffins, cookies.

Basic Recipe: Steel-Cut Oats

4 C water
½ t salt
1 C steel-cut oats

1. Bring water to a boil, add salt, and stir oats in slowly.
2. Return to a boil until mixture thickens slightly, about 5 minutes.
3. Reduce heat and simmer uncovered for 30–35 minutes, stirring occasionally, until soft but a little chewy.
4. Garnish with frozen berries, cinnamon, almonds, walnuts, maple syrup, or agave nectar.

Yield: 1 C dry yields about 2 C cooked

Slow cooker: Our favorite way to prepare whole oats is in a slow cooker, due to the length of time they take to cook. Combine ingredients (1 C groats to 4 C water, plus a pinch of salt) and add them to the slow cooker on low heat overnight. The next morning, the cereal will be ready—wake up to a nutritious, hot breakfast! Add nuts, berries, vanilla, a sweetener (or switch 1–2 C apple cider for cooking water), and any sweet spices. Stir well and serve.

QUINOA

 This was a staple food of ancient South American cultures. Although it is technically a seed, it has been used for centuries like a grain. The seed is covered with saponin, a bitter coating that protects it from birds and insects. Before cooking, rinse or toast in a dry pan to remove any residual saponin. For more information, see Noteworthy Nourisher on page 80.

Taste: Sweet, sour

Benefits: Contains a significant amount of protein and has a lower glycemic load than most other grains. Very high in iron, manganese, B vitamins, and vitamin E. A good source of magnesium, phosphorus, riboflavin, and copper, and rich in antioxidants. Extremely balancing food.

Varieties: White or heirloom red

Accompaniments: Balsamic vinegar, soy sauce, lemon, lemon grass, olive oil, carrots, cucumbers, green leafy vegetables, tomatoes, garlic, onion, dried fruit, coconut milk, curry powder, cumin, nuts, seeds.

Cooking methods/uses: Stovetop. Serve cold or hot, plain or seasoned, as a side dish, or in soups, stews, or salads.

Basic Recipe: Quinoa

1 C quinoa
2 C water or broth
Pinch of salt

1. Rinse quinoa thoroughly in a bowl of cold water and drain through a sieve (grains are small).
2. Optional: Heat unrinsed quinoa gently in a dry sauté pan over a medium burner for 2–3 minutes. This will release a nutty flavor.
3. Bring water to a boil.
4. Add quinoa and salt to boiling water.
5. Lower heat, cover, and simmer for 15–20 minutes, or until liquid is absorbed and the spiral tails of the grains are visible.
6. Let stand for 5 minutes.

   Yield: 1 C dry yields about 3 C cooked

RICE

 White rice is a grain already familiar to most American families. Rice is grown in many places in Asia and the Americas and comes in different lengths and textures. Brown rice is the least refined and contains the most fiber. White rice is more digestible for some, but it has a very high glycemic load. White Asian rice is only partially refined and, as a result, is more nutritious than American white rice, which is heavily processed.

Taste: Sweet

Benefits: Rich in B vitamins and manganese. Helpful for stomach issues, such as nausea and diarrhea. Unrefined brown rice has a rice bran coating, which is higher in fiber.

Varieties:

- *Brown rice:* The husk is only removed during the milling process. The entire bran layer remains, resulting in rice higher in fiber, B vitamins, and magnesium. Basmati brown rice is more fragrant than short-grained brown rice. Toasted brown rice has a nutty flavor and pleasant texture. To adjust to brown rice, some people like to mix half brown rice and half white rice in the beginning.
- *Carolina rice:* Long-grain white rice grown in South Carolina. High glycemic load.
- *Fragrant rice:* Slight floral or nutty flavor. Basmati rice comes from Pakistan, India, and

the Middle East. Jasmine rice comes from Thailand. High glycemic load.

- *Italian and Spanish rice:* Italian rice is called Arborio, and Spanish rice is called Valencia. These short-grain rices are starchy, with a creamy flavor but firm texture that is ideal for paella and risotto. These rices should not be rinsed or drained, because the creamy starch will be washed away in the rinsing/draining process. High glycemic load.
- *Sweet rice:* Asian short, round grain with a lot of starch. Used to make mochi, a Japanese rice dessert. High glycemic load.

Accompaniments: Soy sauce, lemon, lime, garlic, broths, dill, cilantro, parsley, mint, cayenne pepper, chiles, cinnamon, cloves, curry, saffron, dried cranberries, dried cherries, mandarin oranges, raisins, coconut milk, beans, slivered vegetables (bell peppers, carrots, zucchini, onion, etc.), nuts, seeds.

Cooking methods/uses: Stovetop, rice cooker. In patties, pilafs, soups, puddings, salads, sushi, fried rice; serve with beans or vegetables.

Basic Recipe: Brown Rice

1 C brown rice
2 C cold water
Pinch of salt

1. Soak rice for 2 hours to overnight, then rinse.
2. Optional: Toast rice in a dry sauté pan on low heat until golden brown.
3. Transfer to cooking pot and add water and salt.
4. Bring to a boil, cover, and reduce heat to low.
5. Cook for 40–50 minutes, until all water is evaporated.
6. Let stand for 5 minutes, then fluff.
7. Season to taste and serve.

Yield: 1 C dry yields 3 C cooked

Basic Recipe: Simple Fried Rice

1 T olive oil
1 scallion or onion, chopped
2 T finely chopped ginger
1/2 C finely diced carrot
4 C cooked brown rice
1–2 t water
1 or 2 eggs
1–2 T soy sauce

1. Heat oil in a skillet over medium heat, then sauté scallion and ginger for 2 minutes.
2. Add carrots and sauté for 3 minutes.
3. Add rice and water. Cook on low heat until rice is heated, about 10 minutes.
4. In a bowl, combine eggs with soy sauce. Whisk to combine.
5. Make a well in the middle of the grains and add egg mixture. Stir quickly to distribute the egg (it will cook fast).
6. Add more soy sauce if necessary, and serve hot.

WILD RICE

Not a true rice, wild rice is actually a tropical water grass that produces long, dark-colored grains. Wild rice is more expensive because it's a labor-intensive crop. However, when cooked, it makes a large amount because it expands.

Taste: Sweet, bitter

Benefits: A significant amount of B vitamins. Higher in protein than most other rice varieties.

Varieties: No significant varieties.

Accompaniments: Tarragon, parsley, lemon, scallions, mushrooms, dried cranberries, nuts, oils, pesto.

Cooking methods/uses: Stovetop, slow cooker. Combine with other types of rice, use in salads, or as a stuffing.

Basic Recipe: Wild Rice

1 C wild rice
4 C water
Pinch of salt

1. Soak wild rice for 3 hours to overnight, then rinse.
2. Bring water to a boil. Add rice and salt.
3. Lower heat, cover, and cook until rice is al dente, just beginning to burst open, 45–50 minutes.
4. Drain off excess water. Fluff wild rice with a fork.
5. Season with salt.

Yield: 1 C dry yields about 2 C cooked

Beans

Beans are a delicious, inexpensive source of protein and soluble fiber. In fact, while comparable in calories to meat, beans have far more fiber and water. Thus, they provide a lot of protein while helping you feel fuller than if you had a steak or a chicken leg. A recent study found that kids between twelve and nineteen years old who ate beans had a 30 percent reduced risk of being overweight; actually weighed a whopping 7 pounds less than children who did not eat beans at all; and had smaller waistlines by almost an inch! The results were similar for bean-eating adults: they averaged 6.5 pounds less and had a 22 percent less risk of being obese than their peers who ate no beans.[1]

Beans also contain lysine, a necessary amino acid not found in most grains, thus making the combination of beans and grains a complete protein. The type of protein provided by beans helps regulate sugar, water, and other aspects of metabolism, as well as promote proper growth and development of the body, including the brain.[2] Beans are rich in magnesium, potassium, iron, calcium, and several

B vitamins. Sprouted beans are a superb source of enzymes and vitamin C. Think of beans as a power food for balancing the SAD state.

This section provides information and instruction for cooking dry beans from scratch. Cooking your own beans is less expensive than buying canned beans. Home-cooked beans taste fresher, and no vitamins, minerals, and enzymes are destroyed by precooking, freezing, or canning. However, we feel that canned beans are also a fine choice for busy individuals or families. If you are buying canned beans, reading labels is important. Select beans that are organic, low in sodium, and free of MSG or other additives and preservatives. Rinse canned beans before using.

Some people avoid beans because they have difficulty digesting them. Your system may simply need time to adjust to this new food. You can avoid digestive issues by adding beans to your weekly diet slowly. Undercooked beans produce more gas, so follow our instructions for cooking tender, digestible beans. Chewing them slowly and thoroughly will also help. So will drinking plenty of water between meals. You might also try a helpful product called Beano, a natural, over-the-counter aid that helps prevent gassiness. Adding digestive spices or a few strips of kombu will aid digestion. Over time, your system will improve its ability to digest beans.

BEAN BASICS

When to eat: Autumn, spring, and summer. Seasoning beans in the winter makes them more warming and digestible. Some of the best bean spices include cumin, fennel, onion, salt, and pepper.

Varieties: Adzuki, anasazi, black, black-eyed peas, cannellini, cranberry, fava, great Northern, kidney, lentils (brown, red, and French), lima, mung, navy, pinto, split peas, red beans, and soybeans. See below for some of our favorite choices.

Purchasing: Dried beans last a very long time, but you want to avoid buying old beans. Before buying in bulk, find out if there is a good rate of turnover in the bean bins. Otherwise, you can buy them in 1-pound bags. Avoid beans that are split, chipped, or cracked; these are signs that the beans are older. Dry, brittle beans like this require longer cooking time.

Portions: One pound (2 cups) of dry beans makes 4 to 6 cups cooked, depending on the variety. An average adult serving is about ½ cup, and ¼ to ⅓ cup for children.

Storage: Dried beans should be stored in an airtight container in a cool cupboard. They also look pretty displayed in glass containers on a countertop, a good way to remind yourself to use them.

Sorting: Most beans need to be sorted before soaking or cooking. They are cleaned and sorted before packaging, but small stones, sand, or discolored beans may still find their way into your bag. Spread them out on a cookie sheet and discard any pieces that should not be there. After sorting, rinse thoroughly.

Soaking: There are many benefits to soaking your beans. It shortens their cooking time and removes some of the complex sugars that cause indigestion. Also, during soaking, old or immature beans will float to the top and can be discarded. Avoid adding baking soda to soaking beans; it destroys nutrients and affects their texture and flavor. If using a pressure cooker, it's desirable, but not necessary, to soak the beans first. Lentils, split peas, black-eyed peas, and mung beans do not need to be soaked at all.

Beans and Babies

Beans are difficult to digest because of the oligosaccharides—large sugar molecules that aren't broken down and absorbed by the lining of the small intestine as easily as other sugars are. The beneficial bacterial flora of the colon aid in the digestion of these molecules. These flora are not fully developed in very young babies. Thus, it is best to refrain from feeding infants any beans. Slowly introduce small quantities to older babies until they are eighteen months to two years old and their intestinal flora are more fully developed. In small amounts, beans can supply protein, vitamins, and minerals to older babies and toddlers. You can begin introducing the more digestible varieties, such as lentils and split peas, at around eight to ten months. Offering beans to children when they are very young will help them grow to like their unique taste and texture.

Overnight soak: Place beans in a large pot and cover with plenty of water—at least four times the volume of the beans. Beans can absorb three to four times their size in water and expand to two to three times their original size. This takes about 4 hours and can be left to happen overnight.

Quick soak. This is a time saving method to soften and increase the size of your beans. Place beans in a large pot and cover with plenty of water, at least four times their volume. Bring to a boil for one full minute, then turn off the heat, cover, and let stand for 1 hour.

After either method of soaking, pour off soaking water, cover beans with fresh water, and bring to a rolling boil for 5 to 10 minutes. This helps get rid of the sugars that cause indigestion. During this parboiling, scum forms on the surface. Skim it off with a spatula or wooden spoon and discard in the sink. If you forget this step, it's okay; the scum will also disappear on its own as the beans cook, but removing it will improve their digestibility.

Cooking methods/uses: Beans can be cooked on the stovetop, in a pressure cooker, or in a slow cooker. Usually soaked beans take about 90 minutes to cook. Actual cooking time depends on some additional factors: old beans, hard water, and high altitude all add to cooking time. Size does not indicate length of cooking. Large beans, such as lima beans, actually take less time to cook than some tiny beans do. Because small beans can take more time to prepare, we encourage cooking larger batches so that you can eat them for your next meal or freeze them for a later time.

Ideally, a cooked bean is soft and creamy inside, with pliable but intact skin outside. Do not salt the cooking water. Salt and acidic foods prevent beans from softening.

For easier digestion, faster cooking time, and added flavor and nutrients, soak a few strips of kombu in water, then add to the bottom of your cooking pot. Kombu is a sea vegetable that acts as a bean tenderizer. Use 2 inches of seaweed for 6 or more cups of cooked beans. (Kombu is added to Eden canned beans)

Stovetop: Follow sorting and soaking instructions above. After removing scum, add herbs, spices (except salt), and vegetables. Lower the heat and let simmer. Cooking time varies depending on the bean. (See cooking times for different bean varieties below.)

Pressure cooker: This device makes it possible to cook beans quickly. It turns out very tender beans.

Put soaked or unsoaked beans in a pressure cooker with herbs and spices, a teaspoon of oil, and water (at least five times the amount of beans). The oil prevents loose skins or foam from clogging the pressure gauge. Bring to high pressure for 25 minutes unless otherwise instructed. Lower the pressure by quickly releasing the steam. Taste the beans. If they are not quite ready, replace the lid and bring to pressure for 5 minutes more, or simmer until done. Check manufacturer's instructions: soaking beans reduces the amount of time beans need to cook.

Slow cooker: The extended heating of the slow cooker can work well for beans. Soaking beans reduces cooking time, but is not necessary. Boil beans on the stovetop for 10 minutes, pour off the water, then put them in a slow cooker and cover with three to four times their volume of heated water. Cook on high heat for about 5½ hours, or on low heat for about 7½ hours. Check for softness. If still firm, continue cooking for another half hour. Add herbs, spices, and salt during the last hour of cooking. You could use some of the bean liquid for soups or stews. *Note:* Do not cook red kidney beans in the slow cooker because it does not reach a high enough temperature and could produce the toxin phytohemagglutinin (see Kidney Beans for more information about this).

Baking: Beans baked in the oven exude a wonderful aroma in the kitchen. Begin with presoaked beans. Boil on the stovetop for 10 minutes to loosen the skins. Drain the beans and pour into a baking dish. Cover beans with boiling water, cover with a lid, and place in the oven at 350°F. Check after 15 minutes to make sure the beans are simmering, not boiling, and lower the temperature to 325°F if necessary. Baking time and amount of liquid will be about the same as for stovetop cooking time for each type of bean. Add salt at the end of cooking. Uncover and let them cool in their liquid.

Note: If using canned beans in a recipe, always drain and rinse before use unless otherwise indicated in directions.

Seasoning: To flavor your beans, it's important to add herbs and spices during cooking, rather than afterward, so that their flavors are absorbed into the beans. Cumin, fennel, and ginger help reduce the sugars that cause indigestion. See note on page 168 about adding kombu to increase digestibility.

- Onions and carrots add sweetness.
- Cinnamon or allspice helps bring out the flavors in black and red beans.
- Whole bay leaves, dried thyme, rosemary, and cilantro add flavor to white, fava, and lima beans.
- Sea salt, miso, or soy sauce, all salty flavors, can be added toward the end of cooking.

GUIDE TO BEANS

ADZUKI BEANS

See Noteworthy Nourisher on page 156 for more information.

Taste: Sweet, sour

Benefits: High in fiber, folic acid, and manganese; beneficial amounts of phosphorus, potassium, and copper. Detoxifying to the body. Helpful in relieving diarrhea and edema, and aiding in weight loss.

Accompaniments: Soy sauce, ginger, cumin, coriander, rice, kale, winter squash, carrots.

Cooking methods/uses: In soups, quesadillas, rice and beans, salads, fillings for burritos and corn tortillas.

- *Stovetop:* 1 C dried beans with 4 C water for 1½ hours
- *Pressure cooker:* 1 C dried beans with 3 C water for 45 minutes

  Yield: 1 C dried yields 4 C cooked

Basic Recipe: Adzuki Beans

4 C water
1 C dried adzuki beans
(no presoaking required)
1 t ginger
1 t cumin

1. Boil water.
2. Add beans, ginger, and cumin.
3. Simmer for about 1½ hours, until beans are tender.
4. Serve with rice or corn tortillas.

BLACK BEANS

Black beans are popular in Mexican, Caribbean, and South American cooking. They are small dark beans with a creamy color and texture. This is a favorite bean with most children, and is great mixed with rice or added to sprouted corn tortillas with tomatoes. Black beans do not need to be soaked.

Taste: Sweet

Benefits: High in fiber and folic acid; beneficial amounts of thiamin, magnesium, manganese, and phosphorus; contains molybdenum, which helps to remove sulfates from the body. Helpful in kidney and reproductive health.

Accompaniments: Balsamic vinegar, cumin, onion, garlic, wine, cayenne pepper, chili powder, cilantro, parsley, lemon, cumin, cinnamon, allspice.

Cooking methods/uses: In soups, quesadillas, rice and beans, salads, fillings for burritos and corn tortillas, or mashed into patties.

- *Stovetop:* 1 C dried beans to 4 C water for 1½–2 hours. Nutrient-dense cooking liquid can be used to make rice.
- *Pressure cooker:* 1 C dried beans to 3 C water for 35 minutes

  Yield: 1 C dried yields 2½–3 C cooked

Basic Recipe: Flavorful Mexi-Beans

2 T olive oil
½ onion, finely diced
1–2 cloves garlic, minced
1 (15-oz) can, rinsed and drained, or 2 C precooked black beans
⅓ C water or chicken broth
3 T balsamic vinegar
½ t coriander
1 t cumin
½ t ground ginger

1. In medium sauté pan, warm olive oil and sauté onion over medium heat for about 4 minutes, until very fragrant.
2. Add garlic and sauté for 1 minute.
3. Add beans, water, vinegar, coriander, cumin, and ginger.
4. Stir to combine and simmer for 8–10 minutes over low heat until heated through.
5. Serve with rice or in a corn tortilla with salsa and a little cheddar cheese.

BLACK-EYED PEAS

These are a popular bean in the southern United States. They don't have to be soaked because they have thin skins. When fresh, they can be eaten right in the pod. Black-eyed peas are delicate: be careful not to overcook.

Taste: Sweet

Benefits: High in selenium; cooling to the body.

Accompaniments: Garlic, thyme, marjoram, allspice, red pepper flakes, cayenne pepper, onions, carrots, red and yellow bell peppers, hearty leafy greens.

Cooking methods/uses: In soups or combined with vegetables and rice, cooked greens, or salad greens.

- *Stovetop:* 1 C dried black-eyed peas in 4 C water for 45–60 minutes
- *Pressure cooker:* 1 C dried black-eyed peas in 3 C water for 10 minutes

  Yield: 1 C dried yields about 4 C cooked

Basic Recipe: Black-Eyed Peas and Greens

2 T olive oil
1 medium onion, peeled and diced
1 clove garlic, minced
1 carrot, peeled and finely diced
1 stalk celery, diced
½ t thyme
2 C water or vegetable broth
1 bunch collard, escarole, or Swiss chard, rinsed and torn into pieces
1 (15-oz) can, rinsed and drained, or 2 C precooked black-eyed peas
1 bay leaf
1 T red wine vinegar
½ t red pepper flakes (optional)
Salt and pepper

1. In large sauté pan, warm the olive oil and sauté onion over medium heat for about 4 minutes, until very fragrant.
2. Add garlic and sauté for 1 minute.
3. Add carrot, celery, and thyme and cook for 3–4 minutes.
4. Add water, then stir in greens.
5. Bring to a boil.
6. Add beans and bay leaf, reduce heat, and simmer until the greens are tender, 10–15 minutes.
7. Add vinegar, red pepper flakes, and salt and pepper to taste.

FAVA BEANS

 These are also called horse beans. They are available fresh in the spring, and dried and canned year-round. They require a long soaking before cooking because they have thick skins.

Taste: Sweet

Benefits: Very high in folic acid; beneficial amounts of phosphorus and manganese. Has diuretic properties. The sprouts aid in good digestion.

Accompaniments: Bay leaf, cilantro, parsley, rosemary, thyme, garlic, shallots, lemon, hard cheeses, pesto.

Cooking methods/uses: In salads, in soups, tossed into pasta, puréed for dips.

- *Stovetop:* 1 C dried beans in 3 C of water for 30–45 minutes. Remove skins before cooking unless very young and fresh. Can also remove them after cooking and cooling.

  Yield: 1 C dried yields 2½ C cooked

Basic Recipe: Fava Bean Dip

3 T olive oil
1 T freshly squeezed lemon juice
1 clove garlic, minced
1 stalk celery, diced
¼ C finely chopped cilantro or parsley
1 (15-oz) can, rinsed and drained, or 1½ C precooked fava beans, puréed or mashed with a fork
¼ t chili powder
Salt and pepper

1. In a medium bowl, whisk together olive oil and lemon juice.
2. Add garlic, celery, and cilantro and stir to combine.
3. Add mashed or puréed beans and mix well.
4. Season with chili powder and salt and pepper to taste, and serve with raw vegetables.

GARBANZO BEANS

 These are also called chickpeas. Presoaking is very important to help these beans soften. They tend to foam a lot while cooking.

Taste: Sweet

Benefits: Very high in manganese and folic acid; beneficial amounts of copper and iron. Beneficial to heart health.

Accompaniments: Cardamom, chili, cumin, coriander, garlic, ginger, paprika, turmeric, red pepper flakes, parsley, cilantro, capers, lemon, tahini, eggs, pasta.

Cooking methods/uses: In salads, stews, soups; puréed as hummus; cooked with greens.

- *Stovetop:* 1 C dried beans to 8 C water for 1½–2 hours
- *Pressure cooker:* 1 C dried beans to 6 C water for 25 minutes—release pressure, check for tenderness, add salt, and continue to

cook for about 5 more minutes until tender. Important to add 1 T of oil to water before pressure cooking in order to reduce foam. If beans are presoaked: pressure cook for 15 minutes, then check for tenderness. The size and quality of the bean differs, so it's best to cook for less time and check for tenderness to avoid overcooking.

Yield: 1 C dried yields 4 C cooked

Basic Recipe: Hummus

¼ C sesame tahini
¼ C cold water
2 T freshly squeezed lemon juice
½ t ground cumin
1 clove garlic, crushed
1 (15-oz) can, rinsed and drained, or
2 C precooked garbanzo beans
1 T olive oil

1. In a blender or food processor, blend together tahini, cold water, lemon juice, cumin, and garlic. Set aside in a bowl.
2. Purée the garbanzo beans and process until smooth, adding a little cooking liquid or water if too thick.
3. Add the tahini mixture and process until mixed.
4. Put in serving bowl, add olive oil, and mix.
5. Serve with carrot and red pepper sticks or other veggies.

KIDNEY BEANS

Kidney beans are very versatile and are available dried or canned.

Taste: Sweet

Benefits: High in folic acid; beneficial amounts of phosphorus, manganese, and iron. Helpful for swelling and edema.

Accompaniments: Cumin, ginger, cayenne pepper, chile pepper, rice, quinoa, pine nuts, avocado, jicama, corn, tomatoes, salad greens.

Cooking methods/uses: In chili, soups, salads, purées.

- *Stovetop:* 1 C dried beans to 4 C water for 1–1½ hours
- *Pressure cooker:* 1 C dried beans to 3 C water for 30–40 minutes

Warning: Red kidney beans should not be cooked in a slow cooker because it does not reach high enough temperatures to kill the toxin phytohemagglutinin. Most slow cookers studied did not reach temperatures higher than 165°F—not high enough to kill the toxin. Cases of this type of food poisoning are more prevalent in the United Kingdom than in the United States. Eating red kidney beans is quite safe if they are prepared properly: Soak the beans for a minimum of 5 hours, then pour off the water. Add enough fresh water to reach 2 inches above tops of beans. Bring to a full boil and boil rapidly for at least 10 minutes, stirring occasionally. Reduce to a simmer and cook for 1½ hours, until tender. Skim off any foam. Undercooked beans may be more toxic than raw beans. It only takes four or five undercooked beans to cause toxicity. A pressure cooker reaches a high enough temperature to kill the toxin.[3]

Yield: 1 C dried yields 3–4 C cooked

SIMPLE FOOD FOR BUSY FAMILIES

Basic Recipe: Kidney Bean Salad

**1 (15-oz) can, rinsed and drained, or
2 C precooked kidney beans
5 C green-leaf lettuce, cleaned and torn into
pieces
1 C chopped avocado
1 C chopped jicama
2 T corn
1 C cooked brown rice (optional)**

1. Mix all ingredients gently together in a large salad bowl and dress with Italian Salad Dressing on page 194.

LENTILS

 Lentils are one of the planet's earliest cultivated crops. They are grown all over the world and are quite popular in India, where they are cooked into traditional dal, a thick, stewlike soup. Lentils come in many different varieties and colors. Green French lentils hold their shape well. Black beluga lentils are also quite delicious. Red and yellow lentils lose their shape in cooking and are thus the best for making thick, porridgelike dal. Both green and black lentils can be found in bulk bins. Soaking is not necessary.

Taste: Sweet, mildly astringent

Benefits: High in fiber, folic acid, and manganese; beneficial amounts of copper, phosphorus, and iron. Mild diuretic. Valuable for heart health and circulation. Energizing.

Varieties: Brown, green French, black, red, yellow.

Accompaniments: Rice, pasta, tomatoes, cilantro, mint, parsley, tarragon, coconut milk, garlic, ginger, turmeric, cumin, curry, red wine vinegar, balsamic vinegar, carrots, celery, tomatoes, onion.

Cooking methods/uses: In soups, in salads, as Indian dal, as veggie burgers, over rice with vegetables.

- *Stovetop:* 1 C dried beans to 4 C water for 20–30 minutes (red lentils) or 30–45 minutes (brown and green lentils)

Yield: 1 C dried yields 4½ C cooked

Basic Recipe: Our Favorite Lentils

**1½ C brown or green lentils, sorted and rinsed (do not presoak)
4 C water
1 onion, halved
2 cloves garlic
1 bay leaf
1 carrot, finely diced
1 stalk celery, finely diced
½ t cumin
1½ t salt, plus more to taste
Pepper
2 T olive oil
Red wine vinegar
Cilantro or parsley, chopped**

1. Put lentils in a soup pot. Cover with water and bring to a boil.
2. Skim off any foam.
3. Add onion, garlic, bay leaf, carrot, celery, cumin, salt, and pepper to taste.
4. Lower heat and simmer until lentils are tender but slightly firm (not mushy), about 25 minutes.
5. Strain lentils through a fine mesh strainer. (Optional: Catch drained liquid and reserve to use as rice cooking water or in another soup later.)
6. Remove and discard onion halves, garlic cloves, and bay leaf.
7. Transfer lentils to a serving bowl. Add salt and pepper to taste.
8. Stir in oil and a few drops of vinegar to bring out flavor.
9. Garnish with cilantro (or, for most children, leave it plain).
10. Serve with brown rice or your favorite whole grain.

LIMA BEANS

 These flat, green, kidney-shaped beans with a smooth, creamy texture are also called butter beans. Kids enjoy their fun shape and buttery texture. They are available fresh or frozen. Pressure cooking is not recommended because the skins could clog the drain.

Taste: Sweet

Benefits: Very high in molybdenum, a trace mineral that helps detoxify sulfates from the body. High in manganese and fiber; beneficial amounts of vitamin C, iron, phosphorus, potassium, and copper. Highly nutritious and balancing.

Accompaniments: Bay leaf, cilantro, paprika, rosemary, thyme, carrots, corn, green beans, onions, tomatoes, salad greens.

Cooking methods/uses: In succotash, salads, spreads.

- *Stovetop:* 1 C dried beans to 4 C water for 45 minutes. If not yet soft, cook for 15 minutes more.

  Yield: 1 C dried yields 2 1/2 C cooked

Basic Recipe: Simple Succotash

1–2 T olive oil
2 C frozen lima beans, cooked
3 C frozen corn
1 C frozen green beans
1/8 t paprika
Salt and pepper

1. Heat oil in a large sauté pan over medium heat.
2. Add limas, corn, and green beans and cook for 2–3 minutes, stirring to mix and thaw.
3. Cover and cook on low heat until all ingredients are hot but not mushy.
4. Add paprika and salt and pepper to taste and serve.

NAVY BEANS

 These are smaller, white, kidney-shaped beans.

Taste: Sweet

Benefits: High in fiber (19 grams per 1 C) and folic acid; beneficial amounts of thiamin, manganese, phosphorus, and iron.

Accompaniments: Basil, thyme, marjoram, tomatoes, garlic, onions, root vegetables, leafy green vegetables, applesauce.

Cooking methods/uses: In stews, casseroles, salads, purées; cooked with greens.

- *Stovetop:* 1 C dried beans to 4 C water for 1 1/2 hours
- *Pressure cooker:* 1 C dried beans to 3 C water for 25 minutes

  Yield: 1 C dried yields 3 C cooked

Basic Recipe: Mom's Mellow Navy Beans

1 C dried navy beans (do not presoak)
4 C water
Ham bone (optional)
1 medium onion, peeled and chopped
1/2 t red pepper flakes
Salt and pepper

1. Put beans, water, ham bone, and onion in a large soup pot and bring to a boil. Skim off any foam.
2. Reduce heat to low simmer and cook slowly for 2–3 hours.
3. Add spices to taste in last 15 minutes.
4. Discard ham bone and serve with applesauce and cornbread.

PINTO BEANS

Pinto beans are a relative of kidney beans, but slightly smaller. The pink, heirloom variety is slightly larger and more kidney-shaped. They are available canned or dried.

Taste: Sweet

Benefits: High in fiber and folic acid; beneficial amounts of protein, phosphorus, and manganese; contains molybdenum, which helps to remove sulfates from the body.

Accompaniments: Cilantro or parsley, scallion, chiles, Parmesan cheese, tomatoes, onion.

Cooking methods/uses: As refried beans; in chili.

- *Stovetop:* 1 C dried beans to 4 C water for 1 hour
- *Pressure cooker:* 1 C dried beans to 3 C water for 25 minutes

  Yield: 1 C dried yields 4 C cooked

Basic Recipe: Mashed Pinto Beans

2 T avocado oil or grapeseed oil
1 small onion, diced
2 or 3 cloves garlic, minced
2 (15-oz) cans, rinsed and drained, or
4 C precooked pinto beans
1/2 C water or broth
1/2 t salt
1 t cilantro, minced (optional)

If you are pressed for time, you can skip these steps and and prepare everything at room temperature: reduce the garlic to 1–2 small cloves, and use remaining ingredients in amounts that are indicated.

1. In a large sauté pan, heat oil and sauté onions over medium heat until brown, 6–7 minutes.
2. Add garlic and sauté for 1 minute.
3. Add 1 C of beans at a time and mash with a potato masher or back of a fork. Add a few tablespoons of water after each batch of mashed beans. This process should take 10–15 minutes.
4. The beans should be a little soupy because they thicken as they sit.
5. Season with salt and cilantro.
6. Serve with chips and any desired accompaniments, or as a filling in a Mexican-style wrap.

Mixed Veggie Combo Sandwich (see page 188) and Navy Bean and Vegetable Turkey Chili (see page 192)

Mix and Match: Making the Meals

Flexible Family Cooking

After years of making meals for our families, we have found that the best tools for quick, healthy, everyday cooking are *organization* and *flexibility*. Although a faultless, delicious recipe is a beautiful thing, nothing beats a well-stocked pantry and the confidence to "mix and match" ingredients in tasty ways. In this section, we will help you build that confidence by sharing tools and simple instructions for creating endless combinations of easy meals from the dependable staples in your pantry. This way of cooking is far faster and more flexible than having to match the right ingredients to the right recipe every time you want to feed your family.

Our basic rule of thumb is: "the pantry before the recipe." If you are disciplined about keeping staples of grains, beans, and favorite condiments in your pantry or fridge, all you will need on your weekly shopping trip is fresh produce, herbs, meats, and other special foods that appeal to you that week. As you practice with the tools and suggestions in this chapter, you will become more adept at whipping up meals from a combination of your stocked basics and some special, seasonal choices. The focus of your cooking will change from recipes to groups of foods that go well together and ingredients that can be used interchangeably.

To support you in becoming more skilled at this kind of flexible cooking, we have designed a collection of "formulas" for basic dishes such as pastas, soups, stews, and salads. Each formula shows you the basic ingredients (grain, vegetable, water, fat, protein, etc.) in each dish and how much of each you will need. Then you can choose which of your favorite staples and fresh foods to combine according to the formula.

To help you get creative about combining ingredients, we follow each formula with a Mix and Match chart. These charts will educate and inspire you about the many ways you can build your dishes. With a quick glance at your pantry and a short perusal of a Mix and Match chart, inspiration is sure to strike! We've built a lot of freedom into these charts—there's no right or wrong way to cook from them. We want you to become confident in cooking to your own taste and in a style that works for you.

Finally, the Mix and Match charts are followed by lists of sample dishes that follow the formulas. We call these Great Combos rather than recipes. This is to help you wean off the idea that you have to use a *specific* ingredient in a *specific* amount to get the meal "right." In fact, you can make all kinds of ingredient substitutions, vary the amounts, add

Fresh Tofu

- Processed soybean curd, first created in China more than 2,000 years ago
- Was created to improve the digestibility of the highly valued soybean
- Is an inexpensive, low-calorie source of vegetarian protein; look for sprouted
- Is best to buy certified organic tofu to ensure the soybeans have not been genetically engineered
- Research indicates that the best soy products for health are those that have been fermented in the traditional way: fermented tofu, miso, soy sauce, tempeh, etc.
- Contains easily digestible protein; vitamins A, B, D, and E; calcium; iron; phosphorus; potassium; and sodium
- Naturally bland; takes the flavor of what it is marinated and cooked in
- Can be baked, broiled, sautéed, stir-fried, added to soups, puréed into pudding, or mashed into tofu salad (similar consistency to egg salad)
- Eat in small quantities due to its cooling qualities
- Cover with water and seal in an airtight container or jar. Change water every few days for optimal freshness

foods in, and leave others out, and your end result will probably taste just as good as the base idea—better, in fact, because it will be based on *your family's* palate and *your personal* intuition.

In some sections you will not find a Mix and Match chart. For the simplest meals, we provide some basic directions, helpful tips, and our favorite Great Combos.

Getting the Most from Mixing and Matching

The Mix and Match charts display columns listing food items in general amounts or proportions. If you choose one item (or sometimes more than one) from each column and combine it as directed, you'll be custom designing your own meals.

These charts have also been set up so that the dishes themselves can be mixed and matched to be breakfasts, lunches, or dinners. For example, the hot cereal grains do make terrific breakfasts, but they can also be used as dinner side dishes or even as main meals if you fill them out with proteins and lots of veggies. Train yourself to become more and more flexible, even adventurous, with both your ingredients and your meal ideas. What kid doesn't like having breakfast for dinner? How about a Naked Quiche? A breakfast smoothie for a 3 P.M. snack? Leftover dinner stew in a lunch box thermos? Think outside the box. It's very freeing and can be a lot of fun. With a small amount of experimentation, you will find your confidence and skills increasing very quickly.

If anyone in your family has any food allergies, sensitivities, or limitations, these Mix and Match charts provide plenty of substitution options. For example, wherever it says milk or flour, if you can't use cow's milk or wheat flour, select an ingredient from that column that is healthier for your family. Likewise, the charts provide plenty of choices for vegetarians, vegans, or those following other special diets.

To work effectively with the Mix and Match charts, you will need a whole-food pantry stocked with high-quality ingredients and some basic cooking equipment (see chapter 9 for tips on stocking an efficient, healthy kitchen). As you design your meals, keep the Whole Life Nutrition guidelines we discussed in mind: quality, balance, seasonality, quantity, and routine. But please don't let *any* of the guidelines become a limitation. Even if you are not using the highest quality ingredients in season, if you are cooking something fresh rather than grabbing fast food or defrosting a pizza, that is a great improvement!

Enough explanation, let's play!

Breakfast

Breakfast is a vital component of Whole Life Nutrition, especially for school-age children. Yet statistically we know that many children skip breakfast on a regular basis. We encourage you to find breakfast options that your children will eat in the mornings, and to wake them early enough to eat them. It may take a period of trial and error to find the options that are quick and palatable enough to become regular choices for your family. Below are four breakfast options—cold cereal, hot cereal (savory and sweet), smoothies, and eggs—with which our families and our clients' families have had good success.

COLD CEREAL

Cold cereal is one of the quickest and easiest options for breakfast. There are literally hundreds of varieties to choose from in the supermarket, but most have too much sugar, added chemicals, and artificial flavors and colors. To make cold cereal a high-quality breakfast, choose a low-sugar variety with

Pancakes and Waffles

Kids love pancakes, waffles, and French toast, but they take time to prepare and can be too sweet or too processed. Healthier pancake and waffle recipes are easy to find online, and many quick whole grain mixes are available in supermarkets. You can add a fiber boost with wheat germ, ground flax, or fruit such as apples, pears, or blueberries. There are also some good frozen options, especially for waffles. See appendix A for the brands we like best.

A time-saving option is to make a double batch of these breakfast goodies. Feed one batch to your family, then freeze the others individually for later. Simply cool the waffles or pancakes by laying them out three in a row on a long piece of wax paper. When cool, fold the end of the wax paper over the first three pancakes, and then add another layer of three. Repeat until you have a stack of pancakes three long and three high. Pop them into a freezer bag and put the bag directly into the freezer (refrigerating them first makes them too chewy). Defrost and warm in a toaster on another morning when you want a quick breakfast.

all-natural, whole grain ingredients. We like Bear Naked High Protein Granola, Sam's Flakes, Barbara's Shredded Spoonfuls, and Ezekiel Sprouted Grain Cereals. See appendix A for more options.

Because cold cereals are store bought and not made from scratch, you don't need a Mix and Match chart for this one. But follow our tips for improving the quality of your typical cold cereal breakfast:

- Be a label detective. Avoid brands with added sugars or artificial ingredients. Look for 4–5 grams or less of sugar, a minimum of 4 grams of fiber, and any quantity of protein.
- Add additional fiber with berries, flaxseed, or wheat germ.
- Add additional fat and protein with a sprinkling of chopped nuts or seeds.
- Try occasionally using options other than cow's milk, such as unsweetened almond, rice, or soymilk. Plain or lightly sweetened yogurt is another tasty option.
- Beef up the protein in any milk or yogurt by whisking in a scoop of whey protein before adding cereal.
- Add a separate protein, such as a boiled egg, on the side.

MIX AND MATCH: **SAVORY HOT CEREAL** *Serves 6-8*

GRAINS (1 C grains & 2 C water) *choose one*	COOKING TIME	COOKING METHOD
amaranth (1 C grains to 3 C water)	30 min.	Do not rinse. Combine with veggies and water. Bring to a boil and simmer until done. Top with condiments.
millet (1 C grains to 3 C water)	35–40 min.	Rinse first. Combine with veggies and water. Bring to a boil and simmer until done. Top with condiments.
quinoa, whole	15–20 min.	Rinse first. Combine with veggies and water. Bring to a boil and simmer until done. Top with condiments.
quinoa, instant flakes	3 min.	Precook veggies. Boil water, stir in dry flakes, and cook for 3 minutes. Add vegetables. Top with condiments.
rice, medium grain brown	40 min.	Soak overnight. Rinse. Combine rice, veggies, and water in rice cooker and let cook, or bring to a boil in saucepan and simmer until done. Top with condiments.
rice, brown basmati	45 min.	Soak overnight. Rinse. Combine rice, veggies, and water in rice cooker and let cook, or bring to a boil in saucepan and simmer until done. Top with condiments.

HOT CEREAL

Hot cereal is one of the most versatile, satisfying, and hearty breakfasts you can make for your family. It can be made from oats, rice, quinoa, or other grains. These whole grain varieties take some time to cook, but once you have a batch prepared, you can use it in other meals, or freeze it for "instant" cereal later on.

If you like hot cereals, it is good to know about time-saving tools. Our favorite tool is a rice cooker. We both use one all the time. It works best for the longer-cooking grains, such as rice and millet. Also, a slow cooker is a terrific option for cooking oats. In the evening, put 1 cup of steel-cut oats, 4 cups of water (or apple cider), 1 teaspoon of cinnamon, and some whole raw almonds in the pot, set it on low, let it cook for 8 hours or overnight, and wake the next morning to the wonderful aroma of spiced cereal. Give it a good stir, add any sweeteners, fats, or fruits you'd like, and serve it up hot.

Nowadays, there are more and more "instant" versions of whole grain cereals on the market, which can be used in a pinch. You can find plain cream of wheat, cream of brown rice, even cream of buckwheat. Our favorite is Ancient Harvest Quinoa Flakes—it takes all of 90 seconds to cook and tastes delicious, with 2.5 grams of fiber and 4 grams of protein in one serving. We recommend that you avoid buying presweetened instant cereals—they contain too much sugar and too many additives. Plain instant cereal is so easy to flavor and sweeten

CHOPPED VEGGIES (1–2 C) choose any	SPICES AND CONDIMENTS (to taste) choose any	FAT (1t–1T) choose any	PROTEIN (to taste) choose any
bok choy (add in last 10 min. of cooking) broccoli (add in last 10 min. of cooking) carrots collards daikon kale onion pumpkin, canned (1/4–1/2 C) (add in last 10 min. of cooking) sea vegetable (kombu, wakame, 2 in.) sweet potato winter squash	Bragg Liquid Aminos miso paste pepper salt soy sauce (low-sodium tamari or shoyu)	butter (1 t) margarine, nonhydro- genated (1 t) flaxseed oil (1 T) (add after cooking) ground flaxseed (1 T) olive oil (1 t–1 T)	nuts seeds tofu (cubed, add in last 10 min. of cooking)

MIX AND MATCH: **SWEET HOT CEREAL** *Serves 6-8*

GRAINS (1 C grains & 2 C water) *choose one*	COOKING TIME	COOKING METHOD
amaranth	30 min.	Do not rinse. Bring to a boil and simmer until done.
millet	35-40 min.	Rinse first. Bring to a boil and simmer until done.
oats, steel cut	30 min. on stovetop or 7 hours to overnight in slow cooker	Combine with water in slow cooker. Cook on low until done.
oats, rolled	6-10 min.	Do not rinse. Bring to a boil and simmer until done.
oats, instant	3 min. to boil water	Boil water, remove from heat, and stir in dry flakes.
quinoa, whole	15-20 min.	Rinse first. Bring to a boil and simmer until done.
quinoa, instant flakes	3 min. to boil water	Boil water, stir in dry flakes, and cook for 3 min.
rice, sweet brown	40 min.	Soak overnight. Rinse. Combine with water in rice cooker and let cook.

yourself that it's not worth it to "cave in" to a lower quality breakfast.

If you or your children are caught in the SAD blood sugar cycle, we recommend avoiding all instant cereals, as they tend to have higher glycemic loads. Instead, serve small portions of intact (whole) grains and add extra protein and fiber. We have found that kids who have "bouncy" blood sugar generally don't do as well on oats and rice; they have better "staying power" and fewer blood sugar crashes with quinoa or kasha (buckwheat).

USING THE HOT CEREAL MIX AND MATCH CHARTS

Choose a grain and read across the first three columns from left to right for cooking instructions. Add any ingredients you wish from the last four columns in any combination (note separate options for sweet and savory versions). Add the heartier vegetables, fruits, and nuts right at the start of the cooking time. If you want your grains to have a soupier or porridgelike texture, add more hot water to individual servings.

Hot Cereal Formula

1 C grain
2 C water
1/3-1 C fruit (sweet) or 1-2 C veggies (savory)
1/2-1 t spices
1 T fat
Protein, to taste
A healthy sweetener, to taste (optional in the Sweet Hot Cereal)

FRUITS	SPICES	OPTIONAL FAT	PROTEIN
choose any; add apples, pears, and dried fruit at the beginning, all others at very end	(1/2–1 t) *choose any, add at the beginning of cooking*	(1 T) *choose any*	*choose any, add at the end*
apple (1, seeded and chopped into bite-size pieces) berries (1/2–1 C) banana (1/2, peeled and sliced) mangoes (1/2 C, peeled, pitted, and cut into bite-size pieces) peaches (1/2–1 C, pitted and cut into bite-size pieces) pears (3/4 C, cored and cut into bite-size pieces) any dried fruit (1/3 C chopped)	allspice cardamom cinnamon clove ginger mint nutmeg	coconut milk (add at end) flaxseed oil (add at end) ground flax-seed (add at end) butter margarine, non-hydrogenated	plain protein powder, whey, soy, hemp (1 scoop) nuts and seeds: pumpkin seeds, sliced almonds, ground brazil nuts (1/4 C, add anytime) nut butters: tahini, cashew, almond, organic peanut (1 T) plain yogurt (1/3 C) unsweetened milk: almond, cow, rice, soy (1/2–1 C)

Method One: Fresh Morning Grains

1. Select a breakfast grain.
2. Cook grain according to the Mix and Match chart above.
3. Add fruits, veggies, spices, fats, and proteins according to the Mix and Match chart above. (Start with smaller amounts and increase to your taste.)
4. Enjoy fresh and warm.
5. Freeze leftovers in individual serving sizes for later.

Method Two: Leftover Plain Grains Dressed for Breakfast

Note: The following instructions make one serving. When adding the spices, fruits, veggies, etc. to individual portions, remember to scale down amounts proportionately.

1. Take any leftover plain grains out of the fridge.
2. Following the Savory and Sweet Hot Cereal Mix and Match charts on page 180 and above, select vegetables or fruits to add to your grains.
3. Boil 1/2–3/4 C water with fruits or vegetables until they're tender.
4. Turn heat down to medium-low and stir in 3/4 C of leftover grain.
5. Add additional ingredients from the last three columns of the chart to taste, and simmer for a few minutes until everything is warm.

TRY THIS GREAT COMBO

Morning Miso Rice (Savory): brown rice, chopped broccoli, shredded carrots, sweet onion, miso paste, sesame seeds

MIX AND MATCH: **SMOOTHIE** *Serves 3-4*

MILK (2 C) *choose one*	FRUIT/VEGGIES (1–1½ C, fresh or frozen), *choose any*	PROTEIN *choose any*
almond, unsweetened cow rice, unsweetened soy soy/rice blend, unsweetened (more digestible than straight soymilk)	berries mango melon, cubed orange peaches pumpkin, canned (1 C; best with no fruits except banana) sweet potato, baked, cooled, and skin removed (1 C; best with no fruits except 1 orange)	nuts: sliced almonds, walnuts, hazelnuts, brazil nuts (¼ C) nut butters: tahini, almond, cashew, etc. (2 T) plain Greek or European yogurt (1 C; omit 1 C milk) protein powder: plain whey, rice, hemp, etc. (1 scoop or to taste)

FAT *choose one*	SWEETENER *choose one*	GROUND SPICES/HERBS to taste *choose any*	EXTRAS *choose any*
avocado (¼ C) coconut milk (freeze in ice cube tray and use 1 cube) flaxseed oil or ground flaxseed (1–2 T)	agave nectar (1 T) banana (½; fresh or frozen, peel before slicing) frozen apple juice concentrate (1–2 T) fruit juice: orange, apple, pineapple, grape etc. (¼ C) ginger, crystallized (1 t) stevia, powdered (¼ t) or liquid (3 drops)	allspice cardamom cinnamon ground or grated fresh ginger mint nutmeg	bee pollen (1 t) coconut, raw or shredded (1 T) ice (2–5 cubes) nutritional yeast (1–2 t) oat bran (1–2 T) raw oats (1–2 T) wheat germ (1–2 T)

Freezing Bananas

Are your bananas over-ripening? Peel, halve, and wrap them in wax paper. Put them in a plastic freezer bag and store them for smoothies later!

SIMPLE FOOD FOR BUSY FAMILIES

SMOOTHIES

Smoothies make a great breakfast-on-the-go or mini-meal. Whipped up in a flash, they are a healthy "fast food," perfect during warm weather and when the kids are running out the door for school. They also work well for children who have a light morning appetite. A breakfast smoothie feels more like drinking than eating and can be more palatable to kids than a big steaming plate of eggs and vegetables. Let your children experiment and develop their own favorite combinations.

USING THE SMOOTHIE MIX AND MATCH CHART

Choose one ingredient from each of the first three columns. If you wish, choose one or more ingredient from the last four columns. Combine all selected ingredients as directed above.

Smoothie Formula

2 C any milk
1–1½ C fruit, canned or cooked pumpkin, or sweet potato
Protein, varying amounts (see Mix and Match chart)
Optional: fat, sweetener, spices, extras

1. Put all ingredients into a good (sturdy) blender and blend until smooth.
2. Think about combinations that you like when mixing and matching, such as nut butter and chocolate, or pumpkin and apple pie spices, or tropical fruits and coconut.
3. If you use presweetened milk or tropical fruits, omit extra sweeteners. Add sweeteners last, in any case, and taste smoothie before adding them, as you may find them unnecessary.
4. Don't ignore the extras or fats—smoothies are a great place to add extra fiber and/or omega-3s.

Freezing Advice

Here's some good, old-fashioned freezing advice, handed down from Jeannette's grandmother: Cool any hot liquids you wish to freeze, such as soup, sauce, or cereal grains, almost to room temperature. Then transfer to containers and put them in the refrigerator overnight. In the morning, wipe away any condensation from the containers and transfer to the freezer for storage. This will avoid freezer burn and preserve the best tastes in your homemade frozen foods.

Hot cereals freeze beautifully. Make a big batch, serve in the morning, separate what's left into individual portions in sandwich-size zip-closure bags, and store it all in the freezer. Voilà: instant cereal your kids can heat and eat anytime!

TRY THESE GREAT COMBOS

Classic Berry Smoothie: rice milk, plain yogurt, fresh or frozen strawberries, whey protein powder, ground flaxseed, frozen banana, agave nectar (optional)

Pumpkin Pie Smoothie: almond milk, canned pumpkin, rice protein powder, raw oats, fresh banana, pumpkin pie spices (cinnamon, allspice, nutmeg, etc.), agave nectar (optional)

EGGS

We love eggs as a balanced source of protein. Our favorite eggs are from cage-free organic hens that have been fed with an omega-3-rich diet. The added omegas help balance the naturally occurring cholesterols in eggs. There are many ways to prepare your eggs. Our favorite quick and easy methods are: boiled, as a veggie scramble, or in a crust-free (naked) quiche.

BOILED EGGS

Serve your eggs poached, soft-boiled, or hard-boiled. Kids love soft-boiled eggs over toast. A Bessinger family favorite is "egg in a cup," made by cutting up a piece of whole wheat toast, putting it in a coffee cup, and mixing it gently with a soft-boiled egg. Hard-boiled eggs are great to have on hand for a fast protein.

To boil your eggs, put them in a pan and cover with cold water. Set the burner on high and cook for the following amounts of time:

To poach: 3–5 minutes
To soft-boil: 7 minutes
To hard-boil: 15 minutes

VEGGIE SCRAMBLE

This is a great way to increase your children's vegetable servings for the day. Heat 1 to 2 teaspoons of olive oil, avocado oil, butter, or nonhydrogenated margarine in a medium sauté pan, and add 1 to 2 cups of whatever chopped vegetables you have in the fridge. Sauté them until they are softened (for harder veggies such as broccoli or peppers, you may want to put the lid on and steam them for a minute or two to speed the cooking process). Crack and whip 3 or 4 eggs, and pour over the veggies. As the eggs begin to harden, turn the mixture all over until the veggies are coated and the eggs are cooked through. The dish serves 2 to 4 kids, depending on their ages. This is so easy and intuitive that you don't need a Mix and Match chart, but here are some Great Combos to try:

- Tomatoes with broccoli, asparagus, or spinach
- Combined greens such as baby spinach, chard, or collards cut into ribbons
- Mushrooms, onions, and red or yellow bell peppers

NAKED QUICHE

Although a "quiche" might conjure up scary images of gourmet kitchens, it's actually a very easy dish to make. The crust is, of course, delicious and simple to buy premade or frozen. Unfortunately, most premade crusts are loaded with hydrogenated oils and other undesirable ingredients. To reduce the fat content of quiche, here's a way to prepare it "naked" (without a crust).

USING THE NAKED QUICHE GREAT COMBOS CHART

Instead of a Mix and Match chart, we're giving you our four favorite Naked Quiche combinations. Each column gives you one quiche: read from the top down. Once you get comfortable with these combos, branch out and try your own!

GREAT COMBOS: **NAKED QUICHE** *Serves 6-8*

VEGETARIAN	SALMON	GREEK	MEXICAN
5 eggs 1/3 C cow's milk 1/3 C rice milk (unsweetened) 3/4 C asparagus, chopped 1/2 C tomato, chopped 1/2 C cheddar cheese, grated 1/2 t pepper sprinkle of paprika on top	5 eggs 2/3 C rice milk (unsweetened) 1 C onion, chopped, or 1/2 C shallot or leek, chopped (white and light green parts) 1/2 C fresh mushrooms, chopped (porto- bellos are great) 4-8 oz smoked salmon (lox-style or canned) dill (1 t dried or 2 T fresh) mustard (1 t dry or 1 T Dijon)	5 eggs 2/3 C rice milk (unsweetened) 1 1/2 C baby spinach or frozen spinach 1/2 C sun-dried tomatoes 1/4-1/2 C black olives, chopped 1/4 C feta cheese	5 eggs 2/3 C soymilk (unsweetened) 1 C beans (kidney, black, or pinto are good) 1/4 C salsa 1/2 C frozen corn 1/4 C Jack cheese, shredded 1/4 C fresh cilantro or 1 t dried

Quiche Formula

5 eggs

1/3-2/3 C unsweetened milk (cow's, soy, rice, etc.)

Herbs and spices

1 C chopped veggies

1/4-1/2 C meat, soy sausage, or cheese (optional)

1. Preheat oven to 375°F.
2. Oil or butter a 9" pie pan.
3. Chop veggies and meats into bite-size pieces.
4. Whisk eggs, milk, and spices together.
5. Put veggies and meat into the bottom of the pan and spread out evenly.
6. Pour egg mixture over veggies, taking care to leave about 1/2" of space under the lip of the pan.
7. Sprinkle additional spices over the top, if desired.
8. Cook for 30-50 minutes, or until set and lightly browned on the top. If, at 30 minutes, the top is browning too quickly, cover lightly with foil.

MIX AND MATCH: **SANDWICH** *Makes 1 sandwich*

WRAPPER *choose one*	VEGGIE FILLING (½ C) *choose one category*	PROTEIN FILLING (2–3 oz) *choose any*	CONDIMENTS (to taste) *choose any*
2 slices of bread (whole grain or sprouted) 1 wrap (whole grain or sprouted) 1 corn tortilla (whole grain or sprouted corn) 2 leaves of lettuce (big, hearty leaves such as romaine or Boston) 1 pita pocket (whole grain or sprouted)	**Mixed Veggie Combo:** red peppers, mushrooms, onions, zucchini, eggplant (raw, roasted, or baked) **Salad Veggie Combo:** lettuce, sprouts, tomatoes, cucumbers, peppers, shredded carrots **Pickled Veggie Combo:** pickles, cherry peppers, olives, banana pepper rings **Create Your Own Single Veggies or Chopped Fruit**	**Meat:** steak, pork loin, roasted turkey, chicken, or protein sandwich filling (see below) **Vegetarian:** cheese (Monterey Jack, cheddar, muenster, Swiss, havarti, goat, boursin, fresh mozzarella, etc.) egg (scrambled, hard-boiled, fried) **Vegan:** beans (any variety, mashed or patties) hummus (plain or flavored) nut butters (peanut, almond, cashew, etc.) tofu sandwich filling (see below) veggie patties, store bought	avocado bean dip, fat free cranberry sauce (no added sugar) fruit spread (no added sugar) horseradish, prepared mayonnaise mustard pesto red hot pepper salad dressing (any variety) salsa Veganaise or other vegan mayonnaise

MIX AND MATCH: **PROTEIN SANDWICH FILLING** *Yields 1 sandwich*

PROTEIN (2–3 oz) *choose one*	SWEETNESS/CRUNCH (1–2 T, or to taste) *choose any*	BINDER (1–2 T, or to taste) *choose one*
egg, hard-boiled and sliced chicken, shredded or cubed salmon, flaked (freshly cooked or from a can) tofu, cubed tuna, flaked (freshly cooked or from a can)	almonds or walnuts, sliced or crushed apples, sliced or cubed apricots, dried celery, chopped cranberries, dried cucumber, sliced or cubed raisins sprouts	cranberry sauce horseradish mayonnaise mustard oil and vinegar salad dressing soy mayonnaise

Lunch

Here we feature three American classics: sandwiches, soups, and salads. If you've done a good job stocking your pantry, sandwiches and salads are the ultimate fast foods: endless varieties, made up in a flash, and very portable for lunch boxes. Our soups are made from scratch with many precooked ingredients, so they take a minimum of time to prepare and freeze like a dream for later.

SANDWICHES

When Jeannette was in grammar school, she ate exactly the same sandwich every day for nearly five years: peanut butter and bread. Although there's nothing wrong with this sandwich (the bread was whole wheat, even in the '70s!), the fact that she ate it every day is an example of how many of us get caught in the rut of the "same old thing" when trying to come up with lunch box meals. The Mix and Match sandwich chart is designed to inspire you to invent more creative and tasty combinations.

USING THE SANDWICH MIX AND MATCH CHART

Choose one ingredient from each of the first two columns. If you would like to include protein, choose one ingredient from *either* the protein filling column *or* a serving of protein sandwich filling, which you can make yourself using the smaller Mix and Match chart below it. Choose any combination of condiments from the last column. Follow Sandwich Formula to assemble.

Sandwich Formula

½ C veggie filling
Condiments to taste
1 wrapper
2–3 oz protein or protein sandwich filling

1. Chop veggies into bite-size portions.
2. Spread condiments onto sandwich wrapper.
3. Combine protein and vegetables in wrapper, and enjoy!

TRY THESE GREAT COMBOS

Mexican: corn tortilla, salsa, mashed beans, avocado, shredded lettuce, tomatoes

Any-Day Thanksgiving: sprouted grain bread, cranberry sauce, roasted turkey, spinach or lettuce leaves

Grilled Veggies: whole grain wrap, hummus, grilled veggies, romaine lettuce leaves

Salmon Salad: whole grain pita pocket, Trader Joe's wild boneless, skinless salmon, ginger salad dressing, diced cucumber, onion, celery, tomato

SOUP

Most canned soups contain far too much salt, fat, and unwanted additives. Plus, they are fairly flavorless. You can get the convenience of canned soup with fresher, heartier ingredients if you make a big pot of soup at home. If you use precooked protein and grains, you can assemble your soup in no time and freeze individual portions of the leftover soup for future use. Our Mix and Match soups are *very* easy to make. Use the chart and invent one of your own!

MIX AND MATCH: **SOUP** *Serves 6–8*

LIQUIDS (8 C) *choose one*	VEGGIES (3–4 C, chopped or diced) *choose any combination*		PRECOOKED GRAINS/PASTA (1–2 C) *choose one, add in last 10 minutes of cooking*
low-sodium beef broth low-sodium chicken broth coconut milk (1/2–3/4 C only) low-sodium vegetable broth water	broccoli cabbage carrots cauliflower celery corn fennel green beans kale leeks mirepoix (2:1:1 ratio of onions, celery, and carrots) onions	parsnips turnips red or green bell peppers snow or sugar snap peas spinach summer squash sweet potatoes tomatoes, canned, whole, or crushed with basil winter squash zucchini	barley bulgur wheat pasta, uncooked (1/2 C small pasta: alphabets, elbows, small shells, orzo; or up to 1 C medium pasta: ziti, penne, fusilli, bowties, etc.) (will cook in soup) quinoa, rinsed, uncooked (1/2 C; add in last 15 minutes, as it will cook in soup) rice, cooked (any variety)

USING THE SOUP MIX AND MATCH CHART

At the top of each column, you will see amounts listed. Choose any combination of the ingredients in each column to get the *total amount* for each category. For instance, you might want to make a root soup by combining a mix of leeks, parsnips, carrots, and sweet potatoes, totaling 3 cups. Or you could make a carrot soup using 3 cups of just carrots. Combine ingredients from each column into a soup according to the directions.

Soup Formula

1–2 T fat (less if using whole fat animal broth)
3 C chopped vegetables
8 C broth or soup stock (2 [32-oz] cartons)
2–3 T combined herbs and spices
Extra flavorings

1 1/2 C chopped precooked protein
1 1/2 C cooked grains or whole grain pasta
Salt and pepper (optional)

1. Heat fat in a soup pot over medium heat, then sauté any onions or garlic until they are fragrant, 2–3 minutes. (This step is optional, but will heighten the flavors of your soup.)
2. Combine vegetables, broth, herbs, and extra flavorings in a soup pot and heat on medium-high until soup reaches a low boil.
3. Reduce heat to medium-low and simmer, covered, until hardest vegetables are tender, 10–30 minutes.
4. Add protein and grains for last 10 minutes only, so they don't overcook.
5. Sample the soup at the end of the cooking time, and add salt or pepper to taste if it needs a boost.

PRECOOKED PROTEIN (1½ C) choose one—if beans, use precooked or canned and rinsed, add in last 10 minutes of cooking	FAT (1-2 T) choose one	SOUP SPICES (2-3 T) choose any—see appendix C for ideas	EXTRA FLAVORINGS (to taste) choose any
beef, cubed, or ground and browned black beans black-eyed peas chicken, precooked and cubed or shredded garbanzo beans kidney beans lamb, precooked and cubed lentils navy beans Northern beans pinto beans refried beans seafood, raw, (any variety; will cook in soup in 10-20 minutes) split peas turkey, precooked and cubed, shredded, or ground white beans	full-fat yogurt ghee olive oil (or any others) sour cream	basil bay leaf cardamom cayenne pepper (very spicy, start with ½-1 t) chili powder (very spicy, start with ½-1 t) cilantro coriander cumin curry powder dill dry mustard fennel seeds or spice rub marjoram mustard seeds or powder paprika parsley pepper rosemary saffron sage sea salt tarragon thyme	balsamic or other flavored vinegar beer Better Than Bouillon chili oil Dijon mustard garlic ginger hot pepper sauce kombu (sea vegetable) miso shallots sherry (dry) soy sauce wine

TRY THESE GREAT COMBOS

Lentil Soup: vegetable broth, hearty greens (kale or collards work nicely), onion, celery, carrots, diced tomatoes, cooked brown or wild rice (optional), brown lentils, olive oil, garlic, parsley, thyme, bay leaves, Dijon mustard, balsamic vinegar, salt and pepper

Directions for Slow Cooker

1. Wash greens, remove the thick ribs, and tear or chop into 2" pieces.
2. Chop onion, celery, and carrots into small, thin rounds.
3. Put all ingredients except cooked grains in the slow cooker.
4. Cook on low heat for 6–7 hours.
5. Add optional cooked grains 15 minutes before serving.
6. Add salt and pepper to taste.

Directions for Stovetop

1. Wash greens, remove the thick ribs, and tear or chop into 2" pieces.
2. Chop onion, celery, and carrots into small, bite-size rounds.
3. Heat oil in a soup pot with onions and garlic over medium-high heat for about 3 minutes, stirring frequently.
4. Add remaining ingredients and bring to a boil.
5. Lower heat and simmer, partially covered, for 25 minutes.
6. Add optional cooked grains for last 10 minutes.
7. Add salt and pepper to taste.

Navy Bean and Vegetable Turkey Chili: olive oil, onion, turkey (raw ground or cooked breast), chili powder, garlic, cumin, oregano, salt, pepper, canned or precooked navy beans, low-sodium chicken broth, diced tomatoes, red bell pepper, carrots, baby portobello mushrooms, fresh cilantro, fresh lime juice

Directions for Stovetop

1. Wash the carrots. Wash the bell pepper and remove core and seeds. Stem the mushrooms. Chop all into small, bite-size pieces.
2. Heat oil in a large Dutch oven with onion over medium-high heat for about 4 minutes.
3. If using raw ground turkey, add it and brown for 5–6 minutes.
4. Add all remaining ingredients, except cooked poultry, cilantro, and lime juice, and cook for about 25 minutes.
5. If using cooked poultry, add in the last 10 minutes until thoroughly heated.
6. Mix, add fresh cilantro and lime juice, and serve.
7. Optional: garnish with lime wedges.

SALAD

Salads make a great meal for lunch or dinner. In the United States, we typically add too much fat and sugar at the "salad bar" in the form of heavy dressings, cheeses, croutons, etc., and ignore the proteins and higher fiber items. However, it is possible to modify the American salad to turn it into a very healthy meal.

In general, we recommend salads be eaten during the warmer months, since that's when, seasonally, your body is most primed to digest raw foods. However, for many families, salads make up most of their daily vegetable consumption, so we don't want to discourage you from eating them at any time of year that feels good to you. One way to improve salad's digestibility in colder months is to add cooked greens to the raw ones. For instance, lightly boiled kale or steamed escarole or spinach can be added to the lettuce base, or even replace it.

USING THE DINNER SALAD MIX AND MATCH CHART

At the top of each column, you will see an amount listed. Choose any combination of the ingredients in each column to get the *total amount* of each category. To complete your salad, see the next section, Salad Dressing.

MIX AND MATCH: **DINNER SALAD** *Serves 4-5*

GREENS BASE (4-5 C)	VEGGIES (2 C, raw or cooked)	PROTEIN (1/2-1 1/2 C)
arugula Bibb lettuce Boston lettuce butterhead lettuce cabbage, red or green dandelion greens (raw or cooked) escarole (raw or cooked) green-leaf lettuce mesclun greens red-leaf lettuce romaine lettuce	avocado asparagus (blanch first) beets (cooked) bell peppers broccoli carrots cauliflower celery cucumber daikon eggplant (cooked) green beans jicama mushrooms peas radish sprouts summer squash sweet potatoes (cooked) tomatoes zucchini grilled vegetables of any variety	beans (all varieties, cooked or canned: drained and rinsed) cheese (any variety) chicken, grilled or roasted eggs, boiled fish (cooked, smoked, canned, precooked shellfish) hummus lamb, grilled or roasted pork, grilled or roasted steak, grilled turkey, grilled or roasted

GRAINS/PASTA (1/2-1 C, cooked)	OPTIONAL FRUITS (to taste)	GARNISHES (1 T-1/2 C)
millet quinoa rice (any whole grain variety) whole grain pasta (small noodles, e.g., bow ties, shells, twists)	apples, fresh or dried apricots, fresh or dried berries, fresh or dried cherries, fresh or dried cranberries, dried figs, fresh or dried grapes mango, fresh oranges (navel, mandarin, blood, etc.) papaya, fresh peaches, fresh pears, fresh or dried raisins	almonds cashews corn fennel, shaved flaxseeds, ground or soaked (1/4 C max) hazelnuts mustard greens (strong and spicy, use sparingly) peas pine nuts pumpkin seeds sunflower seeds walnuts

GREAT COMBOS: **SALAD DRESSING** *Dresses about 4 salads*

ITALIAN	BALSAMIC	HONEY MUSTARD
(dresses 1 salad) 1 t dried oregano 1 t dried basil 1 t garlic powder 1/2 t pepper 1 whole lemon 1–2 T olive oil Sprinkle herbs over salad. Squeeze lemon juice over all, toss with olive oil.	1/4 C balsamic vinegar 1/4 C olive oil 1/4 C water 1/4 C fresh basil 1/2 clove garlic 1/2 t pepper 1/2 t agave nectar (optional) Emulsify all in a blender.	1/4 C apple cider vinegar 1/4 C olive oil 1/4 C water 1–2 T Dijon mustard 1 t honey Whisk together in a bowl.
GINGER SNAP	**CURRY LEMON**	**TAHINI**
1/4 C rice wine vinegar 1/4 C sesame oil (raw or toasted) 1/4 C water 1 t minced ginger 1 T orange juice 1 T soy sauce Whisk together in a bowl.	Juice from 1 whole lemon or lime 1/4 C water 1 t minced ginger 1 clove garlic, minced 1 t curry powder 1/2 C plain yogurt Whisk together in a bowl.	2 T cider vinegar 1/4 C sesame oil (raw with 1–2 T toasted, for flavor) 1/4 C water 1 t soy sauce 1/2 clove garlic, minced 1/4 C tahini Whisk together in a bowl.

Dinner Salad Formula

4–5 C lettuce
2 C mixed vegetables or fruits
1/2–1 1/2 C protein
1/2–1 C grains or pasta (optional)
1 C cooked greens (optional, good for winter)
1 T– 1/2 C garnishes
Herbs and spices to taste
3 T oil or dressing

1. Clean and spin-dry lettuce. Remove any tough stems or cores and chop or tear to desired size.
2. Clean and cut any vegetables, fruits, or proteins into bite-size pieces.
3. Assemble all the ingredients except the dressing in a large bowl.
4. Drizzle with oil or other dressing. Toss and serve.

TRY THESE GREAT COMBOS

Quick Summer Slaw: red cabbage, green cabbage, carrots, celery, rice wine vinegar, flaxseed or olive oil, few drops of sesame and/or chili oil for additional flavor (optional), fresh cilantro

Shred veggies in a food processor and toss with oil, vinegar, and cilantro. Chill before serving. (For a super-quick slaw, you can buy preshredded vegetables in a bag. A broccoli/cabbage/carrot combo works well for this slaw.)

Quick Southwest Salad: baby romaine, chopped avocado, shredded carrots, corn kernels, red pepper strips, canned or precooked black or pinto beans, crushed baked corn chips, salsa, light ranch dressing

SALAD DRESSING

These days there are many natural salad dressings on the market, but it's important to be a label detective to ensure they don't include a lot of unhealthy fat or sugar. It's actually very simple to make flavorful and healthy dressings from ingredients in your pantry. Try our Great Combos here, and check out the Marinades Mix and Match chart in the last section of this chapter—some of them can double as salad dressings.

USING THE SALAD DRESSING GREAT COMBOS CHART

Here are six great dressing ideas. Each box contains a complete dressing. You can easily dress a single salad (see Italian) or make a larger batch (other combos) that will last you a week or two. Including fresh herbs or yogurt will speed the breakdown time in the fridge, so quickly use up any dressings containing those ingredients. For other great dressing ideas, see the ethnic spice groupings in appendix C. Just add spices to oil, vinegar or lemon juice, and water in a 1:1:1 combination.

Dressing Formula

¼ C water
¼ C vinegar or lemon/lime juice
¼ C oil
1 t–1 T herbs
¼ C thickening ingredient (optional)
1 t pungent or salty ingredients (optional)
1 t sweetener (optional)

1. Mix water with vinegar.
2. Slowly add oil and whisk or process until thoroughly blended.
3. Whisk or blend in any other ingredients.

As you can see, our dressing formula is simple: ¼ C oil, ¼ C water, ¼ C vinegar. This won't emulsify (thicken) in the way you might be used to, but it clings well to salad leaves. If you can get used to the runnier texture, you'll find that the flavor is just as good, and the health benefits greater, because you are consuming less fat. If you add any thickening ingredients or pungent flavorings, the dressing will naturally thicken somewhat.

Dinner

Obviously, soups, salads, grains, and even eggs can make great dinners, but in this section we will focus on Mix and Match templates for more traditional dinner entrées: one-pot stews, pastas, and meat or vegetable marinades. For a completely nourishing dinner, we encourage you to prepare one or two green vegetables as side dishes to go along with the main courses that we are highlighting here. Guidelines for choosing and preparing greens are found in chapter 11.

PASTA

Most of us have made a traditional pot of spaghetti at least once in our lives, and for some it may be a weekly dinner staple. But most people have never branched out beyond basic white flour pasta with tomato or meat sauce. This typical SAD pasta dish can easily be transformed into a healthier meal by using a smaller amount of higher quality pasta, and adding more vegetables and good-quality protein.

We encourage you to try many different kinds of pasta. There is a wide variety available, in different shapes and made from different grains. Some of our favorite products include Tinkyada-brand brown rice pasta, Hodgson Mill Whole Wheat with

MIX AND MATCH: **PASTA** *Serves 6–8*

SIMPLE SAUCE (choose one)	PASTA (1 bag or box) choose one	PROTEIN choose any	VEGETABLES (2 C total) choose any	COOKING METHOD
OLIVE OIL BASE 3 cloves garlic, minced ¼ C olive oil ½ C broth or leftover water from any boiled vegetables	angel hair fettuccini fusilli shells spaghetti tortellini any other whole grain pasta	Asiago, Parmesan, or Romano, grated (⅓ C) ½ C feta, crumbled 1 C white beans, cannellini beans, or navy beans	arugula broccoli florets (blanched first) capers (⅓ C only) carrots (thin rounds, blanched) mushrooms olives, chopped (½ C only) peas (frozen or fresh) shallots sun-dried tomato strips, soaked and drained (½–1 C only)	Sauté garlic in large sauté pan with olive oil, 1–3 min. Add vegetables. Sauté until tender. Stir in broth and beans until warm. Cook pasta as directed. Toss with sauce and sprinkle cheese on top. Serve immediately.
TOMATO BASE 1–2 cloves garlic, crushed 2 T olive oil basil (1 t dried or ⅓ C fresh) 1 t oregano ½ C red or white wine (dry) 1–2 cans crushed tomatoes	angel hair fettuccini fusilli shells spaghetti tortellini any other whole grain pasta or lasagna noodles	1 lb chicken or turkey sausage (precook and slice or take out of casing and brown) 1 lb ground beef or turkey ½ (12-oz) bag Italian meatless meatballs (we like Nate's brand)	arugula bell peppers broccoli florets (blanched first) capers (⅓ C only) carrots (thin rounds, blanched) eggplant mushrooms olives, chopped (½ C only) shallots sun-dried tomato strips, soaked and drained (½–1 C only)	Sauté crushed garlic in large sauté pan with olive oil, 1–3 min. Add all other base ingredients and stir over medium heat for 10 min. Brown meats, drain oil, blanch veggies, and add to sauce. Serve immediately over cooked pasta. For a quick lasagna, ingredients can be layered with no-cook lasagna noodles or Tinkyada rice noodles.

MIX AND MATCH: **PASTA** *Serves 6-8*

SIMPLE SAUCE *choose one*	PASTA (1 bag or box) *choose one*	PROTEIN *choose any*	VEGETABLES (2 C total) *choose any*	COOKING METHOD
PEANUT BASE *(no cooking)* 1-2 cloves garlic, crushed 1/2 C fresh cilantro 1/2 C peanut butter (optional: substitute 1/2 C tahini for nut-free version) 2 T rice wine vinegar 1 T toasted sesame oil or seeds 1 T soy sauce 1/4 t ground ginger 1/4 t cayenne pepper (optional) 1/4-1/2 C water as needed for thinning	rice noodles soba noodles udon noodles whole grain fettuccini whole grain spaghetti any other Asian noodle	1 lb steak, cooked and cut into 1" cubes or thinly sliced 2 chicken breasts, cooked and shredded 1 lb tofu (firm)	bok choy or napa cabbage (raw, sliced into thin strips) broccoli florets (blanched first) cucumber (seeded and sliced) scallions, chopped	Blend all base ingredients together in blender or food processor. Cook pasta as directed. Toss with cooked pasta, protein, and veggies. Serve immediately.
PESTO BASE *(no cooking)* 1-3 cloves garlic 2 C basil, fresh 1/3 C olive oil 3 T pine nuts or walnuts 1/4 t salt	ravioli tortellini any other whole grain pasta	Asiago, Parmesan, or Romano, grated (1/3 C) **Optional extras:** chicken tenders (11/2 lbs cooked and shredded) tilapia (11/2-lb fillets, cooked and laid whole over pasta)	broccoli (blanched first) sun-dried tomato strips in oil, drained (1/2-1 C only)	Blend all base ingredients in blender or food processor. Cook pasta as directed. Toss with cooked pasta, cheese, and veggies. If adding chicken or fish, make extra pesto and use as a base for baking: chicken on 375°F for 20-30 min.; fish, 350°F for 15-20 min.

MIX AND MATCH: **MARINADE** *Dresses 2 lbs protein or 2-3 salads*

OIL (1/4 C) *choose one*	VINEGAR/CITRUS (1/4 C mixed with 1/4 C water) *choose one*	OPTIONAL THICKENER (1/4 C) *choose one*	HERBS/SPICES (1 t–2 T, fresh or dried) *choose any*
almond oil avocado oil flaxseed oil (salads only; not for cooking) grapeseed oil macadamia nut oil olive oil, extra-virgin sesame oil walnut oil (salads only: not for cooking)	balsamic vinegar champagne vinegar cider vinegar fresh lemon juice fresh lime juice pomegranate vinegar (note: strong flavor) raspberry vinegar red wine vinegar rice wine vinegar	nut or seed butter (almond, cashew, peanut, sunflower seed, tahini, etc.) plain yogurt tahini	basil cacao powder celery seed cilantro cinnamon coriander cumin dill oregano marjoram mint nutmeg parsley rosemary tarragon thyme

GREAT COMBOS: **MARINADE** *Marinates 1 main dish*

GINGER MARINADE	PEANUT BUTTER MARINADE	MEDITERRANEAN MARINADE	ZESTY YOGURT MARINADE	TANGY MARINADE
1/4 C water 1-2 T sesame oil 3/4 C orange juice 1 T minced ginger 1 t wasabi (optional) 2T soy sauce	1/4 C water 2 T sesame oil juice of 1/2 lemon 1/4 C rice wine or white wine 1/4 C peanut butter 1/4 C fresh cilantro, chopped 1 T agave nectar 1/2 t cayenne pepper 1-2 cloves garlic, minced 1/4 C minced scallions 3 T soy sauce	1 T olive oil 1 C red wine 1 t basil or rosemary 1 clove garlic, minced 1/4 C chopped olives 1/4 C sun-dried tomatoes, soaked, rinsed, and minced	juice of 1 lemon or lime 1 C yogurt (plain) 1 t cardamom 1 t coriander 1 t curry powder 1 t ginger	1 C dry white wine juice of 1 lime 1 t cumin 1 t agave nectar 1/4 C diced onion 1/2 t cayenne pepper 1-2 cloves garlic, minced

OPTIONAL SWEET FLAVORS (1 t) *choose any*	OPTIONAL PUNGENT FLAVORS (1 t) *choose any*	OPTIONAL SALTY FLAVORS (1 t) *choose one*	*NOT FOR SALADS* EXTRA LIQUIDS (1/4–1 C) *choose one*	*NOT FOR SALADS* PROTEIN (2 lb) *choose one*
agave nectar blackstrap molasses fruit juice honey maple syrup rice syrup	cayenne pepper (1/2 t) chili oil or powder curry powder garlic, minced or powdered ginger, minced or powdered horseradish mustard powder or seed onion, minced pepper shallot, minced wasabi	capers miso paste olives, chopped soy sauce (low-sodium tamari or shoyu) sun-dried tomatoes, soaked, drained, and minced tomato paste	beer fruit juice (pomegranate, orange, pineapple, etc.) sherry vinegars (see vinegar column) wine (white, red, rice, etc.)	chicken (breasts, legs, tenders, thighs, wings, parts) fish (firm is best: salmon, snapper, trout) lamb pork cutlets, (lean, tenderloin) scallops shrimp steak tempeh tofu

EASY KIDS' FAVORITE MARINADE	CAPER MARINADE	AROMATIC MARINADE	HOISIN MARINADE	SUPER-QUICK MARINADES
1/4 C olive oil juice of 1 small lemon 1-2 cloves garlic, minced (optional) 2 T soy sauce	1 C white wine juice of 1/2 lemon 1/4 C capers 1-2 cloves garlic, minced pepper, to taste	1 C red wine 1 t basil 1 bay leaf 1 t thyme 1 t rosemary 1 t 100% maple syrup 1 clove garlic, minced	1/4 C rice wine or white wine 1/4 C orange juice 1/4 C hoisin sauce 1 t 100% maple syrup 1 T organic ketchup 2-3 cloves garlic, minced 1 t chili oil (optional) 2 T soy sauce	Annie's brand BBQ Sauce balsamic dressing Island brand teriyaki sauce Italian dressing salsa

Flaxseed Pasta, soba noodles, any spelt angel hair pasta, and Asian rice noodles.

There are endless variations of healthy home-made pasta sauces that are much tastier and more interesting than sauces out of a jar, and they aren't all tomato-based. In this section, instead of a "Formula" we give you four different bases to work with, plus a selection of pastas, proteins, and vegetables that go well with each.

USING THE PASTA MIX AND MATCH CHART

This chart is a little different than the other Mix and Match charts. First choose a base sauce to work with. Then read across that row, left to right, to select other ingredients to "mix and match" into a great pasta dish. All quantities are provided in the chart.

The Water Sauté

Because of the health risks associated with overheating oils and overconsuming fats, it's good to know about water sauté-ing as an alternative to cooking with oil. This is a safe and low-fat way to retain the fresh flavors of sautéed food. Follow these instructions:

1. Just cover the bottom of the sauté pan with water or broth (vegetable or chicken stock adds a nice flavor).
2. Heat over a medium burner until your water or broth just begins to steam.
3. Add your vegetables or meats and a small amount of additional liquid, if needed.
4. Lightly toss the food to brown or wilt all sides.
5. Cover and steam to soften veggies or meats, if necessary.
6. Serve hot.

MARINADES

SAD dinners commonly have a large piece of marinated protein—steak, chicken breast, or even tofu—as their centerpiece. When transitioning to healthier foods, there is no need to give up this favorite style of family eating, as long as you upgrade your quality of protein, reduce the portion size a bit, and properly balance it with vegetables and whole grains.

Marinating is a great way to add healthy flavor and kick to foods using all-natural ingredients. Here, we provide you with a Mix and Match chart for inspiration, and a table of fourteen Great Combos to get you started. These marinades are incredibly versatile. They can be used on meat, fish, tofu, tempeh, or seitan, or as sauces for vegetables or pasta. Many of them also make great salad dressings. Note that the water and oil may be reduced or omitted if using a full cup of vinegar, wine, or juice. See Great Combos for suggestions.

USING THE MARINADE MIX AND MATCH CHART

Choose one item from each vertical column and combine according to the directions. As you gain more experience with combinations, you may want to add more than one ingredient from the Herbs or Flavors columns, but when you're just getting started, it's best to keep it simple. All of these combinations work well as marinades, but not all work as salad dressings, as you will see noted in the last two columns. With the designated amounts of ingredients, each combination in the chart will make enough to marinate 2 pounds of protein or dress 2 to 3 salads, and will last for 1 to 2 weeks in the fridge. Note that including fresh herbs or yogurt in your marinade will shorten its shelf life.

Marinade Formula

1/4 C water (optional for marinade)

1/4 C oil

1/4–1 C vinegar, wine, or juice

1/4 C thickening ingredient (optional)

1 t–2 T herbs or spices

1 t sweetener (optional)

1 t pungent flavor (optional)

1 t salty flavor (optional)

1. Mince all herbs and fresh vegetables finely and combine all ingredients, whisking to combine.
2. Put the protein in a flat Pyrex baking dish or a gallon-size zip-closure bag and pour the marinade on top. The longer you marinate something, the stronger the flavors will be. With even 30 minutes of marinating, you will be able to taste the flavors in a subtle way. Marinating anywhere from 4 hours to overnight will give you the strongest flavor impact.
3. Marinated proteins respond best to baking in a 375°F oven, broiling, or grilling.

USING THE MARINADE GREAT COMBOS CHART

The first nine boxes give you simple ingredients for a variety of flavorful marinades. Each box contains a single marinade. The last box has a few suggestions for "instant" marinades: items from a jar or bottle that you can use in a flash!

STEWS

Stews are classic comfort food. With their rich flavors and hearty texture, they are most digestible in the colder months. But if you find that these simple one-pot meals work for you as a way to get healthy food into your family, then by all means, try them throughout the year.

Stews usually take a few hours to cook, so we like to use slow cookers and clay pot cookers (for details about this equipment, see chapter 9). With these tools, you can do the prep work hours in advance, turn on your slow cooker, enjoy your day, and walk in at dinnertime to a home-cooked meal.

USING THE STEW MIX AND MATCH CHART

Choose one ingredient from each column and combine as directed above. From the Hearty Veggies and Herbs/Spices columns you may choose more than one ingredient, but make sure your total amount equals what is listed in the Stew Formula.

Stew Formula

4 C hearty vegetables

1 1/2–2 lbs protein

2–4 C liquids (less if using a slow cooker)

1–3 T herbs and spices

Extra flavorings, to taste

1. Chop vegetables: larger, coarse-cut pieces are okay for stovetop preparation, while smaller, bite-size chunks or thin rounds are better for cooking in a slow cooker or clay pot cooker.
2. Chop meat into 1–2" cubes.
3. Optional: You can dredge the meat in 3 T of any type of flour or cornmeal spiced with salt, pepper, and paprika: combine dry ingredients in a gallon-size zip-closure bag, add cubes, toss meat around until all pieces are lightly coated, remove pieces, and discard any leftover flour mixture.
4. Combine all ingredients and cook until veggies are tender and meat is at desired doneness. See specific examples below for stovetop cooking, slow cooking, and clay pot cooking.

TRY THESE GREAT COMBOS

Because we are such fans of these one-pot, slow-cooked meals, here we share some of our favorite recipes with you in the more traditional form.

MIX AND MATCH: **STEW** *Serves 4-6; fills a large slow cooker*

LIQUIDS (2-4 C; 1¼-1¾ if using a slow cooker) *choose one*	PROTEIN (1½-2 lbs) *choose one*	HEARTY VEGGIES (4 C) *choose any*
beef broth or stock chicken broth or stock vegetable broth or stock water	beef, cubed chicken parts fish (red snapper, tilapia, or whitefish) lamb, cubed turkey tenderloins	butternut squash (or other peeled winter squashes), in 1½" cubes carrots, in thin rounds celery, chopped corn, frozen green beans, fresh or frozen eggplant mushrooms, sliced (portobello, shiitake, button, etc.) onions, peeled and quartered parsnips, in thin rounds peas, frozen (add for last 10 minutes of cooking) potatoes, in 1" cubes (new or sweet) tomatoes, diced, stewed, or whole turnips, cut into ½" cubes

Almost any stew can be prepared on the stove, in a slow cooker, or in a clay pot cooker, but some dishes are ideally suited to a particular cooking method. Try out the recipes below to get familiar with these three techniques, and then experiment with the formula above to discover the meals that work best for you.

On the stovetop: Stovetop pot stews are easy and versatile. They generally cook more quickly than the same dish in a slow cooker because the heat is higher. But they do take more hands-on time because you have to stand at the stove and tend to them. Because fish cooks more quickly than other proteins, it's our favorite choice for cooking at the stove. Fish is a wonderful, high-quality protein, and the stewing process mellows the "fishy" flavor that can turn many kids off (and some adults!) to the taste of seafood.

Pan Fish Stew

1½-2 lbs any white fish (tilapia) or fish steaks (wild Alaskan salmon)
Juice of 1 lemon
⅓ C olive oil
½ large onion, chopped
2-3 cloves garlic, minced
½ C dry white wine
1 C chopped canned plum tomatoes
2 T chopped fresh parsley or cilantro (optional)
Salt and black pepper (preferably ground fresh)

1. Wash fish with cold water and dry with paper towels. Squeeze lemon juice over fish.
2. In a large sauté pan, add olive oil and onion. Sauté over medium heat until onion becomes translucent, 4-5 minutes.
3. Add garlic and sauté for 1-3 minutes, until it turns lightly brown
4. Add white wine, tomatoes, and parsley and stir.

HERBS/SPICES (1–3 T) *choose any* (see appendix C for ideas)	EXTRA FLAVORINGS (1/2 C) *choose one*

basil
bay leaf
cayenne pepper
cumin
curry powder
herbes de Provence
marjoram
mustard, prepared or
  powdered
rosemary
turmeric
	beer
	burgundy wine
	coconut milk
	  (1/4 C only)
	crushed garlic
	  (1–4 cloves)
	flavored vinegar
	white wine, dry

5. Cook uncovered over medium heat with a uniform simmer, stirring occasionally, for about 5 minutes.
6. Add fish. Season with salt and pepper to taste, cover, and reduce heat to medium-low.
7. Cook each side for about 5 minutes, or more if very thick, until cooked through.
8. Be careful handling the fish. Gently transfer to a serving dish, ladle the sauce over the fish, and serve immediately.

In a slow cooker: Slow cookers are our number one choice for making stews, both for ease of use and for time efficiency. Although you will have to find the time in the morning or at lunch to prepare the ingredients, the slow cooker safely does all the cooking for you whether you are at home or not. The biggest advantage of slow-cooker cooking is that, when you come rushing in late from work and your kids come in starving from soccer practice, dinner is ready to go!

Slow cookers are very inexpensive, generally ranging from $15 to $35, depending on the size you want. You can get them with high, low, and high-low settings. Some even have timers so they can be set to turn off on their own. It may take some time and experimentation to get to know how your own slow cooker works best. For instance, Jeannette's pot cooks cubed meat too fast, so she has to add it after other ingredients. Tracee's pot, on the other hand, cooks meat more slowly—she adds it at the start of the cooking time.

Most hard grains, beans, and hard vegetables are not easily cooked to doneness in a stew. The proteins and more delicate vegetables are cooked more quickly and leave the longer-cooking ingredients undercooked. (See chapter 12 for instructions for cooking grains and beans alone in the slow cooker.) The best ingredients for slow-cooker stews are soft vegetables (winter squashes, potatoes, tomatoes, peppers, celery, etc.) or hard ones cut very small (such as carrots sliced into thin rounds or finely diced turnips). Place onions and the hardest vegetables at the bottom of the pot. Then add the softer vegetables, and top off with the meat. Finally the liquids can be poured over everything. Remember not to go overboard adding liquids. There is very little evaporation, so your dish will tend to get juicier rather than drier.

Slow-Cooked Beef Burgundy Stew

3 carrots, cut into thin rounds

1 small butternut squash, washed and diced (you can get the peeled and precut version to save time)

2 onions, peeled and quartered

1 1/2 lbs cubed beef stew meat (optional: dredge the beef)

2 T flour (whole grain spelt works well; optional—omit if meat is dredged)

1/2 C beef broth

3/4 C burgundy wine or dark beer

1 (14-oz) can whole or diced tomatoes

1–2 cloves garlic, minced

1 bay leaf

1/2 t marjoram

1/2 t thyme

1/2 t oregano

Salt and pepper

1 (10-oz) box or bag of frozen peas or green beans (add in the last 10 minutes)

1. Select 3 1/2-quart or larger size slow cooker.
2. Layer vegetables in order listed.
3. Add beef.
4. If meat is undredged, whisk flour into broth.
5. Add broth and wine.
6. Add tomatoes, garlic, bay leaf, marjoram, thyme, oregano, and salt and pepper to taste.
7. Cook on high for 4–5 hours, or on low for 7–8 hours.
8. Add frozen peas for the last 10–15 minutes until heated through.
9. Serve over a cooked whole grain or pasta, if desired.

In a clay pot cooker: Jeannette owes her discovery of the clay pot cooker to her sister-in-law. She grew up in a home where the clay pot cooker was used on a regular basis, and gave one to Jeannette as a birthday gift. This lidded terra-cotta pot is a staple in many German and other European kitchens. It is an unusual cooking tool and runs a little pricey (around $70 for the larger models, less for used models sold online or at yard sales). But it cooks foods so effectively and deliciously that it's worth the investment.

Most meals take from 1 hour to 90 minutes to cook in the clay pot cooker, so unless you are home with kids after school, this method may be best for weekends. It's especially great for serving company; you can prep the ingredients, throw them in the pot, get yourself and your house ready, and take your delicious meal out of the oven just as your guests arrive.

To use your clay pot cooker, start by soaking the lid in cold water for at least 10 minutes. While it is soaking, start chopping your vegetables. Assemble your ingredients, put them in the pot, and put on the wet lid. Place the pot in a *cold* oven on the lowest rack, then turn the oven temperature up to 425°F. Let your dish cook for between 60 and 90 minutes, depending on what you're making (whole chickens take longer, diced boneless cuts of meat take less time). The wet lid will release moisture while your meal cooks. This combination of the baking and steaming action perfectly browns meat and vegetable skin, while cooking the insides to a tender, juicy softness—it's like magic!

The recipe below comes out perfectly every time, and makes a very generous amount—plenty left over for lunches or for freezing. In addition to stews, the clay pot cooker does great roasts. Give it a try—you won't be disappointed with the results. *Caution:* When removing from the oven, use extra care, as it may be heavy. Also, always open the lid away from your face because the steam inside can get very hot.

Roasted Chicken Apple Clay Pot Stew

1 (32-oz) carton chicken broth

1 t organic chicken bouillon paste (optional; we like Better Than Bouillon)

½ C apple cider or apple juice

4–6 cloves garlic, peeled and coarsely chopped

2 t rosemary

1 Vidalia or other sweet onion, peeled and quartered

1 or 2 sweet potatoes, peeled and sliced

1 (1-lb) bag carrots, peeled and diced

1 (1-lb) bag baby potatoes (blue, fingerling, new, etc.), skins on, washed and halved

2 large cooking apples, skin on, cored and sliced

1 lemon

1 high-quality, whole baking chicken, any size, rinsed, organs removed, and neck fat trimmed

1 t thyme

Salt and pepper

1 T olive oil

1. Select largest clay pot cooker ("turkey size").

2. Put lid into sink and cover with cold water until completely submerged. Soak for at least 10 minutes.

3. Empty chicken broth into clay pot cooker and whisk in bouillon paste, cider, garlic, and 1 t of the rosemary.

4. Add vegetables and apples to broth and mix well.

5. Cut lemon in half, squeeze some juice gently into the main cavity of the chicken, and put both halves inside (works with orange or lime juice as well).

6. In a small bowl, mix together thyme, salt and pepper, and remaining 1 t rosemary.

7. Oil chicken skin and pat with spice mix (if you have fresh rosemary, you can insert the long stems under the chicken skin on the breast).

8. Place spiced chicken atop veggies, cover, and put on lowest rack in a cold oven.

9. Set oven to 425°F and bake for 90 minutes.

Fats and Cooking Oils[1-3]

Do you know how to select a healthy cooking oil? How about the difference between poly-unsaturated and saturated fats? Do you know where to find those much-praised essential fatty acids? Here is a short guide to help you.

SATURATED VERSUS UNSATURATED

Saturated fats: Saturated fats are solid and more stable than unsaturated fats, so they can withstand much higher cooking temperatures. They are found in both plant and animal foods. In the United States, people consume a lot of "long-chain" saturated fats (found in foods such as butter and fatty meats), which come from animals and can clog arteries if consumed in large amounts. Saturated fats from plants are typically "short-chain" and "medium-chain" fats, which are absorbed directly by the body for quick energy and also contribute to immune system health. A good plant source is coconut oil.

Unsaturated fats: There are two kinds of unsaturated fats: *mono-* and *poly-*. At the molecular level, these fats have one or more double bonds along their carbon chain and a rigid kink at the point of the bond. They are softer, or more liquid, at room temperature than saturated fats are.

- *Monounsaturated fats:* These fats have only one double bond along their carbon chain, hence, "mono," meaning "one." These fats are associated with healthy cardiovascular function. Good sources include olive, avocado, almond, sesame, macadamia nut, oleic safflower, and oleic sunflower oils.

- *Polyunsaturated fats:* These fats have two or more double bonds along their carbon chains. This category includes the essential omega-3 and omega-6 fatty acids. They provide the building blocks for a class of "signaling" molecules (eicosanoids) that control some of the most important systems in your body. Good sources include grapeseed, flaxseed, and walnut oils. Fish or krill oil is the best source, but it is better taken in supplement form rather than used as a food oil because of its strong flavor. Look for fish oil supplements that are certified free of PCBs and mercury (toxins in the ocean).

REFINED VERSUS UNREFINED OILS

Refined oils are made in the following ways:

- *Solvent extraction:* A solvent such as hexane chemically reacts with foods at high temperatures and releases their oils. This is followed by treatment with bleach and chemicals to create colorless, tasteless oils with a long shelf life. Many large, commercial companies use this method.

- *Expeller press:* This is a nonchemical method that mechanically squeezes oil from seeds and nuts by applying pressure and heat.

- *Cold press:* This is an expeller-press method that takes place in a temperature-controlled environment to protect the fragile constitution of the oil. The temperature is kept below 120°F. All cold-pressed oils are expeller-pressed, but not all expeller-pressed oils are cold-pressed.

Expeller-pressed and solvent-extracted refined oils are drained of important nutrients, such as calcium, chlorophyll, copper, lecithin, magnesium, iron, phosphorus, and vitamin E. In addition, exposure to high temperatures during the expelling process can cause the formation of free radicals, which are a health risk. Unrefined oils are by far your healthiest choice, but cold-pressed oils can be a good second choice.

Proper storage of your oils plays an important role in preserving their nutritional benefits and preventing the formation of free radicals. See appendix D for information on how to store your oils.

Unrefined oils offer the best nutritional value. Oils are labeled "unrefined" if they are left in their pure state after being filtered, rather than pressed, bleached, chemically treated, heated, or otherwise processed. Unrefined oils have a lower smoke point than refined oils do, and therefore should be used with low or no heat. (See appendix D for more information about "smoke point" and how to cook with different oils.)

Peach Cobbler (see page 214)

Mix and Match:
Snacks and Sweet Treats

Snacks as Mini-Meals

With snacks, just as with meals, quality counts. The fresher and less refined the ingredients in your snacks, the more "life energy" they contain, and the more they will tide you over between meals. So it's worth it now and then to take time to make them from scratch. Snacks with staying power are more like mini-meals than just temporary fillers—they generally have a higher fiber content or contain some significant amount of protein.

The key to quality snacking is to be prepared: keep a regular stock of different kinds of snack foods in your pantry, in your car, and at work. This will help prevent you or your kids from grabbing lower quality options, and from overeating. Kids like to have options, but it is easy to get caught in a rut with the same old boring snack ideas.

Here is a list of savory and sweet snacks that your kids can assemble themselves.

SAVORY SNACK IDEAS

- Veggie sticks (carrots, celery, bell peppers, sugar snap peas, snow peas, broccoli or cauliflower florets, jicama, daikon, etc.) paired with any protein or salad dressing "dip"
- Small handful of raw nuts or seeds with any raw or cooked veggies
- Part-skim mozzarella stick with carrots or celery
- Cubed Swiss cheese with cherry tomatoes
- Baby carrots poked into green or black olives
- Brown rice cakes with hummus or nut butter
- Soy crisps with any raw veggies
- Whole grain pretzels or crackers with any nut butter, meat, fish, or cheese
- Tuna packed in lemon and olive oil, with veggie sticks or rice crackers
- Smoked fish with horseradish on whole grain crackers
- Celery or carrots with nut butter or hummus

- Half of a whole wheat pita pocket with hummus, sprouts, and cucumbers
- Low-fat cottage cheese with tomatoes or bell peppers and sea salt and pepper
- Nonfat, no-sugar bean dip or refried beans with baked tortilla chips or raw veggie sticks
- Edamame (baby soybeans in the shell)
- Salsa and avocado with baked corn chips or a low-fat corn tortilla
- Baba ghanoush with whole wheat pita or veggie sticks
- Shrimp with low-sugar cocktail sauce
- Hard-boiled egg, alone or with veggies

NOTEWORTHY NOURISHER

Walnuts

- 1 oz dried (14 halves) contains 2 grams of fiber and 185 calories
- Keep serving size to a handful or less so that calories and grams of fat don't add up
- Are rich in omega-3 fatty acids (which also makes them likely to go rancid quickly; store in a cold dark space—refrigerator is great)
- Contain nutrients that reduce cancer risks, and help control blood sugar, cholesterol, and triglyceride levels
- Many are high in phytic acid. Soaking the raw nuts for 4 hours at room temperature will neutralize the phytic acid and germinate the walnuts, helping with digestion. Once soaked, rinse walnuts with 3 cups water and 1 T apple cider vinegar (to kill any bacteria). Then roast at 160–170°F for 15–20 min.—low roasting temperature will protect the healthy oils.
- Are cholesterol-free
- Are great on salads, in trail mix, with cooked fruit, in quick breads, in pestos, and in desserts

- Nonnitrate cold cut roll-ups around veggie sticks
- Plain popcorn flavored with sea salt, cheddar cheese powder, and/or garlic powder
- 1 can or cup of low-sodium, low-sugar bean and veggie soup
- Flax Crax crackers with hummus
- Leftovers from dinner

SWEET SNACK IDEAS

- Part-skim mozzarella stick or 1 oz low-fat cheddar with a medium apple
- Cubed Swiss cheese with berries or small handful of dried fruit
- Apple or pear slices with nut butter
- Low-fat cottage cheese with fruit (berries, apples, peaches), sliced almonds, and cinnamon
- Milk (any variety, cow's or other) and high-fiber cereal or oatmeal with sliced almonds
- Smoothies
- Sliced melon
- Fresh fruit cup with 1 oz low-fat cottage cheese
- Stewed fruits with low-fat yogurt
- Dried prunes with part-skim mozzarella stick
- Low-fat yogurt sweetened with agave nectar or any fruit
- Half low-fat sweetened yogurt with half low-fat cottage cheese and cinnamon
- Whole wheat toast slice with nut butter, banana wheels, and cinnamon, or with butter and applesauce
- Trail mix
- Low-sugar, high-fiber, and high-protein (40/30/30) snack bars

Snack and Dessert Mix and Matches

DO-IT-YOURSELF YOGURT

Individually packaged, presweetened yogurt can be a decent option for a super-quick snack. But many packaged yogurts have additives, preservatives, and unwanted quantities of sugar, so we recommend mixing your own. By starting with a base of high-quality plain yogurt and dressing it up yourself, you have much more control over what goes into your body and your children's bodies. Add a few flavors for a healthy snack, or extra sweetener to make a creamy dessert that is much healthier than ice cream.

USING THE YOGURT MIX AND MATCH CHART

Choose one option from each column of the chart and combine.

Yogurt Formula

1 C plain low-fat yogurt
1–2 T nuts or seeds
½–1 C fresh fruit or a few T dried fruit
1 T sweetener (or to taste)
1 t flavor boost
Optional extra crunch to taste

Gently combine all ingredients and enjoy!

TRY THESE GREAT COMBOS

Nutty Chocolate Cherry Delight: Greek yogurt, crushed hazelnuts, dried cherries, agave nectar, cacao powder

MIX AND MATCH: **YOGURT** *Serves 2–3*

PLAIN YOGURT (1 C) *choose one*	NUTS/ SEEDS (1–2 T) *choose any*	FRUIT (½–1 C) *choose any*	SWEETENER (1 T or to taste) *choose one*	FLAVOR BOOST (1 t) *choose one*	OPTIONAL EXTRA CRUNCH *choose any*
buffalo's milk cow's milk goat's milk (easier to digest than cow's milk yogurt) Greek (thick and creamy) soy	almonds, sliced brazil nuts, crushed hazelnuts, crushed pecans, crushed pistachio pieces sunflower seeds walnut pieces	applesauce bananas, sliced berries, any cherries, dried (¼ C only) cranberries, dried (¼ C only) mangoes, pitted and chopped peaches, pitted and chopped pears, fresh or canned with no added sugar, chopped	agave nectar frozen apple juice concentrate honey maple syrup, 100% rice syrup	cacao or cocoa powder extract (½ t) (almond, chocolate, orange, vanilla, etc.) instant pudding mix (high-quality please!)	dry cereal (½ C) granola (½ C) ground flax-seed (1–2 T) oat bran (1 T) trail mix (½ C) wheat germ (1–2 T)

Quick and Tasty Protein Blast (great for breakfast!): plain low-fat cow's milk yogurt, plain low-fat cottage cheese, diced fresh or unsweetened canned peaches or pears, agave nectar, cinnamon

TRAIL MIX

Trail mix is a fantastic snack for kids: it's an excellent source of fiber, easy to make, portable, and great tasting. By making your own batches, you'll be in control of what goes into the mix. Kids can also easily make trail mix on their own, once you show them how.

USING THE TRAIL MIX
MIX AND MATCH CHART

Trail mix is so easy to make: just choose your ingredients from the chart and stir together gently in a bowl. It requires no cooking and can be prepared quickly.

Sugar Substitutions for Healthier Baking

Try replacing the white sugar in your favorite recipes with these more natural options. For each cup of regular table sugar, you can substitute:

- 3/4 C agave nectar, blackstrap molasses, honey, or 100% maple syrup and reduce the liquid in your recipe by 1/4 C. If no liquid ingredients, add an additional 1/4 cup flour.
- 1 1/4 C barley malt or brown rice syrup and reduce the liquid in your recipe by 1/2 C. If no liquid ingredients, add an additional 1/3 C flour.
- 3/4 C date sugar or Sucanat (unrefined sugar cane).
- Or simply reduce the amount of table sugar in your recipe by 1/4–1/3 C.

Trail Mix Formula

1 C shelled nuts
1 C shelled seeds
1/2–3/4 C dried fruit
1/2–3/4 C dry cereal
Extras to taste

1. Measure out all ingredients and combine in a big bowl.
2. Once it's all mixed together, you can put it in single-serving zip-closure snack baggies for convenience.

TRY THESE GREAT COMBOS

Easy Peanut Butter Apple Snack: whole raw cashews, dried apples, Mother's Peanut Butter Bumpers cereal, whole wheat pretzel sticks

Salty Sweet Treat: tamari almonds or pumpkin seeds, raw sunflower seeds, dried apricots, puffed rice cereal, Sunspire-brand grain-sweetened dark chocolate chips

Soy-Sensitive Snack Bars

When selecting snack bars, watch out for chemicals, artificial ingredients, and too much processed sugar. Also look out for soy. Soy protein isolates are a common form of protein used in many "natural" snack bars. But many people are sensitive to this form of soy and have trouble digesting it. There are plenty of whole food bars without it; we like Odwalla, Lärabar, and TLC Pumpkin Granola bars. If you need a higher protein count, look for bars with whey protein instead of soy isolates.

MIX AND MATCH: **TRAIL MIX** Serves 5–6

NUTS, SHELLED (1 C) choose any	SEEDS, SHELLED (1 C) choose any	DRIED FRUIT (1/2–3/4 C) (no added sugar) choose any	CEREAL (1/2–3/4 C) choose any	EXTRAS (1/4 C or to taste)
almonds, plain or tamari cashews hazelnuts macadamia nuts peanuts pecans, halved pistachios soy nuts walnuts, halved	pumpkin seeds sunflower seeds	apples, chopped apricots, chopped banana chips or crisps (Trader Joe's brand) blueberries cherries cranberries dates, chopped goji berries mango, chopped papaya, chopped pineapple, chopped raisins strawberries	flaked cereal (Uncle Sam brand, Amazon brand Gorilla Flakes, etc.) Kashi Mighty Bites Mother's brand Peanut Butter or Chocolate Bumpers puffed millet puffed rice Whole Grain Chex	candy-coated chocolate pieces (Sunspire brand) grain-sweetened dark chocolate chips (Sunspire brand) coconut, dried and shaved pretzels, whole wheat, spelt, or gluten-free (1/2 C)

FRUIT COBBLER

Almost everyone craves something sweet with meals. This is a normal human response. Our bodies recognize gentle sweetness as nourishment, because it is the flavor of carbohydrates, our main fuel, and of mother's milk, our first food. So go ahead and offer your family small amounts of dessert, but choose gentler, less extreme sweets to satisfy.

Any of the sweet snack ideas, sweet trail mixes, or yogurts above can be a tasty, healthy dessert. There is also plenty of information available in books and on the Internet about healthier baking with whole grain flours and gentle sweeteners. Here we share with you one of our favorite, flexible sweet treats, fruit cobbler. Cobbler is a versatile dessert that can work in all four seasons. Simple to prepare,

it is always a hit after dinner (and sometimes for breakfast, too!).

Cobbler has two parts, the crumble top and the fruit filling.

USING THE FRUIT COBBLER MIX AND MATCH CHARTS

On the next page are one mix and match chart for the crumble top and another for the fruit filling. The charts allow you to select the best flour, nuts, sweeteners, and fruits for you and your family. Assemble and bake your cobbler according to the instructions.

MIX AND MATCH: **COBBLER CRUMBLE TOP** *Serves 6–8*

PASTRY FLOUR (1/4–1/3 C) *choose one*	CRUNCH (3/4 C rolled oats plus 1/2 C nuts) *choose any*	FAT (3 T) *choose one*	SWEETENER (1/4 C) *choose one*
gluten-free baking blend (we like Bob's Red Mill) spelt whole wheat	almonds, sliced hazelnuts, chopped walnuts or pecans, roasted or toasted, chopped	melted butter grapeseed oil walnut oil	agave nectar honey maple syrup, 100% rice syrup

MIX AND MATCH: **COBBLER FRUIT FILLING** *Serves 6–8*

FRUIT (2–3 lbs fresh, cored or pitted, skin left on and chopped into bite-size pieces; or 2 10–14-oz bags frozen) *choose any*	SWEETENER (1/4–1/2 C) *choose one*	FLAVORINGS *choose any or a mixture*	OPTIONAL LIQUID (1/4–1/2 C) *choose one*	OPTIONAL THICKENER (1 t–2 T) *choose one*
apples (Gala, McCormick, McIntosh, Macoun, Granny Smith, etc.) blackberries blueberries peaches pears strawberries (alone or with chopped rhubarb)	agave nectar date sugar fructose honey maple syrup, 100% rice syrup	allspice (1 t) cardamom (1 t) cinnamon (1 t) cloves (1/2 t) ginger (1/2 t) lemon juice (1 t) nutmeg (1/2 t)	apple cider or juice (use less if using wet fruit such as berries) fruit juice (orange, pineapple, cherry, etc.) (1/4 C; use less if using wet fruit such as berries) water (2 T; use less if using wet fruit such as berries)	kudzu (1 T) (premix and dissolve in 2 T cold liquid before adding) cornstarch (2 t)

Crumble Top Formula

1/4–1/3 C pastry flour

3/4 C rolled oats

1/2 C nuts

3 T fat

1/4 C sweetener

Combine all ingredients by hand or in blender or food processor. Blend well and set aside.

Fruit Filling Formula

1/4–1/2 C sweetener

1 t–2 T thickener (optional)

1/4–1/2 C liquid (optional)

Up to 4 t spices

2–3 lbs fruit, cored or pitted and cut into bite-size pieces (or use frozen)

Combine sweetener, thickener, liquid, and spices in a large bowl. Add chopped fruit and stir well to coat. Put filling in a lightly oiled 8" x 8" pie plate. Crumble topping ingredients

Sugar

Everyone's body depends on sugar for fuel. Its sweet flavor signals our brains that food is coming in and that our calorie needs are being met. This is part of the reason sugar is such a common craving. However, it can be detrimental to consume sugar, frequently or in large amounts, because the more we eat, the more we tend to crave.

While getting off the Standard American Diet, it is important to pay attention to your sugar intake. It can be difficult to determine the amount of sugar you are taking in simply by reading food labels because sugar is called so many different things. Also, the grams of sugar listed on a label aren't usually an accurate measure, since they only reflect sugars legally classified as "simple sugars," such as sucrose. Other sugars, such as dextrose, are classified as "complex carbohydrates," even though they taste and behave like simple sugars. They are not included in the total sugar count on labels. This can make things very confusing for consumers.

Here are some of the different forms of sugar found on food labels:

Glucose: Also called dextrose, glucose is found in fruits, honey, and corn syrup. It is less sweet compared to table sugar or sucrose.

Fructose: Also called levulose, this is the sweetest of common sugars, also found in fruits and honey.

Sucrose: This is the scientific name for table sugar, and it is a combination of one molecule of glucose and one molecule of fructose. The second sweetest sugar after fructose, it is very soluble.

Lactose: Lactose is the sugar found in milk. A simple combination of glucose and galactose, it is the primary cause of many people's intolerance of milk and dairy foods.

For healthy sweetener choices, see the sugar substitution chart on page 212 or the pantry lists in chapter 9.

---

evenly over the top of fruit filling. Bake at 375°F for 40 minutes, or until fruit is tender and topping is browned.

TRY THESE GREAT COMBOS

Summer Blues and Peaches Cobbler: *Crumble top:* whole wheat pastry flour, oats, almonds, cinnamon, powdered ginger, melted butter, agave nectar. *Fruit filling:* peaches, blueberries, agave nectar, cinnamon, orange juice, kudzu

Autumn Apple Walnut Warmer: *Crumble top:* whole wheat pastry flour, oats, walnuts, cinnamon, nutmeg, grapeseed oil, maple syrup. *Fruit filling:* apples, lemon juice, water, honey, cinnamon

Appendix A: Our Favorites

As natural and organic foods become popular, more and more packaged natural foods are showing up on the shelves of both regular grocery stores and specialty markets. Although it's great that our choices are increasing, it can be tricky (not to mention overwhelming) to sort through all the options and figure out which products are healthiest and best tasting.

To help reduce confusion, here is a list of some of our favorite, high-quality, brand-name food items. We use these products often and find them reliable and satisfying. You'll be able to locate most of them in regular supermarkets, as well as in higher quality stores such as Whole Foods Market, Wild Oats Market, Trader Joe's, and smaller health food stores.

Many of the companies included feel strongly about producing sustainable, fresh, delicious, healthy food and hold themselves to high standards. For example, Eden Foods has deliberately chosen not to use the USDA Organics labels, because they believe their own standards to be even higher than those set by the government. To find out more about these companies, check out their websites. Many of them have online coupons you can print out to reduce your cost of sampling a new product.

Keep these brands in mind as you stock your Whole Life Nutrition pantry, and you'll be good to go. Enjoy!

BREAD

The Baker, Rudi's Organic Bakery, Vermont Bread Company
www.charterbaking.com
Multigrain oat bread, cinnamon raisin bread, spelt ancient grain bread

Ezekiel Sprouted Grain Products
www.foodforlife.com
Sprouted grain breads and tortillas

CHOCOLATE

Endangered Species Chocolate
www.chocolatebar.com
Chocolate bars, cacao nibs

Green & Black's Organic
www.greenandblacks.com
Dark chocolate bars, hot chocolate

Lake Champlain Chocolates
www.lakechamplainchocolates.com
Fair trade chocolate, hot chocolate

Sunspire
www.sunspire.com
Chocolate bars, grain-sweetened chocolate chips, baking sundrops, Ococo's baked chocolate and cinnamon crisps

DAIRY AND SOY

8th Continent
www.8thcontinent.com
Soymilk, soy refresher shakes

Alden's Ice Cream
www.aldensicecream.com
Organic ice cream, lower in sugar than many other brands

Applegate Farms
www.applegatefarms.com
Cheese slices and cold cuts without nitrates, antibiotics, or chemical preservatives (also bacon, hot dogs, and chicken nuggets)

Bufala di Vermont
www.bufaladivermont.com
Water buffalo's milk yogurt, buffalo mozzarella

Fage USA
www.fageusa.com
Authentic Greek yogurt, tzatziki dips, feta cheese

Lightlife
www.lightlife.com
Organic tempeh, grab'n go tortilla wraps, smart pretzel dogs

Nasoya Organic Tofu
www.vitasoyusa.com
Tofu

Natural by Nature
www.natural-by-nature.com
Grass-fed, organic dairy products: ricotta cheese, butter, milk, and sour cream

Organic Valley
www.organicvalley.coop
Stringles (string cheese), cream cheese, milk (also prairie meats)

Redwood Hill Farm
www.redwoodhill.com
Goat's milk yogurt, goat's milk cheeses (most organic, not 100%)

Rice Dream
www.tastethedream.com
Rice drink, nondairy frozen desserts

Seven Stars Farm
www.sevenstarsfarm.com
Yogurt

Silk
www.silksoymilk.com
Soymilk, creamer

Stonyfield Farm
www.stonyfieldfarm.com
Organic yogurts, all-natural yogurts, smoothies, ice cream, frozen yogurt, milk

Wallaby Organics
www.wallabyyogurt.com
Flavored yogurt

FROZEN DINNERS

Amy's
www.amys.com
Rice-crust pizza (gluten-free), California burgers, pizza, rice bowls, enchiladas, burritos

Boca Burgers
www.bocaburger.com
Vegetarian burgers and breakfast patties

Dr. Praeger's
www.drpraegers.com
Veggie burgers, breaded fish fillets

Health Is Wealth
www.healthiswealthfoods.com
Antibiotic-free chicken nuggets with whole wheat breading

Morningstar Farms
www.morningstarfarms.com
Soy crumbles, meatless grillers, other meat alternatives

Wellshire Farms
www.wellshirefarms.com
Gluten-free chicken bites

FROZEN VEGETABLES

Alexia
www.alexiafoods.com
Sweet potato fries, oven crinkles

Cascadian Farm
www.cascadianfarm.com
Frozen fruits and vegetables (also fruit spreads, chewy granola bars, Clifford Crunch Cereals)

GRAINS, RICE, PASTA, FLOUR, AND CEREALS

Annie's Homegrown
www.annies.com
Whole wheat pasta, whole grain macaroni and cheese

Arrowhead Mills
www.arrowheadmills.com
Ancient grains, beans, pancake mix, nut butters

Back to Nature
www.backtonaturefoods.com
Cereals, granola

Barbara's Bakery
www.barbarasbakery.com
Whole grain, low-sugar kids' cereals (also low-sugar animal crackers, granola, and cereal bars)

Barilla
www.barillaus.com
Barilla Plus Penne (enriched multigrain pasta)

Bionaturae
www.bionaturae.com
Gluten-free pasta (also tomatoes from Italy, olive oil, balsamic vinegar, fruit spreads, fruit nectars)

Bob's Red Mill
www.bobsredmill.com
Organic steel-cut oats, 10-grain hot cereal, whole grains, gluten-free flour mix

Country Choice Organic
www.countrychoiceorganic.com
Steel-cut oats, quick old-fashioned oats

Eden Foods
www.edenfoods.com
Organic grains (also canned beans, miso, tea, dried fruit, traditional Japanese ingredients)

Health Valley
www.healthvalley.com
Cereals, cereal bars (also soups, chilis, and crème sandwich bars)

Hodgson Mill
www.hodgsonmill.com
All-natural flours and cornmeals, baking mixes, pancake mix, whole wheat pastas, veggie pastas

Kashi

www.kashi.com

Kashi Mighty Bites, TLC crackers and bars

Lundberg

www.lundberg.com

Assorted whole grain rice, rice cakes, rice chips

Nature's Path

www.naturespath.com

Pasta, granola bars, waffles

Pamela's Products

www.pamelasproducts.com

Wheat-free and gluten-free baking and pancake mixes

Seeds of Change

www.seedsofchange.com

Quinoa mixes (also vegetable seeds, salsas)

Shiloh Farms

www.shilohfarms.net

Grains, rice, beans (also cereals, spelt pretzels, raw goat's milk cheese, gluten-free foods)

Texmati Rice

www.riceselect.com

Organic and nonorganic rice products

Tinkyada

www.tinkyada.com

Wheat free, gluten-free pasta

MEAT AND POULTRY

Aaron's Gourmet Emporium

www.aaronsgourmet.com

Chicken, turkey, duck, grass-fed meat, wild salmon

Coleman Natural

www.colemannatural.com

Antibiotic-free, hormone-free, preservative-free, vegetarian-fed beef, chicken, pork sausage

Eberly Poultry

www.eberlypoultry.com

Free-range chicken and turkey

Grateful Harvest

www.albertsorganic.com

Grass-fed beef

Murray's Chicken

www.murrayschicken.com

Antibiotic-free, hormone-free, growth-drug-free chicken, turkey, and sausage

Wholesome Harvest

www.wholesomeharvest.com

Organic chicken, turkey, beef, pork

OILS AND FATS

Nutiva

www.nutiva.com

Organic hemp seed and flaxseed bars, organic hemp seed, organic hemp shake, coconut oil

Spectrum Organic Products

www.spectrumorganics.com

Wide variety of healthy oils: avocado, grapeseed, olive, etc.

SNACK BARS

Clif Bar
www.clifbar.com
Fruit and nut bars, Clif Kid ZBar

Lärabar
www.larabar.com
Blend of unsweetened fruits, nuts, and spices

Odwalla
www.odwalla.com
Cereal bars with no soy protein isolates

SOUPS

Edward & Sons
www.edwardandsons.com
Miso soup cups (also brown rice snaps, organic sauces, native forest organic coconut milk)

Imagine Foods
www.imaginefoods.com
Free-range chicken broth, soups, low-sodium chicken and vegetable broths

Pacific Natural Foods
www.pacificfoods.com
Low-sodium vegetable broths, iced tea, soymilk

MISCELLANEOUS

Newman's Own Organics
www.newmansownorganics.com
Olive oil, balsamic vinegar

Frontier Natural Products Co-op
www.frontiercoop.com
Spices, seasoning blends, teas

Santa Cruz Organic
www.scojuice.com
Peanut butter, juice, applesauce blends

Walnut Acres
www.walnutacres.com
Fruit squeezers (berry, wild fruit, and wild apple), soups, juices, salsas

Appendix B:
Less Familiar Ingredients

You may not recognize all of the ingredients mentioned in the pantry staples list or in the Mix and Match recipe chapters, so we provide some details about them here. These ingredients are less common in the Standard American Diet but often come in very handy for everyday whole foods cooking. They can be found at large grocery stores in their natural foods sections, at your local natural food store, or at Whole Foods markets.

Agave nectar: A sweetener derived from one of two types of cactuslike plants originating in Mexico. Can be used in baking. Low glycemic load.

Better Than Bouillon (Organic): A line of concentrated organic soup pastes. Use as an alternative to conventional bouillon cubes or canned or boxed broths. You can control the strength of the broth with the amount of paste used. All flavors are gluten-free. Be aware of the sodium content.

Bragg Liquid Aminos: A liquid soybean base that combines sixteen amino acids. Can be used in place of soy sauce, as it is lower in sodium and has a milder flavor.

Cacao powder: Natural, unprocessed chocolate extremely high in antioxidants.

Daikon: Mild white radish used in Asian cooking; appearance is similar to a white carrot. May be served raw in salads or grated (with a cheese grater) as a condiment. Sweeter than red radishes. Mildly pungent taste. Gently detoxifying to the body.

Date sugar: Made from dehydrated, crushed dates. Does not dissolve as easily as table sugar, but fine for baking. High in fiber and many minerals, including iron.

Flaxseed oil: Rich source of the essential fatty acid alpha-linoleic acid (precursor to omega-3s). Good for healthy skin and hair and regularity of digestion and elimination. Very perishable; must be refrigerated in dark containers and should never be heated.

Fructose: The sweetest naturally occurring sugar. Healthier from beets than from corn. Lower impact on blood sugar if used in dry (baked) goods than in liquids.

Goji berries: Rich in nutrients and antioxidants, dried goji berries make a healthy snack, cereal topping, or addition to many recipes.

Gomasio: A Japanese condiment that is a mixture of ground sesame seeds and sea salt.

Grapeseed oil: A neutral-tasting oil, suitable for high heat cooking. Look for alcohol-extracted grapeseed oil that has been refined at low temperatures.

Hemp protein powder: Easily digestible protein powder; rich in fiber, vitamin E, and omega-3 and omega-6 essential fatty acids. Use in smoothies and baking. Has been used for thousands of years.

Jicama: A sweet and crunchy South American root, like a cross between a carrot and a white potato. Low in calories, low glycemic load, high in fiber. Very tasty and satisfying. Frequently eaten raw. Use in salads, crudités, and stir-fried dishes.

Kombu: A flavorful ocean sea vegetable. The minerals released in cooking can increase the digestibility of beans.

Kudzu: Starchy root (powdered) used as a thickener for sauces, stews, and gravies. More nutritious than cornstarch and soothing to the digestive system. Dissolve in cold water before adding to foods: 1 part kudzu to 2 parts water.

Mirin: Mild cooking wine made from rice, used primarily as a sweetener. Great for soups, sauces, dips, salad dressings, and stir-fried dishes.

Miso paste: Fermented soybean paste. The darker the miso, the longer it has been fermented, and the saltier and stronger the flavor. Calming and alkalizing for the body. Great as a salty seasoning for soups or vegetables. One teaspoon in a glass of hot water makes a soothing broth that can help calm food cravings. Unpasteurized miso should be added to food when it is off the stove; it contains live cultures and high heat kills the beneficial bacteria. Store in the refrigerator.

Pomegranate vinegar: A combination of red wine vinegar and pomegranate juice, with a strong, sweet-tangy taste. High in antioxidants.

Seitan: Prepared from the gluten of wheat with a small amount of whole wheat flour. Very high in protein. A good meat substitute. Can taste salty. Use in salads, stir-fries, soups, and stews.

Shoyu: Japanese fermented soy sauce made with wheat. Fermentation breaks down soy to make it more digestible. In the United States, commonly referred to as simply soy sauce. Tamari is a variation of this sauce made with soy only.

Tahini: A spread made of ground sesame seeds. High in fat (mostly poly- and monounsaturated), protein, and fiber. Great to use in salad dressings, marinades, sauces, dips, and desserts.

Tamari: Wheat-free soy sauce. *See* Shoyu.

Tempeh: Unsalted, quick-fermented soy product. Very perishable. Used as a meat substitute in chili and soups, or flavored with strong seasonings such as smoky barbecue. Cook thoroughly.

Veganaise: Egg-free, vegan mayonnaise, made from four different oils: canola, expeller-pressed canola, grapeseed, and organic soybean.

Wakame: Brown sea vegetable, very high in calcium, niacin, and thiamine. Use like a leafy green; great in grains, salads, soups, stews, and dressings.

Xylitol: Sugar alcohol used as a sweetener. Very low glycemic load, so it's a suitable sweetener for diabetics. Not as sweet as table sugar. Helps prevent cavities. Use in small quantities, because larger quantities may cause diarrhea and other gastrointestinal discomforts, especially in children.

Appendix C:
Great Seasoning Combos

When you are ready to expand beyond your basic Spice Rack, this appendix introduces you to groups of herbs and spices that work well together, in particular, ethnic seasoning combinations. Some of these herbs and spices may be new to you, but don't be intimidated. They are not difficult to work with, and they add a lot of flavor to food. These lists are just to get you started—if a seasoning here is unfamiliar, look it up online or ask your local ethnic grocer about it. It can be fun to explore new flavors and to branch out into new cuisines.

A good way to expand your seasoning collection is to check your pantry before you shop and buy one new herb or spice each shopping trip. Remember to buy small quantities; you might not use them up and seasonings are perishable.

CHINESE SEASONINGS

agar
black bean sauce
chile pepper
Chinese five-spice powder
Chinese hot mustard
curry sauce
fermented black beans
ginger, powdered, grated, or pickled
hoisin sauce
hot bean paste
oyster sauce
plum sauce
rice wine vinegar
sesame oil
shoyu or tamari
star anise, ground or whole

FAVORITE FLAVOR COMBINATIONS

- Shoyu or tamari, lemon, garlic, olive oil or sesame oil: with quinoa, rice, tofu, and stir-fried vegetables
- Shoyu or tamari, rice wine vinegar, ginger, chili oil or sesame oil: as a protein marinade and a base for a dressing
- Fermented black beans, garlic, ginger, soy sauce, water, dry wine, and citrus juice: with tofu, fish, and shrimp
- Equal parts hot bean paste and soy sauce: warming to the body, great with tofu, fish, and seafood
- Tamari, ginger, sesame oil, and agar: warming to the body, great with tofu, fish, chicken, and seafood

INDIAN SEASONINGS

cardamom pods

cilantro

cinnamon

cloves

coriander seeds

cumin

curry powder

fennel seeds

ginger

mint

nutmeg

paprika

pomegranate seeds

red or green curry paste (pungent)

star anise seeds

tamarind

turmeric

FAVORITE FLAVOR COMBINATIONS

- Yogurt, lemon or lime juice, ginger, garlic, curry powder: with chicken
- Ginger, garlic, cumin, coconut milk, curry powder, tomatoes: in soups and stews
- Cloves, cinnamon, nutmeg, coriander, cardamom: with rice dishes
- Whole mustard seed, cumin, onion, ghee: brown spices in ghee until mustard seeds pop, use on vegetables and lentils
- Cumin, coriander, turmeric, mustard seeds, grated coconut: with carrots, root vegetables, soups, and stews
- Cumin, coriander, red and black pepper, ground mustard, cinnamon, cardamom, cloves, ginger, onion, tomato paste: with all types of beans, especially garbanzo and kidney
- Coriander, cumin, cayenne pepper, bay leaf, Celtic sea salt: with lentils, rice, soups, and stews

ITALIAN HERBS AND SPICES

basil

bay "laurel" leaves

garlic

oregano

parsley

rosemary

sage

FAVORITE FLAVOR COMBINATIONS

- Fresh chopped basil, minced garlic: to sprinkle over fresh tomato and arugula salad, or for bean salads
- Garlic, basil, oregano, marjoram: to flavor tomato sauce and tomato-based stews
- Parsley, rosemary, sage, garlic, olive oil, balsamic vinegar: to marinate chicken, turkey
- Parsley, sage, olive oil, red wine vinegar: in bean dishes
- Sage, bay leaves, parsley, garlic: in soups and stews or with rice, beans, chicken, or turkey

JAPANESE HERBS AND SPICES

ginger, grated or pickled

mirin (sweet sake)

miso

red soybean paste

rice vinegar

sake (rice wine)

sesame oil

seven-pepper spice

shoyu or tamari

white soybean paste

FAVORITE FLAVOR COMBINATIONS

- Fresh ginger, rice vinegar, sesame oil, miso: in noodle dishes
- Fresh ginger, garlic, mirin, sesame oil, shoyu: in salad dressings
- Red soybean paste, mirin, sesame oil, toasted sesame oil: for marinating tofu, tempeh, chicken, and turkey
- Red or white miso, mirin or sake, agave or honey, splash of water: warm in a pan until they thicken with a nice sheen; use a small amount on vegetables, squashes, and sweet potatoes
- Ginger, garlic, sesame oil, red pepper flakes, shoyu, splash of orange juice: for marinating tofu or tempeh

KOREAN SEASONINGS

dried anchovy

garlic

ginger

hot chiles (threads, powder, paste)

Korean sesame oil

mung beans

radish

red pepper paste

rice wine

shiso/perilla leaves (kkaennip)

shoyu or tamari

soybean paste

FAVORITE FLAVOR COMBINATIONS

- Maple syrup, soy sauce, garlic, pepper, sesame oil: with beef
- Garlic, soy sauce, sesame oil, red hot chile powder: on tofu, fish, and seafood

MEDITERRANEAN SEASONINGS

aniseed

basil

capers

cooking wine

fennel

garlic

harissa

marjoram

olives

oregano

savory

sun-dried tomatoes

FAVORITE FLAVOR COMBINATIONS

- Rosemary, thyme, red wine: pungent combination for red meats
- Marjoram, oregano: on zucchini or salad
- Olive oil, garlic, basil: on pasta, salads, and cooked green vegetables
- Capers, lemon or white wine, garlic, pepper: on pasta, used as a marinade for tofu, shrimp, fish, and chicken
- White wine, garlic, fresh basil, tomatoes: on pasta, as a marinade for white-flesh fish, and with chicken
- Olive oil, garlic, basil, oregano, black pepper, fresh tomatoes, with a bit of real maple syrup to make the tomatoes less acidic: on pasta and with chicken
- Bay leaf, oregano, thyme, basil, rosemary: for stews, soups, and braising
- Olives, sun-dried tomatoes, garlic, basil: on pasta and lentils

- Olive oil, shallots, fresh thyme or tarragon, vinegar or lemon juice: as a dressing, or sautéed with fish or chicken
- Bed of sliced fennel and onion: under fish for baking
- Bouquet garni: an herb bouquet of bay leaf, fresh thyme, a few parsley sprigs, and a few celery leaves tied together and added to stocks, soups, and stews

DESSERT SEASONINGS

You can also use herbs, spices, and other seasonings to make tasty and creative desserts:

- Cinnamon, nutmeg, vanilla extract, maple syrup or agave nectar: great for yogurt, smoothies, fruit crisps, sweet grain "pudding"
- Powdered ginger, cardamom, cinnamon: for sweet, warming foods such as hot breakfast cereals, winter snack cookies, and spiced teas or ciders
- Cloves, cardamom pods, cinnamon, gingerroot, maple syrup or honey: in tea with milk, soymilk, rice milk, or goat's milk (hot chocolate alternative)
- Ginger, lemon, honey or agave nectar: a hot beverage to warm you up and soothe your stomach
- Mint, honey: steeped together into hot or iced tea

Appendix D:
Best Oils for Best Purposes

When choosing an oil, it's helpful to know its smoke point. Oils should never be allowed to smoke, because that indicates that the heat for that oil is too high. The smoke point is the temperature at which a heated oil or fat breaks down and is no longer healthy to eat.

It is believed that once an oil begins to smoke it produces free radicals, which contribute to the risk of cancer and other degenerative diseases.

HIGH-HEAT OILS

Stable at high temperatures. Safe for frying, popping popcorn, and other high-heat cooking.

ALMOND OIL

- Smoke point: 430°F
- Monounsaturated fat
- High in omega-3 essential fatty acids
- Ideal for baking, stir-frying, sautéing, drizzled on vegetables and pasta

AVOCADO OIL

- Smoke point: 510°F
- Monounsaturated fat
- High in vitamins A, B1, B2, D, and E
- Mild, neutral flavor
- Ideal for popping popcorn, on meats for grill or high-heat sautéing

SESAME OIL (RAW, NOT TOASTED)

- Smoke point: 510°F refined, 350°F unrefined
- Almost equal in monounsaturated and polyunsaturated fats
- High in vitamin E; detoxifying properties
- Does not easily become rancid due to sesamol, an antioxidant naturally present in the oil
- Sesame smell, mild sesame flavor
- Good for stir fries and salad dressings

SUNFLOWER OIL

- Smoke point: 460°F
- Polyunsaturated oil
- No nutritional benefits
- Sesame oil or rice bran oil sometimes added to sunflower oils for antioxidant benefits
- Good for sautéing

MEDIUM-HIGH-HEAT OILS

Stable at medium-high heat. Best for sautéing, wok stir-frying, and baking at 350°F–425°F.

CANOLA OIL

- Smoke point: 425°F
- Monounsaturated fat
- No nutritional benefits
- Becomes rancid easily

- Heavily engineered oil from the rapeseed plant. Loses most of its health benefits through refining and deodorizing. Choose organic to avoid genetically engineered rapeseed.
- Neutral flavor
- Good for sautéing and baking

CLARIFIED BUTTER (GHEE)
- Smoke point: 375°F–475°F
- Saturated fat
- Butter with the milk solids removed. Ayurveda describes it as one of the finest cooking oils
- Can be stored for a few weeks without going rancid
- Increases "digestive fire"; improves assimilation and enhances nutritional value of foods[1]
- Slight nutty flavor
- Great for sautéing spices to release their flavors and health benefits

COCONUT OIL
- Smoke point: 350°F
- 90% saturated fat
- Contains 45% lauric acid, which has antiviral, antibacterial properties
- Mild, distinct smell; great for baking
- Coconut flavor is not distinct if oil is used in small quantities
- Good for baking, sautéing vegetables, and cooking breakfast eggs

GRAPESEED OIL
- Smoke point: 425°F
- 68% polyunsaturated, 11% saturated, 16% monounsaturated fat
- High in linoleic oil
- Many grapeseed oils are extracted using the chemical hexane, which may be unhealthy; however, Spectrum-brand oils are alcohol-extracted, which is safer
- Neutral flavor
- Good for sautéing, searing; great for salad dressings and homemade mayonnaise due to its emulsification properties: won't separate when refrigerated

MACADAMIA NUT OIL
- Smoke point: 390°F
- High in monounsaturated fat, low in polyunsaturated fat
- High in antioxidants and vitamin E
- Mellow, nutty flavor
- Good for baking, salad dressings

HIGH OLEIC SAFFLOWER OIL
- Smoke point: 390°F
- Polyunsaturated fat
- High oleic properties; acts like monounsaturated oil, which contributes to lowering cholesterol
- Neutral flavor
- Good for baking, sautéing; works well with dips and mayonnaise with its mild flavor

MEDIUM-HEAT OILS

Stable at medium heat. Ideal for cooking in which you want to impart the full flavor of the oil to foods. Good for sauces, salad dressings, sautéing, stir-frying at medium heat.

OLIVE OIL

- Smoke point: extra-virgin 350°F (unrefined extra-virgin 320°F)
- Monounsaturated oil
- High in antioxidant-rich polyphenols, which are destroyed during high-heat cooking
- If extracted by natural means without chemical solvents it does not become rancid easily
- Extra-virgin olive oil should only be used at room temperature or for low-heat cooking because the heat will change the composition of the oil, creating free radicals
- Refrigerate for extended shelf life and freshness
- Nutty or fruity flavor depending on type and locale of olives
- Good for low-medium-heat cooking and salad dressing; great as fresh bread dip in place of butter

PEANUT OIL (UNREFINED)

- Smoke point: 320°F (refined 450°F)
- High in monounsaturated, polyunsaturated, and saturated fats
- Resistant to rancidity
- Peanut flavor
- Good for stir-frying and sautéing

WALNUT OIL (UNREFINED)

- Smoke point: 320°F
- Polyunsaturated fat
- High in omega-3 fatty acids
- Walnut flavor
- Good for salads, drizzled on veggies or fruits

FINISHING OILS

These oils should not be exposed to direct heat. Add to salad dressings, drizzle on cooked vegetables, add to cooked rice or eggs, or use in yogurt, smoothies, or oatmeal.

FLAXSEED OIL

- Polyunsaturated fat
- High in omega-3s that the body can convert to healthy fatty acids DHA and EPA
- For full nutritional benefits, should be fresh, cold-pressed, and kept refrigerated; will keep for 8 weeks
- Nutty flavor
- Good for salad dressings and drizzling on cooked veggies

TOASTED SESAME OIL

- Best for flavoring only
- Sesame smell, mild sesame flavor
- Add to cooked veggies, stir fries, or use in salad dressings

Appendix E:
Animal Protein Safety

With the current increase in reported food-borne illnesses, it is important to make sure your meat and poultry are cooked to an internal temperature high enough to destroy harmful bacteria such as *E. coli*, salmonella, and trichinosis. According to the USDA, temperature is the only way to tell whether food is cooked sufficiently. USDA research says that looking at the color of meat does not accurately determine its safety, because color varies significantly, especially if a food has been frozen and thawed.

Learn how to use a thermometer to check for the proper doneness of animal protein dishes. It is important that the thermometer be inserted properly. It should be placed in the thickest part of the meat, not near the bone, because bone is generally hotter and could give a false reading.

HOW TO KNOW WHEN CHICKEN AND TURKEY ARE DONE

- When piercing the wing, breast, and thigh with a fork, clear juices should run. A thermometer reading taken at the leg (not touching the bone) should read 165°F. The meat will be firm, but the joint will be slightly pink. If this is unappealing, cook up to 170°F.

- To test the breast meat, stick the thermometer into the neck end of the breast where the meat is the thickest. It should read 165°F.
- Whole chicken should read 180°F.
- For stuffed poultry, you should check the internal temperature of the stuffing, too. It should read at least 160°F.

HOW TO KNOW WHEN BEEF AND PORK ARE DONE

- Ground meat is safest if the middle gets cooked to at least 160°F.
- Roasts and steaks should be cooked to 145°F (medium-rare).
- Cook pork to 160°F. This gives you slightly pink, juicy, tender chops and roasts.

OTHER MEAT SAFETY TIPS

- When reheating, bring food to a temperature of 165°F or bring to a rolling boil.
- When holding or serving hot cooked meats, keep at a temperature of 140°F or higher. Cold meats should be kept at 40°F or lower.
- Wash the stem section of your thermometer in hot soapy water after each use.
- After handling meat, wash your hands thoroughly for 20 seconds before rinsing.
- Never put cooked meat or poultry back on the same plate where the raw meat or poultry

was, or allow raw poultry, meat, or seafood to come into contact with cooked foods.

- Don't defrost meat and poultry on the same plate.
- Don't use the cooking utensils (such as forks or knives) that have touched meat before it's been fully cooked to serve the finished meats.
- Never defrost or marinate food directly on the kitchen counter, where bacteria may be lingering; always place it in a bowl or pan.
- Wash your counters with hot soapy water and dry them with a paper towel or clean dish-towel that has been through the hot cycle of the washing machine.
- Keep a separate cutting board for raw meat; clean it thoroughly with hot soapy water after each use and once a week with a small amount of bleach.
- Microwave your wet sponge on high for 2 minutes to kill most food-borne bacteria that has accumulated on it. Microwave it for 4 minutes to kill everything, but make sure it's soaking wet to avoid any risk of fire!

Notes

CHAPTER 1

1. Cynthia L. Ogden, PhD; Margaret D. Carroll, MSPH; Katherine M. Flegal, PhD, "High Body Mass Index for Age Among US Children and Adolescents, 2003–2006," *Journal of the American Medical Association (JAMA)*, Vol. 299, No. 20 (May 28, 2008): 2401–2405.

2. "An Update on Type 2 Diabetes in Youth From the National Diabetes Education Program," *Pediatrics* Vol. 114, No. 1 (July 2004): 259–263, http://pediatrics.aappublications.org/cgi/content/full/114/1/259 (accessed June 26, 2008).

CHAPTER 2

1. US Department of Health and Human Services, Centers for Disease Control and Prevention, "Does Drinking Beverages with Added Sugars Increase the Risk of Overweight?," www.cdc.gov/nccdphp/dnpa/nutrition/pdf/r2p_sweetend_beverages.pdf (accessed June 26, 2008).

2. American Dietetic Association, "Position of the American Dietetic Association, Dietary Guidance for Healthy Children Ages 2 to 11 years," *Journal of the American Dietetic Association* Vol. 104 (April 2004): 660–677.

3. Gladys Block, "Foods Contributing to Energy Intake in the US: Data from NHANES 111 and NHANES," *Journal of Food Composition and Analysis* Vol. 17, Issues 3–4 (June–August 2004): 439–447.

4. Michael F. Jacobson, PhD, "Liquid Candy: How Soft Drinks Are Harming Americans' Health," Center for Science in the Public Interest (January 2005), www.cspinet.org/new/pdf/liquid_candy_final_w_new_supplement.pdf (accessed June 26, 2008).

5. Susan Harrington, "The Role of Sugar-Sweetened Beverage Consumption in Adolescent Obesity: A Review of the Literature," *The Journal of School Nursing* Vol. 24, No. 1 (February 2008): 3–12.

6. Center for Science in the Public Interest, "Cutting Salt in Kids' Diets Reduces Blood Pressure" (October 2006), www.cspinet.org/new/200610311.html (accessed June 26, 2008).

7. Patricia M. Guenther, et al., "Most Americans Eat Much Less Than Recommended Amounts of Fruits and Vegetables," *Journal of the American Dietetic Association* 106:9 (September 2006): 1371–1379.

8. Biing-Hwan Lin, et al., "Away-from-Home Foods Increasingly Important to Quality of American Diet," *Agriculture Information Bulletin* No. 749 (January 1999): 1–21.

9. Center for Science in the Public Interest, "Anyone's Guess: The Need for Nutrition Labeling at Fast-Food and Other Chain Restaurants" (November 2003), www.cspinet.org/restaurant report.pdf (accessed June 26, 2008).

CHAPTER 3

1. Weston A. Price, DDS, *Nutrition and Physical Degeneration* 50th anniversary edition (Chicago: Keats Publishing, 1989).

2. Liz Lipsky, PhD, CCN, "Nutrition Basics," www.innovativehealing.com/free_library/articles/articles_nutrition_basics.html (accessed June 26, 2008).

3. Gary Cummings, "Food Shelf Life Recommendations" (January 1999), www.a1comserv.com/gary/expire.html (accessed June 26, 2008).

4. Janet Star Hull, PhD, "Food Additives to Avoid" (2002), www.sweetpoison.com/food-additives-to-avoid.html (accessed June 26, 2008).

5. Center for Science in the Public Interest, "Food Additives," www.cspinet.org/reports/chemcuisine.htm (accessed June 26, 2008).

6. Judith Jones Putnam and Jane E. Allshouse, "Food Consumption, Prices and Expenditures, 1970–97," *Statistical Bulletin* No. 965 (April 1999): 1–196.

7. David S. Ludwig, et al. "Relation Between Consumption of Sugar-sweetened Drinks and Childhood Obesity: A Prospective, Observational Analysis," *Lancet* 357 (2001): 505–8.

8. Anne Raben, et al., "Sucrose Compared with Artificial Sweeteners: Different Effects on Ad Libitum Food Intake and Body Weight After 10 Weeks of Supplementation in Overweight Subjects," *American Journal of Clinical Nutrition* 76 (2002): 721–9.

9. George A. Bray, et al., "Consumption of High-fructose Corn Syrup in Beverages May Play a Role in the Epidemic of Obesity," *American Journal of Clinical Nutrition* 79 (2004): 537–43.

10. "Fructose-sweetened Beverages Increases Risk Of Obesity In Rats," *Science Daily* (March 2007), www.sciencedaily.com/releases/2007/03/070315123558.htm.

11. Michael Roizen, MD, and Mehmet Oz, MD, *YOU: The Owner's Manual: An Insider's Guide to the Body That Will Make You Healthier and Younger* (New York: Harper Collins, 2005).

12. Organic Trade Association, "US Organic Standards" (2003), www.ota.com/organic/us_standards.html (accessed June 26, 2008).

13. Organic Trade Association, "The O'MAMA Report: How to Read USDA Organic Labels" (2007), www.theorganicreport.com/pages/12_how_to_read_the_usda_organic_labels.cfm (accessed June 26, 2008).

14. Linda Bren, "Genetic Engineering: The Future of Foods?," *FDA Consumer Magazine* (November–December 2003), www.fda.gov/fdac/features/2003/603_food.html (accessed June 7, 2008).

15. Richard Manning, "Super Organics: A Better Future for Food?," *Wired Magazine* Issue 12.05 (May 2004), www.wired.com/wired/archive/12.05/food.html (accessed June 8, 2008).

CHAPTER 4

1. Alam Khan, et al., "Cinnamon Improves Glucose and Lipids of People with Type 2 Diabetes," *Diabetes Care* 26:12 (2003): 3215–8.

2. KidSafe Seafood, "How Do We Select KidSafe Seafood?" (2007), www.kidsafeseafood.org/bestchoices_howdoweselect.php (accessed May 3, 2008).

CHAPTER 5

1. "CDC Issues Warning About Raw Sprouts," *New York Times*, January 15, 2002, http://query.nytimes.com/gst/fullpage.html?res=9502E7DF1538F936A25752C0A9649C8B63 (accessed May 24, 2008).

2. Harold McGee, *On Food and Cooking: The Science and Lore of the Kitchen* (New York: Scribner, 2004).

3. Paul Pitchford, *Healing with Whole Foods: Asian Traditions and Modern Nutrition* 3rd ed. (Berkeley: North Atlantic Books, 2002).

CHAPTER 7

1. Circadian Rhythm Laboratory, "Circadian Rhythms," www.circadian.org/blorhyt.html (accessed June 26, 2008).

2. National Center on Addiction and Substance Abuse at Columbia University, "The Importance of Family Dinners II" (September 2005), www.casacolumbia.org/absolutenm/articlefiles/380-Importance%20of%20Family%20Dinners%20IV.pdf (accessed June 26, 2008).

3. TV Turnoff Network, "Screened In: How Excessive Screen Time Promotes Obesity," www.tvturnoff.org/images/action/AmLivedocsrpt.pdf (accessed October 26, 2006).

4. Ibid.

CHAPTER 9

1. Integrity in Science: A CSPI Project, "Is DuPont Holding Back Data for Teflon Study?," Integrity in Science Watch Week 10/16/2006, http://cspinet.org/integrity/watch/200610161.html (accessed June 26, 2008).

CHAPTER 10

1. Yogeshwer Shukla and M. Singh, "Cancer Preventive Properties of Ginger: A Brief Review," *Food and Chemical Toxicology* (November 2006): 683–690.

CHAPTER 11

1. Yixuan Gong et al., "3,3'Dindolylmethane Is a Novel Topoisomerase II (Catalytic Inhibitor That Induces S-phase Retardation and Miotic Delay in Human Hepatoma HepG2 Cells," *Molecular Pharmacology* 69 (2006): 1320–1327.

CHAPTER 12

1. Physicians Committee for Responsible Medicine, "Eat Beans, Weigh Less" (April 2006), www.pcrm.org/news/archive060410.html (accessed June 26, 2008).

2. Paul Pitchford, *Healing with Whole Foods: Asian Traditions and Modern Nutrition* 3rd ed. (Berkeley: North Atlantic Books, 2002).

3. M. Walderhaug, *Foodborne Pathogenic Microorganisms and Natural Toxins Handbook: Phytohaemagglutinin*, US Food and Drug Administration Center for Food Safety and Applied Nutrition (January 1992).

CHAPTER 13

1. Mary G. Enig, PhD, *Know Your Fats: The Complete Primer for Understanding the Nutrition of Fats, Oils, and Cholesterol* (Silver Spring, MD: Bethesda Press, 2000).

2. Spectrum Organic Products, "Process: Tradition and Innovation," www.spectrumorganics.com/?section=process (accessed June 26, 2008).

3. Ellie Brown, PhD, and Michael F. Jacobson, PhD, "Cruel Oil: How Palm Oil Harms Health, Rainforest & Wildlife," Center for Science in the Public Interest (May 2005), www.cspinet.org/palmoilreport/PalmOilReport.pdf (accessed June 26, 2008).

APPENDIX D

1. Kenneth D. R. Setchell, et al., "Lignan Formation in Man-microbial Involvement and Possible Roles in Relation to Cancer," *Lancet* 2 (1981): 4–7.

Bibliography

Aron, Elaine, PhD. *The Highly Sensitive Child: Helping Our Children Thrive When the World Overwhelms Them.* New York: Broadway Books, 2002.

Aron, Elaine, PhD. *The Highly Sensitive Person: How to Thrive When the World Overwhelms You.* New York: HarperCollins, 1999.

Colbin, Annemarie. *Food and Healing.* New York: Ballantine, 1986.

David, Marc. *The Slow Down Diet: Eating for Pleasure, Energy, and Weight Loss.* Rochester, VT: Healing Arts Press, 2005.

Douillard, John. *The 3-Season Diet: Eat the Way Nature Intended: Lose Weight, Beat Food Cravings, and Get Fit.* New York: Three Rivers Press, 2001.

Enig, Mary, PhD. *Know Your Fats: The Complete Primer for Understanding the Nutrition of Fats, Oils, and Cholesterol.* Washington, DC: Bethesda Press, 2000.

Garcia, Deborah Coons. *The Future of Food: An In-Depth Look into the Controversy over Genetically Modified Foods.* Mill Valley, CA: Lily Films, 2004. Documentary.

The George Mateljan Foundation for the World's Healthiest Foods. www.whfoods.com

Haas, Elson M., MD. *Staying Healthy with the Seasons.* Berkeley: Celestial Arts, 2003.

Johnston, Anita A., PhD. *Eating in the Light of the Moon: How Women Can Transform Their Relationship with Food Through Myths, Metaphors, and Storytelling.* Carlsbad, CA: Gurze Books, 2000.

Madison, Deborah. *Vegetarian Cooking for Everyone.* New York: Broadway Books, 1997.

McGee, Harold. *On Food and Cooking: The Science and Lore of the Kitchen.* New York: Scribner, 2004.

Pennington, Jean A. T., Anna de Planter Bowes, and Helen N. Church. *Bowes & Church's Food Values of Portions Commonly Used.* Philadelphia: Lippincott Williams & Wilkins, 2004.

Pitchford, Paul. *Healing with Whole Foods: Asian Traditions and Modern Nutrition.* Berkeley: North Atlantic Books, 2002.

Price, Weston A., DDS. *Nutrition and Physical Degeneration* (50th anniversary edition). Chicago: Keats, 1989.

Rimm, Sylvia, and Eric Rimm. *Rescuing the Emotional Lives of Our Overweight Children: What Our Kids Go Through—And How We Can Help.* Emmaus, PA: Rodale, 2005.

Roizen, Michael, MD, and Mehmet Oz, MD. *YOU: The Owner's Manual: An Insider's Guide to the Body That Will Make You Healthier and Younger.* New York: HarperCollins, 2005.

Rosenthal, Joshua. *Integrative Nutrition: Feed Your Hunger for Health and Happiness.* New York: Integrative Nutrition Publishing, 2005.

USDA National Nutrient Database for Standard Reference. www.nal.usda.gov/fnic/foodcomp/search/.

Workman, Jennifer, MS, RD. *Stop Your Cravings: A Balanced Approach to Burning Fat, Increasing Energy, and Reducing Stress.* New York: The Free Press, 2002.

About the Authors

Jeannette and Tracee are both passionate nutrition educators committed to improving the daily diets of families everywhere. Together they are the Real Food Moms (www.realfoodmoms.com). Their common experiences as mothers and nutrition professionals, and their shared vision for healthier families, inspired them to write this book.

JEANNETTE BESSINGER, CHHC

Owner of Balance for Life, LLC (www.balancefor lifellc.com), Jeannette is a board-certified holistic health counselor, award-winning lifestyle and nutrition educator, and real foods recipe designer. Author of *Your Baby's Best Food*, she also created the meals and recipes for Dr. Jonny Bowden's *The Healthiest Meals on Earth*. A graduate of Columbia University and the Institute for Integrative Nutrition, she holds advanced certifications in a wide range of holistic wellness modalities, including

stress management and the psychology of nutrition. She currently resides in Portsmouth, Rhode Island.

As a young adult she suffered from an autoimmune disorder and gained a lot of weight after each of her pregnancies. Dissatisfied with conventional treatment options and shocked by a diagnosis of diabetes, she began her exploration of healing with food and natural practices, ultimately going into remission and achieving long-term blood sugar balance without the use of drug therapy. In the course of starting a family and learning more about nutrition and health, she found herself increasingly disturbed by many of the American cultural norms for raising children. She began to see how families can so easily fall victim to the Standard American Diet and lifestyle.

As an experienced "motivational educator," she has designed and facilitated award-winning lifestyle change programs in schools, child care centers, social service agencies, corporations, hospitals, and wellness centers for the past 15 years.

As a resident "lifestyle health expert" on school and hospital health councils, she has consulted with many groups and agencies working toward stemming the tide of childhood obesity. With a grant from a state health department, she helped develop a comprehensive assessment of community-specific barriers to lifestyle health and a subsequent citywide obesity intervention plan for families.

Over time, Jeannette has struggled to balance her work, her social change efforts, and her own self-care, while keeping her family's needs as the first priority. She understands firsthand how challenging it can be to invest time and energy into making healthy lifestyle choices in a consistent way. She is not an abstract "academic" dabbling in the theoretical; she writes from the trenches. She works intimately every day with people of all backgrounds, ages, and walks of life who are working to make healthy changes in their lives.

TRACEE YABLON-BRENNER, RD, CHHC

Tracee is a registered dietician and board-certified holistic health counselor with a certificate of training in the Childhood and Adolescent Weight Management Program through the Commission on Dietetic Registration. Owner of Nutrition Is Healing (www.nutritionishealing.com), she is the RD expert and recipe creator for *Your Baby's Best Food* with Jeannette. She lives in New Jersey.

Tracee became interested in the relationship between high-quality food and personal health as she was growing up in a household with sick parents. When she was six, her mother was diagnosed with Hodgkin's disease. When she was sixteen, her father had a heart attack and quadruple bypass surgery. Her mother was chronically ill for twenty years without receiving advice or support on how to improve her nutrition or self-care. This inspired Tracee to seek out better solutions.

Pursuing an interest in the benefits of healthy cooking, Tracee attended Johnson and Wales Culinary School and Florida International University, followed by a brief career in corporate food service. Passionate to learn more about the role nutrition plays in health, she attended Marymount College to become a registered dietician. Through an internship at New York Hospital-Cornell Medical Center, she worked with diverse groups and make deeper connections about the role of diet in optimal health. Later she completed her holistic health training at the Institute for Integrative Nutrition.

Although generally slim and healthy, Tracee faced health challenges when she went back to work after having her children. Balancing family and career was a challenge. She struggled with fatigue and digestive issues. Through education and experimentation she changed her diet and reduced her stress levels, greatly improving her vitality. Experiences of better health have influenced both her professional work and her parenting of her two vibrant daughters.

Inspired by teachers and other mothers, and concerned about the terrible nutritional offerings in school cafeterias, Tracee joined the school's wellness committee and opened a private counseling practice to support women, especially mothers of school-age children. She has taught a weight-loss behavior modification course in a hospital for the past nine years and speaks to schools, organizations, and corporations about nutrition.

Index

PHOTOGRAPHY CREDITS

Top cover photo and photos on pages vi (quiche and succotash), vii (smoothies and pasta), 38, 78, 92, 106–107, 176, 187, and 208 copyright © 2008 by Leo Gong. Food styling by Karen Shinto. Prop styling by Harumi.

Bottom left cover photo and photos on pages vi (blueberries and eggs), vii (tomatoes and beans), xii–1, 2, 22, 57, 58 (blueberries and peapods), 108, 120, 125, 132, and 154 copyright © 2008 by Jupiterimages Corporation.

Bottom right cover photo and photos on page 105 copyright © by Diamond Sky Images/Digital Vision/Getty Images.

Photo on page 11 copyright © 2007 by Dallas Events Inc. Used under license from Shutterstock.com.

Photo on page 12 copyright © 2007 by Paul Reid. Used under license from Shutterstock.com.

Photo on page 21 copyright © 2007 by iofoto. Used under license from Shutterstock.com.

Photo on page 58 (apples) copyright © 2007 by Sergei Didyk. Used under license from Shutterstock.com.

Photo on page 58 (squash) copyright © 2007 by Dee Golden. Used under license from Shutterstock.com.

Photo on page 63 copyright © 2007 by Daniel Gale. Used under license from Shutterstock.com.

Photo on page 126 (basil) © iStockphoto.com/Jaroslaw Wojcik.

Photo on page 126 (bay leaf) © iStockphoto.com/Juan Monino.

Photos on pages 127 (cardamom and cilantro), 128 (cumin), 136 (beet greens). 137 (bok choy and broccoli rabe), 138 (chard), 139 (Chinese cabbage and collard greens), 141 (kale), 142 (mustard greens), 143 (spinach and watercress), 147 (beets and carrots), 150 (turnips), 152 (delicata squash), 158 (amaranth), 159 (barley), 160 (buckwheat), 162 (kamut and millet), 164 (quinoa and rice), and 169 (adzuki beans and black beans) © iStockphoto.com/Suzannah Skelton.

Photos on pages 127 (cayenne pepper) and 131 (turmeric) © iStockphoto.com/Jean-Yves Benedeyt.

Photo on page 128 (cinnamon) © iStockphoto.com/Matt Trommer.

Photo on page 128 (dill) © iStockphoto.com/Sandra Caldwell.

Photo on page 128 (fennel) © iStockphoto.com/Nina Shannon.

Photo on page 129 (garlic) © iStockphoto.com/Alex Balako.

Photo on page 129 (ginger) © iStockphoto.com/Ewa Brozek.

Photo on page 129 (mint) © iStockphoto.com/Ivan Mateev.

Photo on page 129 (nutmeg) © iStockphoto.com/Walter Matheson.

Photo on page 130 (oregano) copyright © 2007 by Matt Trommer. Used under license from Shutterstock.com.

Photo on page 130 (paprika) © iStockphoto.com/Edyta Pawlowska.

Photo on page 130 (parsley) © iStockphoto.com/Sally Scott.

Photo on page 130 (rosemary) © iStockphoto.com/joannwnuk.

Photo on page 136 (arugula) © iStockphoto.com/Lindy Sherwell.

Photo on page 140 (Dutch head cabbage) ©iStockphoto.com/Norman Chan.

Photo on page 141 (escarole) copyright © 2007 by Leon Forado. Used under license from Shutterstock.com.

Photo on page 144 (asparagus) copyright © 2007 by nfsphoto. Used under license from Shutterstock.com.

Photo on page 145 (broccoli) © iStockphoto.com/jerryhat.

Photo on page 146 (Brussels sprouts) © iStockphoto.com/Victor Murko.

Photo on page 148 (parsnips) © iStockphoto.com/Matt Craven.

Photo on page 149 (sweet potatoes) copyright © 2007 by Rena Schild. Used under license from Shutterstock.com.

Photo on page 152 (acorn squash) © iStockphoto.com/YinYang.

Photo on page 152 (buttercup squash) © iStockphoto.com/Jeffrey Hochstrasser.

Photo on page 152 (butternut squash) © iStockphoto.com/P_Wei.

Photo on page 152 (hubbard squash) © iStockphoto.com/Amma Karwowska.

Photo on page 152 (mini squash) © iStockphoto.com/Jane Norton.

Photo on page 152 (spaghetti squash) © iStockphoto.com/Bronwyn8.

Photo on page 152 (turban squash) © iStockphoto.com/David Powers.

Photo on page 153 (spinach) copyright © 2007 by Elena Elisseeva. Used under license from Shutterstock.com.

Photo on page 160 (bulgur) copyright © by Jennifer Thorpe.

Photo on page 161 (cornmeal) copyright © 2007 by Nathalie Dulex. Used under license from Shutterstock.com.

Photo on page 161 (couscous) © iStockphoto.com/Stephen Rees.

Photo on page 163 (oats) © iStockphoto.com/Daemys.

Photo on page 165 (wild rice) © iStockphoto.com/Paul W. Brain.

Photo on page 170 (black-eyed peas) © iStockphoto.com/Nigel Monckton.

Photo on page 171 (fava beans) © iStockphoto.com/Luís Brás.

Photo on page 171 (garbanzo beans) © iStockphoto.com/Ugur Bariskan.

Photo on page 172 (kidney beans) © iStockphoto.com/edfuentesg.

Photo on page 173 (lentils) © iStockphoto.com/Štepán Ježek.

Photo on page 174 (lima beans) © iStockphoto.com/Graeme Gilmour.

Photo on page 174 (navy beans) © iStockphoto.com/Stephan Hoerold.

Photo on page 175 (pinto beans) © iStockphoto.com/Harris Shiffman.

Photo on page 236 by Faith Dugan.

Photo on page 237 by Paul Florio.